BLUE BUG, RED ROAD

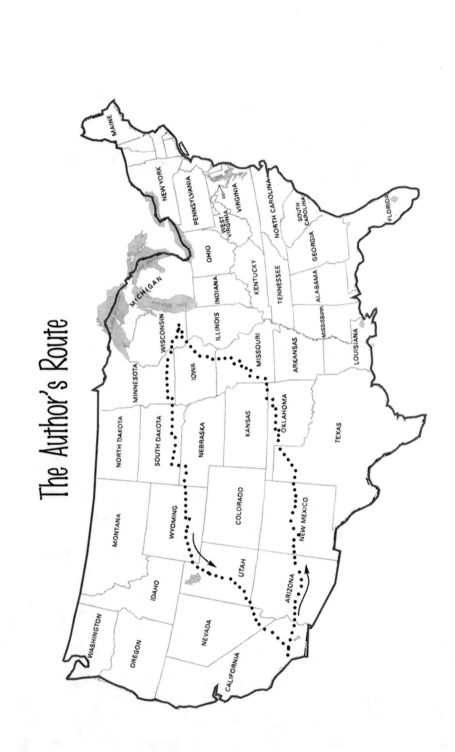

The Author's Route

Also by Gaines Post Jr.:

The Civil-Military Fabric of Weimar Foreign Policy (1973)
Dilemmas of Appeasement (1993)
Memoirs of a Cold War Son (2000)

Blue Bug, Red Road

Gaines Post Jr.

*To Frank + Carol,
old friend + new friends,
with thanks for a lovely day
and evening*

*Gaines
May 20, 2011*

iUniverse, Inc.

New York Lincoln Shanghai

Blue Bug, Red Road

iUniverse books may be ordered through booksellers or by contacting:

iUniverse
2021 Pine Lake Road, Suite 100
Lincoln, NE 68512
www.iuniverse.com
1-800-Authors (1-800-288-4677)

Because of the dynamic nature of the Internet, any Web addresses or links contained in this book may have changed since publication and may no longer be valid.

The views expressed in this work are solely those of the author and do not necessarily reflect the views of the publisher, and the publisher hereby disclaims any responsibility for them.

Photographs by the author (exceptions: photo of author and brother near beginning of chapter five by Andrew Mailer; photo of author on rear cover by Thomas Dean)

Maps by Christopher Schink

ISBN: 978-0-595-46794-5 (pbk)
ISBN: 978-0-595-91084-7 (ebk)

Printed in the United States of America

To my oldest friends, my brother John, and Andrew and Stan Mailer. Had it not been for our first reunion in forty years, the Blue Bug would not have discovered the Red Road.

Contents

Acknowledgments

The cast of characters in this book is too large for me to thank everyone by name. I am indebted to all of them for humanizing the road with conversation, assistance, local history, and simple acts of recognition. More than we could have known at the time, several helped shape this story. I gratefully list them in the order of their appearance: Marlene the waitress in Socorro, New Mexico; Stanley and Wendy Marsh in Amarillo, Texas; Sacred Eagle Woman (Pauline Jones) in Pawhuska, Oklahoma; Dick Ferguson in Carthage, Missouri; Duane Spriestersbach and his late wife Bette in Iowa City, Iowa; Mary Mohs in Madison, Wisconsin; Ansel Wooden Knife in Interior, South Dakota; Dennis and Nancy Daly near Douglas, Wyoming; and Walt and Sandra Whitman near Denver, Colorado.

While I debated whether to fly or drive to Wisconsin, James Custer of Volkswagen of America offered encouragement along with a "birth certificate" for my Bug. Only minutes into my trip, Doug Lashbrook of Connie & Dick's Service Center in Claremont performed the timeliest of all the mechanical feats that readied the old car for a long distance. Three weeks later, when the engine gave out in Wyoming on my way home, Powders Volkswagen in Casper ably replaced it.

For helpful advice at various stages of planning and writing, I am obliged to Bob Fossum, Steve Davis, Bill Sterling, Bob O'Neill, Dick Sylvester, Robert and Marie Christine Gray, Bill Stott, Arthur Latimer, Mike Bryan, Edward Ingraham, Stan Schwartz, Martha Bates, Joe Spieler, Hugh Van Dusen, and Mikel Jollett. Christopher Schink, artist and techie, designed the front cover, prepared the maps of my route, and converted my old-fashioned photos into electronically correct files. Mike Brainard and Bert Lemmo urged me to seek out their Lakota friend, Ansel Wooden Knife. Ansel pointed me toward Red Cloud's grave. After I began to try to make written sense of my journey, he sent me the prayer that he kindly permitted me to use in the afterword.

My courageous wife, Jeanie, has given me unfailing support from the first inkling of the trip to the last page of the book.

Author's Note

Early in 2002, my brother and I quickly accepted Andrew Mailer's invitation to spend a week together in Wisconsin in June. Sixty years before, Andy and his brother, Stan, had moved to a house across the street from John and me in Madison. Stan was now the only one of us still living in Wisconsin, and he had recently been diagnosed with Parkinson's disease. The two sets of brothers had not been together since the early 1960s. Andy thought this might be our last chance.

At first, I thought I would fly to Wisconsin from my home in southern California. I soon changed my mind. Having just refurbished my blue 1966 Volkswagen Bug, I liked falling into conversation with strangers who came over to admire the old car in parking lots or at filling stations. I would soon turn sixty-five, and I had an itch to hit the road. I decided to drive the Bug one more time across America, alone, like the first time.

I presumed the home-state reunion was the purpose of the trip and I would hear a lot along the way about the state of the nation. I was wrong on both counts. Driving slowly, I found quiet layers of time and memory beneath the national clatter. Most of the strangers I met wanted to probe roots, not politics or the War on Terror. Rivers and trails led me into America's past, where westward expansion attracted my ancestors and shaped our national character, for better and for worse. The reunion placed me back in the Wisconsin landscape that helped form the Post and Mailer boys. Returning to California, I understood something even deeper than history and biography. It was something simple and reassuring. We are inseparable from the land if we can escape the noise and listen.

CHAPTER 1

▼

CROSSING THE DIVIDE

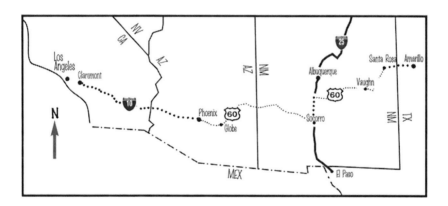

Thursday, May 23

"Doug, you gotta help me. I just kissed my wife good-bye and my car doesn't work."

As soon as I left Jeanie waving from the driveway of our home in Claremont, California, something went wrong with the Bug's combustion. I limped downhill to Connie & Dick's Service Center, where Doug Lashbrook is the Volkswagen expert. He had installed the new engine last year. He had recently become a kind of co-conspirator for my trip, testing and repairing, telling me the Bug was fine and I wasn't crazy.

Doug quickly finds the problem and fixes it. A plug in the casing of the carburetor had blown out when the engine backfired as I started it.

"Did you wash your car this morning?" he asks.

"No, yesterday afternoon."

"That's it. Moisture got into the system and caused the backfire," he says. He replaces the plug, cementing it with epoxy. "Now you should be in good shape. Have a good trip."

About two hours later, on Interstate 10 between Palm Springs and Blythe, the plug is still holding. I begin to believe I'm actually on my way. After all the planning and packing, I'm on the road to Wisconsin in my *seeblau* (sea blue) 1966 Bug. I bought the car in October 1965 in Bonn, the Cold War capital of West Germany. It was the first and only time I have walked into a dealership, plunked down the price—fifty-six hundred deutsche marks, or fourteen hundred U.S. dollars—and left in a new automobile.

The Bug is my backpack. It carries everything I need, all of it readily accessible: the day's maps in the pocket of the driver's door; guidebooks under and behind my seat; camera and snacks on the floor in front of the passenger seat; writing pad and small cassette recorder on that seat; pens, pencils, and film in the glove compartment; and water bottle, carrots, and grapes in the small cooler on the backseat. Thanks to long arms, my left can steer while the right reaches anything inside the car, including duffel behind the backseat.

Several features of the Bug slipped my mind after we bought a second car in the mid-seventies for long drives with babies. I can easily put my left elbow out the window and prop my arm on the sill. There is ample headroom. The no-nonsense windows provide good visibility. I can manage the large steering wheel with a knee if both hands are needed to unfold a map or unwrap a candy bar.

Smog clings to desert sinks well beyond Palm Springs, where signs advertise homes "on the waterfront." Southern Californians living in the desert now produce much of this foul air themselves, though escaping pollution along with other murky features of urban life is one of their reasons for moving out here in increasing numbers. I cruise at sixty miles per hour, passing no one except heavy trucks on grades. A retired-looking couple pass me in a small RV and wave. I return the salute. Anyone who will wave on this trip either once drove a Bug, wishes they had, or admires anyone my age who still does.

At the rest stop just short of Blythe, a man drinking from a plastic water bottle walks over and stops.

"Admiring my car?" I ask.

"Yeah. Sure am. I had one almost just like it. A '67."

He's a tall, slim African American, about fifty years old and balding, and he's traveling with his wife. We discuss Bugs for a few minutes.

"Boy, I sure wish I still had that car," he says wistfully. "But we started a family and had to get something bigger, so we bought a station wagon and got rid of the Bug. But that sure was a beautiful car."

"I decided to restore mine rather than sell it."

"Well, you did the right thing," he replies.

"I'm driving it to Wisconsin and back."

"That's great." He pauses. "Wisconsin and back, huh?"

"Yeah, I hope I make it," I say.

"Oh, you will. You will."

I leave the rest area before he does. He honks as he passes me on the outskirts of Blythe. The cold front that brought light rain to Claremont two days ago has lowered the desert temperature to the tolerable low nineties. An enormous, gas-guzzling RV roars around me a few miles into Arizona. On its side, I read the words, "American Tradition." I fear it is.

Just looking at the town of Quartzsite from the highway, I wonder who trashes the desert the most. Is it those who live there or those who thrash it on weekends with dune buggies, dirt bikes, and off-road vehicles? What a shabby sight: junk, billboards, dilapidated trailers, abandoned cars, containers and tatters made of plastic. No greenery hides this rubbish; no rain helps biodegrade it. I wonder why we profess our love for open space only to declare our right to fill it and our freedom to foul it.

The last time my Bug traveled this highway was in June 1983, when our family moved to Claremont from Austin, Texas. Daniel and I were in the Bug, Jeanie and Kate in the Toyota Corolla station wagon. We would miss our cheerful stone house in the trees of Travis Heights and our proximity to my parents, who had retired to their hometown of Haskell, north of Abilene. But we happily left other things behind, such as my allergic reactions to the educational politics of the University of Texas as well as the horny male cedar trees that pollinated Austin in winter. The future seemed bright and long. We had no idea that Jeanie carried the defective gene that now disables her. We did not know what caused Daniel's disciplinary difficulties back in Austin or dream that they would mushroom into juvenile delinquency in California. I did not foresee all of the land mines awaiting me as dean of faculty at Claremont McKenna College.

Now, memory toys briefly with what might have been. Suppose we had not driven I-10 to Claremont in 1983 but stayed in Austin. No. *Das geht nicht.* That's out of the question. Stick with reality.

In the long run, it didn't matter very much whether we left Austin or which road we took. Jeanie and Daniel could not flee the ailments that had not yet been diagnosed. After the move, I remained the same organic bundle as before. I succeeded and failed according to the same talents and flaws. I had the same dreams and letdowns. But surely it did matter that we took to the road. Just leaving and going gave us the chance to imagine that not everything would be the same. I can still imagine today.

On the flatbed of a passing truck, a large push broom stored upright behind the cab turns in the wind like a small radar antenna. Further on, the wake of four big rigs playing tag pummels the Bug, and I'm heading toward three dust devils. As I squeeze between two of the whirlwinds, three more semis blow past. Arizona has seemed uncongenial since my first sight of it in 1963, when "Impeach Earl Warren" signs discolored the image of the state that I had drawn from the radiant photographs in *Arizona Highways*. Now it's eighteen-wheelers and dust devils.

The sooner I leave this highway, the better. I must get through Phoenix before the late afternoon rush and reach the mountains beyond, driving more than four hundred miles on my first day. Starting tomorrow, I'll settle for a daily average of about two hundred and fifty miles, giving me time to loiter.

Outside Phoenix, a sign advertises a retirement community. "To the age of wisdom," it says. Who, me? I may have gotten smarter, but I don't feel wise. If that sounds Socratic, I don't feel Socratic.

Housing developments spread ever outward into the desert, naked structures with no trees or shrubs around them. A few miles off to my right, the Agua Fria and Salt Rivers enter the Gila River. I waded the New Mexico headwaters of the Gila with my brother, John, and his son, Gavin, when we backpacked in the Gila Wilderness in May 1995, a month after our mother died.

I beat the peak rush in Phoenix and turn east on U.S. 60. Hot, tired, and not in the best condition to generalize about anything, I wonder if it's possible—and what it would take—for a desert city in America to be urbane or cosmopolitan. Beyond Apache Junction, the highway angles southeast and begins climbing toward its status as a scenic road in the arid Pinal Mountains. Off to the left, the jagged ridges and steep bluffs of the Superstition Mountains turn redder as the day wears on. Saguaro cacti dot the terrain, oddly symmetrical with the skeletal white crosses on the highway's curves.

East of Superior, a small copper-mining town nestled at the foot of a prominent butte, the road abruptly ascends a plateau of about four thousand feet in elevation, three thousand feet higher than Phoenix. On the way up, I welcome the cooler air and the green of cottonwoods that cling to a steep creek bed. Among them are the dead relatives left by landslides or floods.

About fifteen miles before Globe, I pass an antique shop. The sign says, "Top of the World—Antiques and Collectibles." I begin to hum "I'm Sitting on Top of the World," the popular song from the fifties. Without a radio or CD player in the Bug, I have to make my own music, and I'm open to suggestions.

Without warning, a huge open pit mine eviscerates the charm of the plateau. Descending toward Miami and Globe, I see more signs of copper mining, pallid shades of gray, beige, and white. The land is violated. Every ounce of animism and pantheism in my feelings about the outdoors comes to the surface. Surely the earth that nourishes life must also feel pain. These mines are death. One of them is named "Bluebird."

Miami looks sad and seedy. It's almost a ghost town, its bars and gun shops surrounded by rigid mineshafts, ravaged bluffs, and gaunt tailings. Smokestacks crown a massive plant that overlooks the town like a gloomy fortress that Vauban built for Louis XIV in the foothills of the French Alps. Globe is a relief by comparison, with several late-nineteenth-century stone and brick buildings located in the old downtown. Silver made Globe a boomtown in the 1870s on land taken from the Apache after the discovery of a large orb of the pure metal. When the silver played out, copper took over. I have always been able to imagine finding a home in or near cattle towns of the Old West, but not mining towns. I might have survived a few weeks in Globe. In Miami, I would have lasted no more than a few hours.

On Globe's east side, I register at a motel and dine across the street. More than half of the restaurant patrons over the age of twenty are obese, but the liver and onions taste good. My waiter is a friendly young man with a limited linguistic menu.

"I'll have the baked potato," I say.

"No problem, sir," he replies.

"May I have some water?"

"No problem, sir."

"Thank you."

"No problem, sir."

I haven't been treated with so much deference since I left the army forty years ago, and I don't need it now.

Back at the motel, I close the window against the witless yapping of a small dog whose owners have left their door open.

Friday, May 24

As I rummage in the Bug after the motel's continental breakfast, a man stands nearby drinking a Coke. He's dressed in shorts, a grubby T-shirt, and floppies.

"Is that a '66?" he asks.

"Yes. How did you know?"

"'Cuz I had one of those when I was in college back in the sixties."

"Where was that?" I ask.

"Georgia."

"Were there many Bugs in the South in those days?"

"No," he says. "Not many. Most guys drove big clunkers, but I couldn't afford a big car. I had to work my way through college, so that Bug was the best car for me, and boy, was it a dandy. Say, are you the fella that was on TV? Went to Germany and bought a '66 way back then, returned to Germany thirty years later, and drove all around the same places?"

"No, I'm not. But that's where I bought mine."

"Sure is nice," he says. "Nice car. Sure looks nice. Nice car."

A few miles north of Globe, a sign warns me not to pick up hitchhikers because of the nearby state prison. That's the third such sign I have seen since entering Arizona. The irony of the warning hits me in open country that I am free to roam. The highway skirts the western boundary of the San Carlos Indian Reservation, which President Grant created in 1872 as part of the White Mountain Reservation. It's now home to about nine thousand Apache. Their forebears thought it a miserable piece of land. The dark women I saw cleaning rooms back at the motel probably live on the reservation, not in town.

A sign says, "Watch for animals next 77 miles."

The possibilities and distance are among the many things I love about driving two-lane roads in the West. Thoreau understood that his small corner of New England was a microcosm full of infinite detail. But when I'm in New England, Europe, or parts of the Midwest, I daydream about landscapes and roads like this. I know that traveling them makes me part of the problem, part of the loud rush of people who occupy the hushed emptiness. But I hope I'm the best kind of intruder, the one who drives small and pitches a tent, who leaves and leaves nothing behind.

It's good to be alone without a cell phone where the land tells layered stories with no end of endings. I'm going through a rough period. I don't know how far back it goes, but it goes deep. Jeanie's muscular dystrophy and my own demons have heightened normal post-retirement quandaries over career and aging. It's silly of me to think I should have accomplished more professionally, but the thought is there. My doubts grew after Dad's death and again after Mom's passing. I don't know why. Perhaps because losing parents takes away your oldest friends and leaves you as the next to die. You wonder whether you have lived up to them, what your best work has been, whether you will be wise before you go, and how your children will remember you.

That's not all. More than by anything else, I'll be judged by how I care for Jeanie. But her decline bewilders me. I'm angry that she's dying. I'm angry at modern medicine for lacking a cure and at myself for failing her. I dislike the word "caregiver" for expecting more than I can offer. How can I give when I need to get away? I'll need help from Kate and Daniel, but of course, they now have their own concerns. Like most children, they underestimate paternal doubt.

After nearly an hour of upland scattered with cedar, I descend the barren, red walls of Salt River Canyon. The highway switchbacks down nearly two thousand feet, then climbs just as steeply. Across the river, I enter the Fort Apache Indian Reservation. The name evokes scenes from the John Wayne movie, which was filmed at a time when Hollywood still depicted Indians as savages, much to the dismay of Wisconsin boys who looked up to Uncas and Tonto.

The Bug thrives on this kind of driving. Except for the steepest grades, third gear easily takes me uphill and brakes me going down. I cruise in fourth at forty-five to fifty-five miles per hour and coast in neutral on long downhills. The steering is tight and the suspension firm. I feel every ripple of road too well to misjudge it.

When vehicles come up behind, I pull over and let them by. It's mostly a selfish act, for I want to enjoy the best pace for Bug and driver. Two guys dressed in black pass me on a motorcycle, their long hair trailing behind black helmets. The passenger looks over at my car, smiles, and waves. I wave back. Most cars, pickups, and SUVs in Arizona have darkly tinted side and rear windows. The occupants can see me, but I can't see them. It's just like transparency in government and business. The windows of the Bug are honest, two-way glass. Closed, they do not falsify the natural look of things. Open, they provide old-fashioned air-conditioning. Either way, they let you acknowledge strangers.

Bugs have been part of my life for over forty years. I've had this one for nearly thirty-seven years. I keep things. I still wear the Omega watch I bought in Germany in 1960. In one room of my Claremont home are the longhorns that hung on my maternal grandmother's wall in Haskell for sixty years and on her parents' wall before that. In another room, I play the same thick records on the 1924 Edison phonograph that I listened to in the old Post house in Haskell. I've had these things for so long that I don't think of what other people might see in them.

Several months after I had this Bug refurbished, I visited a friend at another California college.

One of his colleagues said, "You know what's really authentic about your car?"

"No," I replied. "What?"

"It's not just the car. It's the license plate. You don't have one of those fancy plates that draws attention to yourself."

Many gussied-up old cars do have fancy plates. Joining them hadn't occurred to me, and I would feel foolish now if I had done so. This trip, perhaps my last long one in the Bug, gives me a way back to the years when I explored America in a car that defied behemoths made in Detroit. There wasn't anything very fancy about that younger self. At the end of the day, maybe all I have to hold on to is what's always been there under the repainting, not my profession, possessions, or even family.

I see my first old Bugs of the trip—two of them in rapid succession. One is on the back of a wrecker. The driver of the second, a shiny beige number heading in the opposite direction, does not return my wave. Bad omens?

The road climbs to the forested Mogollon Rim, which marks the southern border of the vast Colorado Plateau. I soon enter the town of Show Low, elevation 6,350 feet. Its name comes from the winning hand in an 1876 poker game between the cofounders of a ranch to decide which one would keep it.

A sign reads, "Fire Danger Extreme." It certainly is. It's awfully dry around here, even for Arizona. The highway dominates the town. Four lanes wide, it's lined with fast-food joints, automobile dealers, real estate offices, and motels.

A sign east of town warns, "Watch for Elk." I encounter none across the treeless, bone-dry plateau over Cerro Montoso Summit (elevation 7,550 feet). In the valley of the Little Colorado River, with headwaters in the White Mountains south of Springerville, there are large lava beds and the remnants of volcanic cones.

I lunch on a good hamburger in Springerville at Booga Red's Cantina, which specializes in Mexican food. Most of the locals fill up on the daily buffet, but I want to avoid afternoon bloat. After paying, I linger next to the Bug while reading a map. The stratagem works. A young man drives up in a GM pickup from the sixties. He has repainted it blue and keeps it well.

"Saw you from the gas station," he says. "Nice Bug. There are more old Bugs around here than you think. A guy in town rebuilds 'em."

"I bought mine in Germany."

"Were you in the army over there?" he asks.

"Yeah, but that's when I bought my first one. I sold that one in '65. Then I went back to Germany and got this one. You live here in Springerville?"

"Yeah. The people are real nice and the summers are about twenty degrees cooler than down below in Phoenix."

We shake hands good-bye. He does not have the pinched look of so many rural Anglos of the Southwest who are wary of strangers. Over the years, I have come to believe that there is more of this suspicion per capita in Arizona than in New Mexico or Texas. This guy has reduced his state's ratio of pinch.

Driving around town after filling the Bug's tank, I see a couple of old stone-fronted buildings. Next to a chiropractor's office, there is a large painting of John Wayne with an eye patch.

I've been here twice before with my brother. In September 1963, we drove west to Berkeley and Stanford in my first Bug. In August 1965, I had just sold the Bug. We passed through while heading east in his swept-back Plymouth Barracuda to see our parents in Princeton. After Princeton, I was bound for Germany and dissertation research in the archives of the German Foreign Office. John would backtrack to Nashville for his first year teaching in Vanderbilt's philosophy department. We drove through St. Johns, north of Springerville, on our way to or from Holbrook and I-40. In those days, I-40 had not completely replaced U.S. 66, which still covered most of the distance between Flagstaff and Needles. On both trips, we stayed with relatives in West Texas.

"What kind of airplane is that?" our Uncle Marvin Post wondered when he saw the Barracuda.

Highway 60 enters New Mexico north of the San Francisco Mountains. Off to my right, the Apache-Sitgreaves National Forest begins along an invisible boundary where grassland and evergreens coexist. Looking up valleys that wind back toward the mountains, I wonder what is around the bends and what sort of place I might have built out of view and tucked up against the trees for shelter.

On a flat stretch west of Pie Town, a motorcyclist speeds around me. He's going about eighty. After reaching the mirage ahead, he looks suspended above the highway, like a character from *Star Wars* in a gravity-defying runabout. Off to my left, cattle of various colors stand around a windmill, colleagues at the water-cooler. I will cross the Continental Divide in another fifteen miles or so, at the elbow of the wide V formed by ridges that close in on my left and right. Their highest points are more like buttes than peaks, except for Alegros Mountain at about ten thousand two hundred feet.

Randomly arranged on both sides of the highway a few miles west of the divide, Pie Town consists of a few homes, two cafés, an all-purpose repair shop, and a post office. I chose this route across New Mexico partly because of Pie Town. Two years ago, friends in Albuquerque served Jeanie and me a delicious goat-milk cheese with "Pie Town" on the label. The name stuck. My short-term memory is still functioning for good cheese, but the town was named after the baking done at the general store opened in the early 1920s by a settler who was unable to make ends meet on the forty acres he had purchased for mining.

I stop at one of the cafés and ask the lone waitress if there is a goat farm around here.

"I haven't heard of one," she says. "But you could ask at the post office."

Of course, I tell myself. If anybody knows of a goat farm in ranching country, it's the postmaster. A middle-aged man and woman approach the café as I step off the front porch.

The woman asks, "You aren't by any chance from Caltech, are you?"

"No. Why?"

"Well, we just passed those telescopes east of here," she says. "Really interesting. I thought you might work there because you have California plates."

"I'm from Claremont, not far from Pasadena, but why did you think I was from Caltech?"

"Your car! I thought that's perfect, you fit the role. You look like you should be a scientist from Caltech, especially driving that car."

We chat a few minutes while her husband goes inside to check the menu. She grew up in Rockford, Illinois. She has been working in theater in Arizona. When I tell her my destination, she says she knows Madison.

"Say hello to my friend in Mazo ... Muzo ...," she says.

"Small town west of Madison?" I ask.

"Yes."

"Mazomanie."

"Yes, that's it," she says. "He's director of the small theater there. Tell him Candace says hello."

"I will if I get there." It's probably a white lie. I'm certain I'll visit Mazomanie, but not for the theater.

A solitary arroyo willow dapples the patched adobe front of the small building which a hand-painted sign over the front door identifies as the post office. Inside, the postmistress tells me there is indeed a goat farm.

U.S. Post Office, Pie Town, New Mexico

"About thirty-four miles from here," she says. "Gravel roads all the way. Never been out that far myself. Probably not a good idea for you to go out there in that old car of yours."

I ask how old this building is.

"Dates from the forties," she replies. "But those old metal postal boxes over there go back to the first post office in the twenties."

The American flag flying outside reminds me that I have seen many more flags on this trip than I would have before September 11, 2001. There are also many more "God Bless America" signs, especially in Arizona, where the number of patriotic symbols per capita has always been much higher than the national average.

Stapled to the willow, a tattered notice dated April 20 advertises, "Dance at Uncle Bill's This Saturday Night. Featuring Russell Burris and the Shadow Mountain Band. Good Fiddlin', Great Fun."

A man appears from the southeast corner of the post office and walks toward me. Grinning, he asks where I'm from and where I'm going. About forty years old, he's either intoxicated or impaired. His speech is slurred, and his mind seems to struggle with my responses. He wears stained work pants, a dirty green T-shirt, and an old cap with a design of crossed elk antlers stitched on the front. He looks lonely.

"Ya oughtta move here," he says. "Lotta city folk do just to get away from it all."

The population of Pie Town can't be much more than fifty. The number of postal boxes suggests few outlying customers.

"Well, how's the weather?" I inquire.

"Just great. Gets down to ten below in the winter. Doesn't snow much. Almost nothing last winter, so we're really low on water around here," he says.

At the Continental Divide, elevation 7,796 feet, I enter Cibola National Forest. John and I often stopped at forest campgrounds on cross-country trips in the sixties, including that of August 1965 when we drove southeast from Springerville into the Gila National Forest to rest our aching bodies after covering nine hundred miles from Berkeley in fifteen hours. In those days, it cost about two dollars per night to camp in national forests. It was the best deal in the country, and there were plenty of spots for tents before RVs took over America's campgrounds. The price has gone up since then. It isn't unreasonable, but tent sites are rare; campgrounds have turned into trailer parks.

Maybe I should have gone back inside the café in Pie Town to stir up a political discussion with the waitress and the couple who took me for a scientist. Although the Bug attracts strangers just as I had hoped, no one has mentioned national security and the War on Terror. That fact in itself is revelatory. Perhaps it's best for me just to see what comes up. If it's not politics, my reading of America will disagree with that of the government and the media, who see conflict everywhere.

I find oddities in the middle of nowhere on the downhill toward Datil. One sign, "Public Library Off to the Left," is soon amplified by another at a dirt driveway that says, "Baldwin Cabin, Public Library."

The cabin is deserted. What is that story? Was it the library's holdings that I saw on the shelves of used books at the café back in Pie Town? Do people still read in the middle of nowhere? They certainly did in the Old West.

The teenage driver of a pickup flashes me the peace sign as he passes going west. He must identify my Bug with the peace movement of the sixties. If we are what we drive, this old car makes me certain things, but vintage flower child is not one of them. His friendly signal, however, cheers me, as have the New Mexico drivers who have lifted fingers from the steering wheel in greeting since I left Springerville. No one did so yesterday in Arizona between Globe and Springerville.

East of Datil, the road drops into an ancient dry lakebed, the Plains of San Agustin, the site of an alleged UFO landing in the forties, thunderstorm research in the fifties, and now the National Radio Astronomy Observatory's VLA (very large array) telescope, where I do not work. I park at an overlook near one of the many large dish antennae that are placed symmetrically across the basin on rails along three axes that form a Y. I estimate about ten miles for each axis and a mile between dishes. This afternoon, they face north.

On a sign at the overlook, I read that the VLA, dedicated in 1980, is "the most powerful, flexible and widely used radio telescope in the world."

Three young men pile out of their car and we chat. One takes a photograph of the Bug, not the VLA. Another got his master's at Cornell and does environmental testing in the nearby mountains. They are on their way to the Sangre de Cristo Mountains near Santa Fe for rock climbing over Memorial Day weekend. I wish them a safe climb.

Nearby, a tall motorcyclist in his forties, I would guess, bends over his bike to work on something. His head is shaved, and he's dressed in black, the same color as his bike. I pause as I leave the parking area to see if he's okay. He walks over to the passenger window.

"Anything serious?" I ask.

"No. Just gotta tie my parking light down so it doesn't flop around and scratch the paint. I'll get some duct tape in Socorro, and everything'll be fine," he replies.

"Duct tape solves everything, doesn't it?"

"You bet. Thanks for stopping," he says.

"Welcome. Safe trip."

"Same to you."

I stop briefly in Magdalena, population around one thousand, elevation around sixty-five hundred feet. Named after the nearby mountain in which Spaniards saw her face, the village was incorporated in 1884, a year before the Santa Fe spur arrived from Socorro. The spur turned the place into one of the largest livestock shipping points west of Chicago, serving the "Magdalena livestock driveway." Ranches used this driveway in the high grazing country that I had come through since leaving Show Low. The former railroad depot houses the town government and public library. Among a few old redbrick buildings, the handsomest is "Salome Store, General Merchandise," which has been in continuous operation since George Salome and his wife opened it in 1910. They had emigrated from Lebanon.

Painted in red on a corrugated metal fence, a sign reads, "Send Fosso after Bin Laden!!" Though the message must relate to local politics, I'm not sure if the messenger wants Fosso elected or banished.

Eight pronghorn antelope graze off to my right, where the highway begins a gradual descent of some two thousand feet into the Rio Grande Valley. The great river drains some of the continent's most beautiful country in northern New Mexico and southern Colorado. It irrigates a narrow strip of green all the way to Texas. Traffic halts at a grade crossing on the outskirts of Socorro for a short Santa Fe freight train. Its old caboose, a rare sight in today's America, is covered with fresh graffiti. Some experts on pop culture would ask me to appreciate this affront to our rolling past.

I have been drawn to Socorro since reading Charles O. Locke's novel, *The Hell-Bent Kid*, on a homesick day in England in 1962. The town owes its name ("help" in English) to Don Juan de Onate, who was grateful to local Pueblo peoples for sharing their corn with his expedition in 1598, twenty-three years before Squanto taught the Plymouth colonists how to grow it. But Don Juan was a conqueror on the move, working his way north from New Spain along the Rio Grande. He proclaimed most of the Southwest a Spanish colony, named it New Mexico, settled colonists along the river, sent parties of soldiers out to look for gold, and brutally suppressed any Pueblos who defied him.

On side streets, I find several attractive Victorian brick houses with wooden porches, dating from the silver mining heyday of the 1880s. The plaza is not as picturesque as I had expected, but its small park is a quiet oasis. Relaxing on a bench, I wonder why I prefer redbrick to brown adobe in old towns of the Southwest. It must have been the childhood lesson on building houses from *The Three Little Pigs*. Adobe was not a fourth option.

I dine at the Val Verde Steak House, which occupies the original dining room off the gardened courtyard of a former hotel built in 1919. The elegant room has wood paneling. Just below the dark ceiling is a narrow band of mural depicting the region. According to Marlene, my waitress, an artist who "worked for food" painted the mural in the 1930s. "Worked for food" is a good subtitle for the Works Progress Administration (WPA) of Roosevelt's New Deal.

Marlene is a kick. Calling me "honey" and "dear," she recommends a local Gewürztraminer, the ten-ounce filet, and the Kendall-Jackson Cabernet Sauvignon.

"I'll take it back if you don't like it, dear," she says of both wines.

I lie about liking the Gewürz.

She pats me on the back on her rounds. "Good, you're doing great," she says. "Guess you like it. You must be hungry! Be sure to save room for the blackberry pie. It's the only pie we make from scratch."

I take her advice, and the pie is delicious.

About halfway through my meal, Marlene asks, "What brings you to Socorro and what's your name?"

I oblige, adding that it's my first time here in over thirty-five years and my given name was the family name of Virginia ancestors.

"Oh, I've heard that name before. There was a boy in my high school in Ohio. G-A-Y-N-E-S," she spells.

"Mine is G-A-I-N-E-S," I correct her.

She takes my credit card to the receptionist in the alcove behind me. "Look at this guy's name," I overhear her say. "Isn't this an interesting name? Gaines Post. Two last names."

When she returns, she says, "I told her your name. It's not a name you forget." What's in a name?

I add a generous tip. As I get up to leave, she says, "Let's have a look at that car."

Outside, streetlamps flicker on, their black posts silhouetted against the late twilight. Marlene walks around the Bug, muttering compliments to the car and me for our endurance.

"I think we ought to do these things while we can," I declare.

"How old are you?" she asks.

"Almost sixty-five."

"Well, I'm sixty-nine, so I'm ahead of you, hon," she says.

"You don't look it."

"Well, I take care of myself."

She does, but she may dye her dark hair. Her slim legs support wide hips. What really counts is her warmth. She's what the French call *sympathique*, just plain likeable.

She asks why my wife isn't with me.

"Because she's disabled, and because I wanted to do this alone," I reply. "What brought you to Socorro?"

"Got here about five years ago, honey," she says.

"Straight from Ohio?"

"No, no. Went to Florida first. Spent about twenty-five years there. Buried two husbands, and then said to hell with it. Decided to pack up and come to New Mexico."

A young Latino parks his bulky Pontiac from the eighties next to the Bug and joins us, cradling an infant in one arm.

"How much do you want for that car?" he asks.

"A million dollars," I reply.

"I can't give you that much," he laughs. "Boy, it's a pretty car. Really nice."

Marlene has to go back to work. We shake hands.

"You take care of yourself, Gaines," she says.

"You too, Marlene. You're good news."

She smiles. She turns at the iron gate into the courtyard. We wave to each other.

The young man asks to see the engine. "I buy and sell old cars," he says.

"Take a look," I say.

"I see you're from California."

"Yeah, Claremont, near Los Angeles."

"I know Claremont," he says. "Grew up in Palmdale and drove all over the LA area."

"So, how much do you think I could get for my Bug?" I ask.

"A '66 in that condition? About thirty thousand. Not around here, though. Out in LA," he says.

I reckon that's way too high, but there's no point in arguing because I'm not selling at any price.

"Are you traveling alone?" he asks.

"Yeah."

"Isn't that dangerous?"

"I don't think so," I reply. "People around here are okay."

"Yeah, they are. It's not like LA."

"No, it's not."

Saturday, May 25

Reading the Albuquerque newspaper over my complimentary continental breakfast in the motel lobby, I come across an article about the state's two U.S. senators, Jeff Bingaman, a Democrat, and Pete Domenici, a Republican. Both will soon travel to Russia to discuss nuclear arms control. Bingaman has been making waves by insisting on an amendment to the defense bill to block spending on so-called bunker-busting nuclear weapons, at least until the Bush administration can give a cogent reason why they're necessary.

Presiding over the Senate's Energy and Natural Resources Committee since Vermont Senator Jim Jeffords left the GOP in June 2001 and Democrats assumed chairmanships, Bingaman is conscientious about environmental issues. So far, he has been able to thwart the administration's campaign for drilling for oil in Alaska's Arctic National Wildlife Refuge. I met Jeff in the late sixties at Stanford where he attended law school while I wrote my dissertation and taught

Western civilization. He has rock-solid integrity, and as long as he's in Washington, I'll have some hope for our political system. I still kick myself for not going backpacking with him in the Gila Wilderness in 1968.

I drive north on I-25, the Rio Grande to my right just beyond large fields, some of them fallow. I acquired my love of early morning drives from my father, who would wake John and me at daybreak on our summer trips to Texas. The air was cool and crisp, we were rested, and birdsong greeted us. Once the cobwebs cleared, I sensed that every day promised something new. That's how I feel this morning.

I called John last night from the motel and told him I had thought of him often between Springerville and Socorro. We reminisced about driving through Socorro in September 1963 after a cold overnight in the mountains near Lincoln, Billy the Kid country. We remembered our first time in New Mexico in the late forties, when our dad drove to Texas by way of Cheyenne and the Colorado Rockies. We met his brother, our Uncle Marvin, and Aunt Gladys at Cloudcroft in the mountains east of the White Sands, whose name I had heard in newsreels about ending the Second World War and beginning something called the Atomic Age.

John says he can't wait to see me in Wisconsin next week. Our reunion with the Mailer brothers seems closer now that I have crossed the Continental Divide. Andy has advised Stan that we're coming, but Stan, always skeptical about promises, won't believe it until he sees us. Stan was a classic misfit for our generation, brilliant with trains but inept at sports and moody in school. I last saw him in August 2000 when I went to Wisconsin for my forty-fifth high school reunion. He looked old and ill, even though Parkinson's disease had not yet been diagnosed. I'm afraid of what I'll find this time.

Andy has grown closer to Stan over the years, regretting he did not give his younger brother more support when he badly needed it. Their father derided Stan as a son unworthy of him, but Andy was the one who eventually suffered a mental breakdown. Both brothers are easily hurt and quick to size up temperaments around them. So are John and I, one of several traits the four of us have in common. We're all over sixty. Andy, the oldest, will soon be seventy-two. We had strong-willed ancestors with firm values, for better or worse. Our families broke apart during and after World War II. We coped with loss. Members of the Silent Generation, we were too young to fight in World War II and too old for Vietnam, but just right for service in the Cold War. Three of us were teachers, and the fourth would have made a good one. We had ambitions that exceeded what we have achieved. We tell stories.

South of Belen, I leave the interstate at U.S. 60 and cross the Rio Grande. The river is startlingly low, reduced to about 20 percent of normal springtime volume by successive dry winters in its watershed. After climbing through the gap between the Los Pinos and Manzano Mountains, I pull off for Abo Ruins, a unit of the Salinas Pueblo Missions National Monument, a few miles west of Mountainair.

In 1598, Don Juan de Onate and his party were the first Europeans to see the Pueblos of the Salinas (salt) Valley, which was named for its precious commodity. About thirty years later, Franciscan missionaries built San Gregorio church here in the Abo Pass next to a Pueblo that descendants of the Mogollon and Anasazi inhabited. The Mogollon had arrived from the southwest in the tenth century, the Anasazi from the west in the fourteenth century. A larger church followed in 1651. Abo became one of the major missions in the Southwest. It was also one of the most syncretic. Its missionaries, unlike many elsewhere, encouraged the Indians to amalgamate the two religions and build a kiva for their ceremonies next to the church. The village and mission were abandoned in 1673, casualties of drought, disease, and Apache raids. This was seven years before the Pueblos of the northern Rio Grande rebelled and drove the Spanish government out of New Mexico for more than a decade.

I walk around the silent sandstone walls of the church and sit on the bank of the dusty arroyo on the west side of the site. Its formerly life-giving flow began dwindling long before the Spanish arrived. I see the creek turning seasonal, springs drying up, and pools in the red rock evaporating.

Beyond Mountainair, I cross the Estancia Basin, a broad depression between the Manzano Mountains and Pedernal Hills. A Pleistocene lake filled it. Laguna del Perro is the largest of the salt ponds that remain. The railroad paralleling the highway breaks the monotony. It's the double track of the Santa Fe's (now BNSF) Belen Cutoff from Amarillo and Clovis to the Rio Grande, which trimmed hours from the Santa Fe's Chicago-Los Angeles schedule by avoiding the steep grades over Raton Pass and the mountains southeast of Santa Fe.

Not far north of here is the trail taken from the Texas Panhandle to the Rio Grande by Tot Lohman, the protagonist in Locke's *The Hell-Bent Kid*, a somber Western. It's the 1880s, and Tot is eighteen. He rides alone, reads the country, keeps a diary, and is a crack shot with his sawed-off Winchester. He lost his mother as a boy after she had "taught me to read and write and counseled me good." Now he goes looking for his father, who has fallen in with a lawless bunch near Socorro. Tot knows the Boyds will follow him to the New Mexico Territory and kill him. He sees "there is a system in the world, and that people like the Boyds have it fixed for you and keep it fixed" (Locke 1958).

An American friend at Oxford University, Arthur Latimer, found the English edition, *Road to Socorro*, during one of his daily browses of Oxford's bookstores.

"You'll like this one," he said.

Years later, Art described Tot as "a competent man-boy who knows something about loss at an early age. He's self-reliant by necessity and struggles with a hostile and corrupt world. He's on a quest. He's a chivalrous sort of character who won't yield to the Boyds around him, and he's headed for trouble. Reminds me of you."

Jeanie agreed. "But you're not hell-bent," she added.

I blame the likeness and Abo's deserted arroyo for the melancholy that has crept in. The reunion has disappeared. What am I doing here alone? Escape? Tot couldn't. Quest? There's no grail. Reading the country? That's more like it, good for the inner nomad, amateur geographer, and historian. But I'm also reading a life. It's a much longer life than Tot had, but death seems closer than it should be for a healthy man of sixty-five. Depression is part of my nature, but now I think my mind is absorbing Jeanie's pathology. Medications, living will, readings on illness and care, and meetings of the support group: we are both dying.

They say that, in your last second, your whole life passes in front of you. Perhaps I'm saying, why wait until then? Hit the road while you still can. See your life in the country. Remember as much as you can. Don't blame the Boyds or be too hard on yourself. Welcome the good memories. Let time and country assuage the bad stuff. Keep a diary. Keep moving.

The pasture on my left looks as large as Rhode Island. Hoofprints riddle the depressions that hold rainwater the longest. They are dry now. On the southern horizon, ridges loom where the Rockies begin their last major uplift in the Lincoln National Forest. When I cross the low divide between the watersheds of the Rio Grande and the Pecos, I leave the continent's cordillera behind me.

My mood brightens where U.S. 285 joins U.S. 60 west of Vaughn. The sign pointing northwest to Clines Corners brings back my most scatological memory of driving across the Southwest. Jeanie and I stopped at Clines Corners in June 1969. We had loaded this Bug with combined belongings from graduate school. We would store everything in Austin on our way to marriage in Boston. We had spent the night in Albuquerque. Jeff and Anne Bingaman drove down from Santa Fe to join us for a late dinner. The next morning, we decided to postpone breakfast until we had some miles behind us.

Clines Corners is one of the West's classic long-haul pit stops. It's not the zoological kind that specializes in rattlesnakes and Gila monsters. It's the interdisciplinary oasis where you can gas up, eat, sleep, and buy glittering rocks and Indian artifacts of dubious provenance. Clines Corners owes its existence to the junction of I-40 (formerly U.S. 66) and U.S. 285, a strategic hour from sleeping, dining, or failing to fill up in Albuquerque, Santa Rosa, Santa Fe, or Vaughn.

We fell into the trap. The gas was expensive. The food was greasy. The coffee was insipid. The curio shop was schlocky. The men's room was filthy. The bacon and eggs went straight through me, and I found a toilet just in time. When I eventually flushed it, a blast of subterranean air erupted from the bowl, smelling primeval and blowing bits of paper into the stall. I fled, tucking and buttoning my way back through the curios to find Jeanie out front.

"Let's get outta here!" I yelled. "The toilets fight back!"

We jumped in the Bug and fled. We have not stopped at Clines Corners since.

Vaughn's post office was established in 1907 when the Santa Fe's Belen Cutoff crossed the El Paso & Southwestern Railroad's line from El Paso to Tucumcari. Preceding the iron horse, traders came through here on a shortcut between El Paso and the Santa Fe Trail at Las Vegas, New Mexico. Then came the Stinson cattle trail, named after the manager of the New Mexico Land and Livestock Company who, in 1882, moved twenty thousand head in eight herds from Texas to the Estancia Basin. My grandfathers may have known some of his Texas drovers.

A bustling railroad town of two thousand in 1910, Vaughn has declined along with the industry. The population has dropped to around six hundred, down 30 percent since 1970. The old main street has died. Shops and motels along the highway are shuttered and peeling. Defying mortality with a drive-through window, Pedro's Burritos occupies part of what was once a gas station. The Las Chaves Hotel has disappeared. It was torn down in the sixties after passenger service ended, according to A. P. Anaya, one of the town's oldest residents. He grew up in Vaughn, where his father worked for the Santa Fe. His grandfather in Fort Sumner had served as a pallbearer for Billy the Kid. The hotel still thrived when Anaya returned from the war, having fought from Normandy to the Rhine.

The Las Chaves was one of the many Harvey Houses built during the Santa Fe's heyday for passenger travel in the Southwest. Before ordering a meal from a high-backed swivel chair at the coffee shop's counter, you could have bought a Cuban cigar at the newsstand along with your choice of papers published from Los Angeles to Chicago. Fred Harvey's brilliant alliance with Santa Fe began in 1870, the same year that George Pullman publicized his new Palace Cars by running a special train of them from Boston to San Francisco on the transcontinental railroad just completed at Promontory by the Central Pacific and Union Pacific companies. Harvey's enterprise survived the subsequent popularity of dining and sleeping cars, thanks to his insistence on good quality and diversification. He began to serve food on trains; expanded to other railroad routes; organized tours; popularized Indian artifacts soon after the word "curio" came into usage; and catered to townspeople and, eventually, automotive tourists.

I turn northeast on U.S. 54, which was built in the mid-twenties along the western half of the major railroad route from El Paso to Chicago. Plotted by railroad engineers who did not have to follow rivers, this became one of the few prominent diagonals of transport between the Midwest and Southwest. The Southern Pacific began to exploit the oblique as soon as the El Paso & Southwestern reached Tucumcari in February 1902. The Chicago, Rock Island & Pacific Railroad's Golden State Route already ran from Tucumcari to Kansas City and Chicago.

Since the 1880s, Collis P. Huntington's Southern Pacific (SP) had commanded the Sunset Route from San Francisco to Los Angeles, Tucson, El Paso, and New Orleans and used complex connections with other lines in Texas to get to Chicago. Now the SP could bolt northeast from El Paso, shortening the distance to Chicago and competing with the Santa Fe's all-Pullman California Limited for the fastest passenger service across the Southwest.

Edward Harriman, whose syndicate had acquired the Union Pacific in 1897 and who became majority owner of the SP after Huntington's death in 1900, welcomed the new route. Controlled by the Moore brothers, the Rock Island Line was happy to oblige. The brothers had cashed in on the biggest corporate merger of the Gilded Age, the sale of Carnegie Steel to J.P. Morgan in 1901 to form U.S. Steel.

The first passenger train along here in 1902, the deluxe Golden State Limited, ran daily in each direction between Chicago and California, taking sixty-seven hours to Los Angeles and eighty-seven to San Francisco. The SP and Rock Island pampered the all-Pullman train and its passengers with upgraded roadbed, new equipment, and excellent service. Sleeping, dining, and observation lounge cars featured burnished mahogany paneling, inlaid woodwork, art nouveau touches around mirrors and windows, soft cushions, lace here and there, marble sinks with silver-nickel hand pumps, and electric lights. You could dine on raw oysters, antelope, lemon sherbet, and French wine. A bottle of Mumm Extra Dry Champagne cost two dollars. Among the California red wines was Alta Vista, a "Chateau Lafite type," for seventy-five cents.

Like the Harvey Houses, everything about the Golden State Limited was designed to prevent Clines Corners. They failed. The Fred Harvey Company closed most of its restaurants by the end of the fifties. Amfac, which preserved the old name for its retail division, eventually purchased it. The SP and Rock Island Line added daily second-class trains to this route, carrying names like "Apache" and "Californian." For the Golden State Limited, they introduced a "finer and faster" daily in 1926, art deco ads accenting citrus and golf as well as air-conditioned cars in the thirties, a streamliner in 1948 that reduced the run between Los Angeles and Chicago to forty-five hours, and Day-Nite coaches in the fifties with tilt-back seats and leg rests. In 1968, it was all over. The Golden State ceased operations. All passenger service ended between El Paso and Tucumcari. Today, I'll be lucky to see one of the occasional Union Pacific freight trains that still use this neglected track since the UP absorbed the SP in 1996.

My father was born in 1902, a few weeks after the El Paso & Southwestern reached Tucumcari. He could not have arrived in a better year for new passenger trains. There was not only the Golden State Limited, but also the New York Central's 20th Century Limited to Chicago and the Pennsylvania Railroad's Pennsylvania Special, later the Broadway Limited, between Chicago and Jersey City. In the same year, a new design of locomotive appeared with a 4-6-2 wheel arrangement, the so-called Pacific. It had four wheels in the leading truck, six drive wheels, and two wheels in the trailing truck under the cab. This became the American standard for passenger service. It was Dad's favorite engine. He gave us an American Flyer electric train for Christmas in 1940. He guessed that America would enter the war in Europe and metal toys would be hard to come by. More importantly, he wanted time to play engineer before we grew old enough to take over. The locomotive was a Pennsylvania Railroad Pacific, model K4.

Dad had been hooked since the first steam engine on the Wichita Valley Railroad's new line south from Wichita Falls whistled into Haskell in 1906. In his stories about going by rail to college in Austin and graduate school in Boston, we could always count on him to spotlight the sign in the Texas & Pacific's dining car that said, "Drink T&P Coffee." On our trips from Wisconsin to Texas, Dad sought highways near tracks, towns with stations, and stations with coffee shops or Harvey Houses. Though partial to Pacifics, we waved toward all engines and cabooses. We usually got waves in return, and we were ecstatic to get a whistle. After Dad found lodgings around mid-afternoon, we would drive or walk to the station, check the schedule, and wait. John and I sat on baggage wagons, imitating cartoon characters or slugging arms while Dad read the paper and told us to keep our voices down … even if we drew blood.

Dad's social conscience, liberal for his time, took a holiday around railroads. So I did not worry about coal mining to fuel the engines; class and ethnic distinctions in building and riding the rails; the extermination of buffalo on the Great Plains; government giveaways of land and credit; the sins and cutthroat rivalry of railroad magnates and their conglomerates; and the Southern Pacific's lock on California politics by 1910. I cared about headlights, steam, whistles, wheels thundering, valve gears spinning, trainmen waving, and cabooses and observation cars inviting before leaving me behind in the anticlimactic silence. We dropped everything to watch steam engines, from the smallest switch engine to the massive articulated locomotives (2-6-6-2, and 2-8-8-2) waiting their turn in Cheyenne to pull Union Pacific freight trains over the Continental Divide. I miss Dad's trains.

The terrain rolls gently as I approach the Pecos River. Cirrus clouds have moved in, or I have moved into them. I have entered the overlap between climate systems. The more humid of them is ahead. In this part of the country, the overlap extends from the Pecos River Valley to Amarillo, roughly speaking. Along and west of this "dry line," afternoon heating builds up summer thunderstorms. East of it, Canadian cold fronts, unimpeded by mountain ranges, can produce spring tornadoes and drop winter temperatures twenty degrees in less than an hour. Texans still call them "blue northers."

In or near Santa Rosa, I cross Coronado's trail of 1540 to 1542. Having conquered the Seven Cities of Cibola, the Zuni villages south of today's Gallup, but finding no gold in them, he and his expedition slowly made their way east and northeast. They got as far as central Kansas before giving up on gold and returning to the Rio Grande, leaving behind bits of armor that plows still unearth from time to time. They were the first Europeans to anticipate the route of the Golden State Limited and Highway 66 from Santa Rosa to Tucumcari, and to walk the ancient path along the Arkansas River that became part of the Santa Fe Trail. According to legend, they gave the Llano Estacado its name when they drove tall stakes into the treeless plateau so they could find their way back after prospecting. Today, they could drink High Plains Merlot from the Cap Rock Winery in Lubbock.

I gas up at the first opportunity in Santa Rosa and check the mileage. The Bug has made twenty-nine miles per gallon since Socorro and twenty-eight point seven since Claremont. Not bad, but I expected at least thirty-one because I had tail and quartering winds much of the way and did enough downhill coasting to compensate for climbing the Mogollon Rim and Continental Divide. I assume I have not broken in the new engine yet, and it will never equal the thirty-four to thirty-five highway miles per gallon of the smaller engine that powered the 1300 series. Although I had never been a good mechanic, I grew so familiar with the original engine that I could detect its slightest cough. When I had it rebuilt in

Austin and when I replaced it in Claremont, I grieved. I don't know this new engine yet, and I have to remember that the fuel gauge sometimes registers a quarter of a tank when it's almost empty. So recording gallons and miles is precautionary common sense, as it was with my first Bug, which I purchased shortly after arriving in Germany in early 1960 as an artillery lieutenant. That Bug had no gas gauge at all, just a lever that tapped a small reserve unless you forgot to reset the lever after gassing up.

I park in town near a bridge over the Pecos and lunch on dried apricots and peanut butter crackers. Several pedestrians stare at the Bug, but none stop to talk. Maybe it's because I'm eating with one hand while the other rummages and my left leg stretches out the open door. I drive on through town on old Highway 66, over rough pavement and past main street decay. Most of Highway 66 in New Mexico is buried under I-40, but you can find portions in bypassed towns like Santa Rosa, Tucumcari, and Gallup.

I recognize a filling station where Jeanie and I stopped on trips from Austin to the Pecos Wilderness east of Santa Fe. New Mexicans seemed to forgive our license plates because no Texan of the kind they loathed would drive a Bug. To that kind, especially owners of mountain property around Ruidoso and Santa Fe, they said on a bumper sticker, "If God had wanted Texans to ski, he would have given them a mountain," and on a poster I saw in Santa Fe, "Ski Lubbock!"

We introduced our children to backpacking in the Pecos Wilderness. On one such outing, Daniel and I came alone. Crossing a sloping snowfield, we lost our footing one after the other. We slid until we hit dirt and began laughing as soon as we realized we were silly and safe. During the hard years of raising him that lay ahead, I drew hope from the memory of that delectable moment.

Seconds after turning onto I-40, I regret having decided to take it the rest of the way to Amarillo. I am surrounded by semis. They nuzzle up behind the Bug as if sniffing a morsel. They turn up their noses and roar around me, monstrous and relentless. Five pass without a car among them, then eight more. They travel in pods, even though they fear nothing.

Between Santa Rosa and Tucumcari, low red buttes reveal the western edge of the caprock that keeps the High Plains flat across the Panhandle. "Historic Route 66" signs indicate remnants alongside I-40 that are maintained for tourists. More interested in ruins, I note an unusable stretch with a low concrete bridge like the kind we saw on the way to Texas in the forties. On one of these trips, I figured out that the large oil spots on concrete highways coincided with dips or cracks in the road. When I pointed this out to Dad, his praise of my inference was so high that I can still see the stretch of road where I heard it.

Near the Texas state line, Amarillo's Big Texan Restaurant advertises its famous seventy-two-ounce steak. If you can eat the whole thing, it's free. Off to the left, where old Highway 66 intersected a county road, are the shells of a café, a filling station, and a first-generation "motor court" with detached cabins that competed with hotels for auto travelers. Certain things change as soon as I enter Texas. Most of the place names are Anglo-Saxon. Hardly any of the others are Hispanic, let alone Indian. The nine counties surrounding Amarillo are called Hartley, Moore, Hutchinson, Oldham, Potter, Carson, Deaf Smith, Randall, and Armstrong. The land is flatter than eastern New Mexico, the fields larger, and the mirages more frequent.

The old grain elevator several miles ahead in Adrian reminds me of seeing the towers of Chartres cathedral across French farmland. Mesquite trees cram lean pastures where Coronado walked through thick buffalo grass. Livestock spread the mesquite seeds north from Mexico and the lower Rio Grande. When ranchers eliminated prairie dogs to gain grazing, they lost the critter most likely to devour the seedlings.

South of the highway on Amarillo's west side, Stanley Marsh's Cadillac Ranch has become the city's landmark. The ten cars from the period of 1949 to 1963 are planted nose first with their fins angling skyward. Volkswagen's invasion of America had a lot to do with the demise of the fin and the education of Detroit. I shall ask Stanley what he now thinks of old Bugs. He and Wendy have invited me to stay. I look forward to a day of rest with them at Toad Hall. Interstate 40 has worn me out.

CHAPTER 2

▼

TRAILS

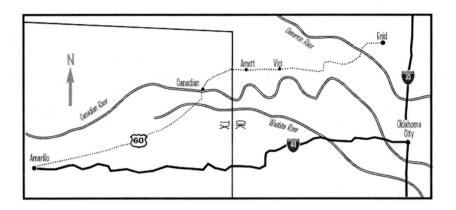

Toad Hall is the Marsh home on the northwest fringe of Amarillo. I park my Bug about twenty feet from a newer old Bug that plunges into the front lawn at the same angle as the famous Cadillacs. But there are fewer frivolities on the grounds than when I first met Stanley Marsh 3 and Wendy about thirty years ago—no toy monkey with its tail wrapped around the flagpole and no sign pointing to "International Airport," the makeshift airstrip that nature has reclaimed.

One of my graduate students at the University of Texas, John Rhinehart, had worked for Stanley. Stanley invited Jeanie and me to stop by on our way to the Rockies one summer. After John left grad school to return to Stanley's employ, Stanley telephoned me annually at salary time to ask what UT would pay me the next year.

"I'll pay John a thousand dollars more than that!" he'd exclaim. "Who needs a PhD?"

Toad Hall's front porch uses stone from the original house that Wendy's grandfather, William Henry Bush, built on this spot in 1912. His business career had begun in and around Chicago. He married the daughter of entrepreneur Joseph Glidden of DeKalb, who patented barbed wire in 1874 and co-founded the Barb Fence Company. With his partner Henry Sanborn, Glidden bought and fenced the Frying Pan Ranch west of Amarillo with its quarter-million acres. Bush acquired the ranch in 1892.

Stanley was wealthy before he married Wendy. His father had purchased mineral rights to thousands of acres of land around Amarillo in the twenties when he noticed how often drillers for water hit pockets of natural gas.

Stanley greets me warmly at the door. Wendy soon joins us. We exchange fleeting looks of surprise at the aging since our last mental photos of twenty years ago. Wendy offers me a soft drink.

"No, thanks," I say. "But I'd love some cold water."

"Ah," she replies, "we have wonderful water from our own well, straight from the Oglala aquifer."

It's as good as she says.

Both have had near-fatal illnesses and adopted a largely vegetarian diet. At supper, Wendy fills the round table with large bowls of artichoke, asparagus, baked potato, and tamales. As articulate and irreverent as ever, Stanley is quick with puns and associations across an array of topics. He's loaded with stories about his career, friendships, and notorious gags. In the best of the latter, he and members of his staff, including John, flew to Washington in April 1975 to attend the second day in the trial of John Connally. The former governor of Texas and treasury secretary under Nixon was charged with accepting an illegal gift of ten thousand dollars from the dairy campaign in return for urging Nixon to increase federal price supports for milk production. Before entering the U.S. District Court, Stanley and company, dressed like cowboys from hats to spurs, paused on the sidewalk to stomp their boots in manure they had brought from Amarillo in plastic-lined lunch pails. Once inside, they carried on as if they were just good ol' boy friends of Connally's, standing, waving, and voicing encouragement when he appeared with his lawyer, Edward Bennett Williams. Then they nodded and winked as the trial got underway.

At the time, Stanley had already appeared on Nixon's list of enemies. He attributes this honor to having written to Mrs. Nixon, introducing himself as "Curator of the Museum of Decadent Art." He asked if she would be kind enough to donate some of her pillbox hats. Stanley joined the longer of Nixon's two enemies' lists. He still regrets not having made the short one.

But Stanley is neither a doctrinaire Democrat nor out of sorts in Amarillo.

"I know a lot of Texas right-wingers," he says. "I disagree with 'em on politics, but they're nice people. They're decent folks who will give you a hand if you need it, and I get along well with 'em."

I interrupt when Stanley expresses admiration for "men of vision, even if they are creeps like Rupert Murdoch."

"How can you call that vision?" I ask.

"Well," Stanley replies, "he gives people what they want."

"Nonsense, Stanley. The word 'vision' ought to be reserved for something other than counting noses and feeding the animals. Or making millions at anything for that matter."

"Well, Gaines, I know you want to spread the wealth around, but that's just not the way things work. It's the entrepreneurs who make things happen. I mean the first generation of 'em. The second are just petty bureaucrats, midgets by comparison."

"What about Enron?" I ask. "How do you classify their executives, first or second generation? What kind of Texans are they?"

"Oh, God, I don't know," he replies. "I don't know any of them. In fact, I don't know anybody who knows them. God, that's a different world."

Wendy asks, "Why didn't you just fly to your reunion?"

"I'm sure there's a long answer," I reply, "but I don't yet know what it is. For now, let's just say I wanted to take one more long trip in my old Bug, sort of like Steinbeck hitting the road with his dog, Charley."

"Tomorrow," Stanley says, "I'll show you Steinbeck's '66."

Buck Ramsey's name comes up. The late Amarillo cowboy poet, he received the National Heritage Award from the National Endowment for the Arts in 1995. Buck collected and recorded cowboy music. He read poetry at Elko, Nevada, and other gatherings. In his sixty-page epic about a boy growing up in the West, he borrowed the stanza format from Pushkin and much of the text from his own life.

"A horse tougher than me ended all that," he said about his youth, "and I have since been a stove-up cowpuncher trying to figure out how to write about the cowboy life" (Ramsey 1993).

When we met in 1997, Buck inscribed my copy of his epic, acknowledging my roots in Texas and closing with the words, "Let's keep in touch and talk about these things." He died before we had another chance.

As if the memory of Buck requires a reckoning around the table, Stanley muses about what we do in our youth and why.

"As for me," he adds, "well, I owned a building and some television stations and two hundred square miles and had a good wife and just thought I'd do some crazy things."

Wendy has been a good wife indeed. She let Stanley be Stanley and nurtured their five children. Like him, she gave generously to philanthropy. Shortly after I helped the Rockefeller Foundation publish a report on the state of the humanities in America, she hosted a large party at Toad Hall, distributed copies of the report, and followed up with initiatives in local schools, colleges, libraries, and museums. Several years later, during a statewide fund-raising campaign by the Texas Committee for the Humanities, on whose board she served, the citizens of Amarillo donated the highest per capita amount of any Texas city. That's thanks to Wendy. It's thanks also to one Texas tradition, a high regard for letters and learning, that she is determined to defend against another one, anti-intellectualism.

Also at the table and sharing the guesthouse with me, is Doug Michels, an architect living in Houston. After receiving his master's at Yale's School of Architecture in 1968, Doug co-founded Ant Farm, the San Francisco avant-garde design group that built Cadillac Ranch for Stanley in 1974. Ant Farm broke up a few years later after a fire destroyed their offices. Doug wound up in New York. He shaved his beard and bought a suit for his interview with Philip Johnson in the acclaimed architect's posh offices.

"I want to be your apprentice," he told the formidable Johnson.

"Okay," Johnson said. "You start now."

Doug did anonymous scutwork for nearly a year until he bumped into his boss in the elevator one day and suggested how to fix the angle of three curved surfaces converging in the design of a house that Johnson intended to build in Big Sur. Next day, the plans for the entire project landed on Doug's desk.

He established his own studio in Houston in 1988. Whether designing space stations, government buildings, or homes, he advertised working "where science and imagination converge to create architecture of new millennial grace." But his mission in Amarillo this holiday weekend is to supervise a repainting of old millennial, beat-up Cadillacs. The Hampton Inn chain will foot the bill. The company adopted Highway 66 as a pet project, paying every year to renovate landmarks along the route. This year, it has chosen Cadillac Ranch.

Toad Hall's boisterous peacocks scold while Doug takes a few pictures of my Bug and me for a friend who collects pictures of old cars and their owners.

"You're really brave to do this trip," he says.

"Well, thanks," I reply. "I've been wondering how to ask people what they think of a senior citizen driving across the country solo in his old Bug."

"Brave," he repeats.

Doug would die in Australia in June 2003 while advising the production crew of a film about whales.

Sunday, May 26

After breakfast, Stanley, Wendy, Doug, and I drive into town. Sixth Street, which carried Highway 66 from the twenties to the fifties, now tries to cash in on nostalgia with retro stores, cafés, motels, and houses. The effect varies from authentic to corny. There is little business on a Sunday morning. Even on the busiest days, there are few "people in flight," like the Joads and Wilsons in *The Grapes of Wrath*. As we enter the modern business district, an old man dressed for church and wearing a wide-brimmed hat bicycles through an intersection ever so slowly, oblivious to the possibility of motor traffic. He looks proprietary and noble.

Stanley gives us a quick tour of the offices of Marsh Enterprises, located nearly halfway up one of the few buildings in Amarillo that justify an elevator. Only the old Santa Fe Railroad Building interrupts the flat, western skyline. Office décor ranges from African masks to abstract expressionist paintings. As always with Stanley's art, the untutored eye should beware. What looks like Pollock, de Kooning, and Rothko isn't.

"Why pay for originals when you can commission good copies?" he explains.

Stanley and Doug want to scout Cadillac Ranch. As part of Hampton Inn's publicity, a Houston television station will cover the repainting. We park on the I-40 access road and walk two hundred yards to the Cadillacs. A field surrounds them that is large enough to prevent urban development from obscuring their outline against the southern horizon. That happened at the original site, a smaller property a few miles to the east, which Stanley also owned, so he moved the cars here in 1997. They are arranged in chronological order, tracing the rise and fall of the fin after its modest introduction in 1948 by General Motors. Harley Earl, head of GM's Art and Color Section, based the original design on the twin fuselage and tail of the Lockheed P-38 Lightning of World War II, which was my preferred fighter in neighborhood dogfights during the war. The evolutionary excess of fins by the late fifties owed more to Cold War rockets that Wernher von Braun designed.

Stanley figures that unofficial repaintings will resume the day after the televised event.

"But that's okay," he adds. "I don't care who paints it or what colors. I had no idea Cadillac Ranch would last so long and become so popular. Isn't it great?"

He gestures toward the members of a weekend motorcycle club who are returning to their bikes.

Cadillac Ranch is only one example of Stanley's theory that good art is public art that surprises the viewer. Another example, the Phantom Soft Pool Table, has telephone poles for cues. It is best seen from mesas or airplanes and has moved about since its debut in the breaks of the Canadian River north of Amarillo. I should know better than to leave theory behind as we depart Cadillac Ranch.

Stanley says, "Let's go see Ozzie."

We drive south toward Canyon and stop near an intersection. In a pasture beyond a marker are two gigantic, sculpted legs that are at least ten feet high. The marker, impressively official with a Texas star and raised text, commemorates the day in 1817 when Percy Bysshe Shelley and his second wife, Mary Wollstonecraft Godwin, were riding horseback across the Panhandle and stumbled upon these ruins. The sight stirred him to write "Ozymandias." ("… Two vast and trunkless legs of stone/Stand in the desert …" [Shelley 1969])

The fine print below the plaque tells us that the originals, having been vandalized "by students from Lubbock who had lost a football game," can be found in an Amarillo museum. I want to buy the story, so convincing is Stanley's artifice. The city government is not amused. Tourists ask directions to the nonexistent museum and want to track the Shelleys instead of Amarillo's pioneers.

Back at Toad Hall in the afternoon, warnings of severe thunderstorms and hail keep me on the front porch of the guesthouse. From there, I can easily watch the clouds, reach the Bug, and, if necessary, move it to the shelter of a grove of trees. I imagine the front-page photo caption in tomorrow's local paper: "Battered Bug." Just before supper, a slam-banger without hail washes the top of the Bug and speckles its sides with mud.

Memorial Day

Over an early breakfast, I have the kind of talk with Wendy and Stanley that could not be sustained during yesterday's jaunts and mixed company. Soon their morning would fill up with preparations and hoopla for Cadillac Ranch.

We discuss adoption and our good fortune to have done this through the Edna Gladney Home in Fort Worth. In Stanley's case, Christian kindness had nothing to do with it.

"Hell, I adopted my kids because I wanted them, and I wanted five. Just like going through a cafeteria. I'll take that and that and that," he says.

Wendy agrees. But, a devout Catholic, her altruism runs deep. I tell them my daughter, Kate, located her birth mother several years ago.

"The woman still lives in Texas," I continue. "Last year, Kate invited her to Los Angeles. They got acquainted before Jeanie and I joined them for tea one afternoon. Kate presided over the occasion with wonderful sensitivity. I'll never forget how lovingly she said 'Mom' to Jeanie a few days later."

"None of our kids," says Wendy, "ever tried to find their birth parents, but one used to hurt us with words like 'You're not my real parents' and 'I'm not like other kids. I don't belong to you. I belong to somebody else.'"

"Jeanie and I weren't hurt that deeply," I reply. "But Daniel came close several times. Not long ago he said, 'I'll never adopt a kid. It's unfair.'"

As toddlers, both our kids loved to hear their adoption story. It was one of their bedtime favorites because Jeanie and I told it honestly. But unlike Kate, Daniel has never shown the slightest interest in knowing anything about his birth parents. I compliment Wendy and Stanley on their daughter Lizzie, who came by Saturday night with her boyfriend.

"She reminds me of Kate," I observe. "Warms up the room as soon as she enters."

"Exactly," Wendy says.

Lizzie taught English in an Amarillo public school, where the students loved her and she tied for city teacher of the year. But administrators, parents, and other teachers scolded her for wasting time on things that wouldn't prepare kids for the Texas achievement tests. For instance, she would teach Greek mythology to interest her students in ancient literature. She has moved to a private school, where there is less pressure to stifle imagination and close the mind.

I cannot leave without asking Stanley what he thinks of the Bug. I have been looking forward to a colorful quote that I can pass on to Volkswagen's American headquarters near Detroit, where James Custer of the Customer Care office has taken an interest in my trip. He asked me for the vehicle identification number of my Bug so he could determine its date of birth.

About a month ago, he sent me a certificate, "ANNOUNCING A (NOT-SO) NEW MEMBER OF THE VOLKSWAGEN FAMILY."

I'm named as the proud parent. The birth date is September 22, 1965. I called to thank James.

"It was a nice idea to choose September 22," I said. "But how did you know that's my birthday?"

"I didn't!" he said. "That's the day your Bug made it through inspection and got its official papers."

I relate the coincidence to Stanley.

"Isn't that something?" I say. "Now, Stanley, tell me how the owner of Cadillac Ranch looks back on the Bug as icon of the rebellious side of America that thumbed its nose at Detroit in the fifties and sixties."

Stanley's reply is indeed colorful, but VW wouldn't like it.

"Gaines, I admire your ideals, fairness and equal opportunity and all that, even though you sometimes sound like a communist," he says. "But you just reminded me there's something in the American experience I absolutely don't like, and that's you should get by on as little as possible and not be extravagant or flamboyant or have fun. The Bug represents that attitude. They're not built so you can screw in the backseat, and they don't look good at drive-in movies. They're not American. They're an awful foreign import, trying to impose European crowded conditions and uniformity on us. Give me bright colors! Give me doodads! Give me the American dream! Give me movie stars! But don't give me prudence!"

I catch Wendy's eye. She's silently telling me not to worry, the Bug can take it, you know Stanley.

We say good-bye in front of Toad Hall's old stone entrance. "Come back any time," Wendy calls as I turn toward the Bug. "And give our love to Jeanie."

I wish there had been more opportunity to talk only with her, a woman of patient wisdom, about personal quandaries. Stanley is too much the maverick for that.

On Amarillo's east side, I drive under an old metal railroad bridge. The Bug's tires thump over the ridges of tar that cover the gaps between sections of yellowed concrete. The girders, the sound, and the black lines take me back again to driving with Dad before highways were blacktopped. He drove Chevies: the black '35 that he put up on blocks during the war, the cream '46 that took us to Cheyenne and the Colorado Rockies, and the green '52 that celebrated our return from a year in Paris when my mother was with us after a long absence.

What will Daniel remember of me? At breakfast, I recalled the despair of raising a boy who seemed bent on self-destruction. Wendy and Stanley nodded. They have one like him. They already knew that my son had been plagued by severe attention deficit disorder (ADD), and that he defied every conceivable authority after the age of five. I recounted how Dan reversed course last year by moving back to the electrician's job in New York that had briefly kindled his self-esteem a few years earlier.

Leaving Amarillo, I thought of Dan's first trip to New York. After scrapes with parents, police, and employers, he left without telling us and used my credit card number to buy a bus ticket across America. As soon as he came back to southern California, he fell apart, drinking, doing drugs, and losing jobs. Failure and the animal instinct to heal prompted his return to New York.

"Dad," he said, "that's the only place I know how to stay out of trouble. And my old boss Carmine will take me back."

I gave Dan travel money, urging him to take it easy and stay in motels. Three days later, he called from an Ohio jail. He had driven straight through with only an occasional catnap, using speed to stay awake. He got lost, pulled off the highway around midnight to look at a map, and tried to flee when local police, who stopped to see if he needed help, asked him to step outside his pickup because they didn't like what they smelled in the cab. The judge who released him ordered him to leave Ohio and not come back.

When Jeanie and I told my parents that we would not be able to have our own biological children, my mother, as was her way, immediately lightened our burden.

"Oh good," she said. "Now your kids won't have my funny-looking little finger."

We knew nothing then about the alarmingly high percentage of adopted boys who have ADD and need psychiatric help. I should have known that a boy's inner voice changes forever when he is separated from his biological mother, no matter what his age. In my case, family history provided reassuring models and lessons. For Dan, ancestry meant nothing.

Yesterday's storms have cleaned the air and left it distinctly Texan, that is, northern and central Texas. East of the dry line, the prevailing wind retains Gulf moisture as it pushes north. This morning, clouds have appeared far to the south, and the wind is from the southeast. I inherited the habit of watching the weather from West Texas forebears whose lives depended on it and a father who would call John and me out onto our back porch in Madison to see the lightning.

"Dad," my four-year-old brother said on one such occasion during an unusually dry summer, "you asked God for rain, and he brought it."

In Dad's telling, it had not been a request.

There was a story in Haskell, no doubt of regional parentage, about an old-timer who lived in a cabin in the country. A young reporter asked how he could tell the weather if he didn't listen to forecasts on the radio.

He replied, "Well, I just go out back and look around. What I see is what I get."

Just looking around now and remembering what Uncle John Rike taught me about wind from the southeast out on his ranch, I would bet on afternoon thunderstorms.

The Bug wants to drift left as I head northeast toward Pampa. I'm glad to be back on U.S. 60. The land is pancake flat. The slightest rise provides a vantage point. Telephone poles disappear far up the straight highway. Grain elevators, a few of them still in use, loom along the railroad at intervals of about eight miles, staking the plain according to yields and capacities back when wheat replaced cattle as the Panhandle's chief farm commodity.

A long BNSF freight train rumbles past on its way to Amarillo. The line was originally part of the Santa Fe's second route from Kansas to California, from Emporia to Woodward (Oklahoma), Amarillo, Clovis, and, finally, the Belen Cutoff through Vaughn to the Rio Grande. This is another rare Midwest-Southwest diagonal. For nearly five hundred miles, it parallels the more northerly one that the Southern Pacific's Golden State Limited once took. About a hundred miles separated the rivals. Together, these diagonals disobeyed both the artificial and natural topography of this region. Politicians divided the land into territories, states, counties, and townships along vertical and horizontal lines. Rivers do not flow northeast to the Missouri and Mississippi or southwest to the Gulf.

Most of today's highway maps neglect early trails and the railroads that followed them, such as the Santa Fe Trail and the Santa Fe Railroad's route over Raton Pass. The Santa Fe Trail's Cimarron Cutoff foreshadowed the railroad diagonals that could cover even more ground without water as they headed for the Rio Grande south of high passes. Slanting left from the Arkansas River some fifteen miles west of what is now Dodge City, the Cimarron Cutoff rejoined the Mountain Branch of the trail about twenty miles northeast of Las Vegas, New Mexico. Except for the Cimarron and Beaver Rivers, water was scarce along the cutoff, but most travelers took it to shorten the route and avoid Raton Pass, as did traders who were not destined for Bent's Fort on the Arkansas east of La Junta, Colorado. A good map traces history. A good historian needs one.

Near Panhandle City, a marker identifies the home site of Thomas Cree, who worked on the Union Pacific's transcontinental construction crew after the Civil War and later settled here with his wife in the 1880s while he helped the Fort Worth & Denver City Railroad lay track northwest through the Panhandle. The Crees built a dugout. Near it, Thomas planted a bois d'arc sapling. He had traveled many miles to find it after his wife begged to have at least one tree in view. I can hear her reminding him—how often? morning or evening chore?—to haul water from the pond he made out of a buffalo wallow. The tree died in 1970, succumbing to herbicide sprayed on nearby fields. A small plaque next to the marker reads simply, "First Tree, Texas High Plains."

Somewhere since leaving Amarillo, I may have crossed a branch of the Western Cattle Trail. At Albany, Texas, the main trail from south Texas continued north to the Red River, Indian Territory, and Dodge City. Today's U.S. 283 closely follows this route from Brady in central Texas to southern Oklahoma.

In 1883, Jack Potter veered his herd northwest from Albany and through the Panhandle and eastern Colorado on the way to delivery at Cheyenne. About forty miles from Albany, he passed through Rice Springs, renamed Haskell a year later, around the time both sides of my family arrived to help turn a watering hole into a town and provide cattle and cowboys for the Western Trail. I have found no sign of Potter's trail this morning, but I hope to see the main trail commemorated where Highway 60 crosses it east of the Oklahoma border. For the moment, I note the names of early Westerners who had something in common. William and Charles Bent, Thomas Cree, and Corwin Doan, who ran Doan's Store where the Western Trail forded the Red River: all of them stopped in open country and liked company passing through.

Northeast of White Deer, "Home of the Bucks," a roadside marker recalls cattle drives from Texas to Montana and Wyoming. Near here, the N-Bar-N Ranch organized the last large drive to Montana, where the outfit also had extensive holdings. About a hundred cowboys trailed twenty-five thousand head in ten herds from April to September in 1892. Like many stories of large cattle operations in the late nineteenth century, this one has international overtones. The German-born Niedringhaus brothers owned the cattle, having made millions in St. Louis selling graniteware for the home. The N-Bar-N, which had leased range in the 1880s from a British-owned company backed by Cunard Steamship Line, left the Panhandle when the next lessor, the White Deer Land Company, ordered large herds off its property and began selling it to small ranchers and farmers.

In Pampa, American flags line both sides of the highway on this first Memorial Day since September 11. A sign identifies U.S. 60 as Woody Guthrie Memorial Highway. Born in Okemah, Oklahoma, in 1912, he moved with his father to Pampa in 1929 after his mother was committed to a mental hospital. It would have been called an "insane asylum" then, and no son could forgive the name. Woody left Pampa in 1937 for Los Angeles and fame. He sang about the land and said that it's for all of us. His spirit lives around here when drivers wave "Howdy!"

Dark clouds have moved closer from the south. The country rolls gently and turns to pasture between Pampa and Miami, where the drainages of three rivers overlap: the Canadian, the Washita, and the North Fork of the Red. The last two rise in the Panhandle. All three flow east into Oklahoma, but they resist union, as do most of the rivers that have furrowed the central and southern Great Plains. The Washita comes within ten miles of the Canadian east of Miami and again in central Oklahoma before making up its mind to bear south and join the Red. The Canadian is even more independent. With small geological changes around Las Vegas, New Mexico, some of the Canadian's headwaters might have fed the Pecos River and gone south to the Rio Grande. Instead, at a standoffish right angle to the Pecos, they help make the Canadian the southernmost river to rise in the Rockies and meander to the Mississippi. In Oklahoma, the Canadian will have none of the Red, but continues east to meet the Arkansas River upstream from Fort Smith. No estuary between New Orleans and Brownsville contains bits of the Rockies.

I congratulate myself for recognizing divides in the long continental downhill. Then I recall the story about the Prussian staff officer in the Napoleonic wars who eagerly apprised his general of the strategic significance of a summit in eastern France.

"I'll tell you its importance," the general grunted. "If I were to relieve myself on top of it, half of my water would flow into the Mediterranean and half into the Atlantic."

In Miami, the depot of 1888 belonged to the Southern Kansas Railway Company of Texas, which sold the line to the Santa Fe in 1899. The depot remained in service until 1978, and it is now a museum of local history. Next to it stands a stone hut built into the hillside, an early-day dugout that looks much fancier than the norm, except for the grass growing on the log roof.

Stopping in the Miami town park to use the men's room, I fall into conversation with two guys in their early thirties who oversee the place. They are not sure the Western Trail is marked up ahead. But, if so, it's on the right side of the highway near Seiling. When I tell them my ancestors knew that trail, one says, "I love readin' old-time trail cooking. I've been experimenting with a Dutch oven."

"You gotta be patient," he adds. "With a pot roast, you should figure eight or ten hours. Let the meat cook slowly. Then toss in potatoes and carrots with about forty-five minutes to go. Be careful not to seal the oven. Prop it open a bit so the steam and smoke can get out. I don't understand these boys who just slap a piece of meat on a charcoal fire and do it in a hurry. There's just no flavor. You gotta cook beef a long time for the flavor. Same with son of a bitch stew, I was reading in my book."

"Have you ever eaten that?" I ask.

"No," he replies.

"Well, I have," I say. "It will peel your wallpaper. My grandmother made it and called it 'cowboy stew' because even 'son of a gun' was too close to cussing for her."

I ask, "Are there any old Bugs in Miami?"

"Maybe one or two," the Dutch oven cook says, "but you don't see hardly any on the road these days. Boy, that's the simplest car ever made. Sort of an overgrown lawnmower engine. And designed for common people."

I resist the professorial urge to tell him the historical baggage carried by the German word, *Volk*. He laughs at remembering games of slug bug. Whenever a Bug appeared, the person who yelled "slug bug!" first could strike you on the arm. The first time this happened to him, he lived in Oklahoma, but he was slugged in Texas. He had no idea why.

"Boy, we don't do that in Oklahoma!" he protested when the ritual was explained.

"Well, you're in Texas," the slugger said.

A few miles northeast of Miami, I stop near one of North America's largest Pliocene fossil beds, which oil geologists discovered in 1928. According to the historical marker, paleontologists identified fossil bones of "a prehistoric camel, a kind of antelope, horse, bone-crushing dog, mastodon, and wild pig." Some years later, experts named the fossils' geologic age "Hemphillian," after the name of the county. The Texas Highway Department developed the roadside park another half-mile along, where a marker says the department launched its roadside program in 1933 "to provide safe places for motorists to relax and eat during their travels. Native stone and plantings were often used to create a natural park atmosphere." I reckon New Deal work programs funded the construction of this one, which was completed in time to accommodate travelers on their way to state centennial events in 1936.

The sky is overcast, increasing my comfort and, I hope, reducing the likelihood of afternoon thunderstorms. The Marcy Trail is commemorated where Highway 60 intersects U.S. 83, but the sign should read "Gregg-Marcy Trail" or "Fort Smith-Santa Fe Road."

In 1849, Captain Randolph Marcy and Lieutenant James Simpson of the United States Army Corps of Topographical Engineers guided a wagon train of California-bound emigrants from Fort Smith to Santa Fe. Most of their route had already been mapped by Josiah Gregg, who led a party of traders up the Canadian to Santa Fe in 1839, one of many frontier examples of trade preceding the flag. The primary mission for Marcy and Simpson was surveying and mapping. After America's conquest of the Southwest in the Mexican War, citizens of Fort Smith had ambitious plans for turning their town into a center for emigration and commerce across the Southwest. Their pressure got to the War Department. To the disappointment of such promoters in Arkansas and Texas, however, the Civil War dashed chances for the first transcontinental railroad to come this way. The Pacific Railroad Act, which President Lincoln signed in July 1862, chose the Omaha-San Francisco route.

The highway turns north and downhill into the valley of the Canadian River. Since prehistory, the river has been a trading and hunting route from the Sangre de Cristo Mountains of New Mexico to the Arkansas River, a crow-fly distance of six hundred miles. The Spanish were the first Europeans to explore the Canadian in the sixteenth century. The French followed in the eighteenth century. Americans came after the Louisiana Purchase: Major Stephen Long (1820), who traveled south from Pike's Peak in search of the source of the Red River but got it wrong when he followed the Canadian; Gregg; Lieutenant James Abert in 1845, by order of Captain Frémont at Bent's Fort, before Frémont's third Rockies expedition entered the mountains; Marcy; and cattlemen and other settlers after the army drove the last Comanche and Kiowa from the Panhandle in the Red River War of 1874 to 1875. Before Marcy and America's westward migration, most European and American explorers had followed the Canadian downstream, having found its sources along the eastern slope of the Rockies.

The town of Canadian grew at the site of a ford and early bridge. One historical marker refers to trails, another to the town's most famous son, Robert Young, who was born in 1897 in a house built by the son of Sam Houston, president of the Republic of Texas. Young dropped out of the University of Virginia and, in 1916, married Anita O'Keeffe. That was the same year that her older sister, Georgia, teaching art in Texas, had her abstract drawings shown for the first time in Alfred Stieglitz's gallery in New York City. Young predicted a stock market crash in 1929 and sold in time to make a fortune. He went into railroading, where he advocated modernization and advertised himself as a champion of the people against corporate mismanagement. He used populist slogans such as, "A hog can cross the country without changing trains, but you can't."

With the help of Clint Murchison and Sid Richardson, both Texas oil millionaires, Young gained control of the New York Central Railroad in 1954. Four years later, severely depressed, he killed himself.

A light rain falls as I cross the brown-red river. A turtle has found its way onto the highway beyond the bridge. I remember how Granddad Post said "terrapin," a marvelous word that evokes more than "turtle." For me, the marvel is in the saying. Highway 83 bears northwest toward the Oklahoma Panhandle. I continue northeast on U.S. 60. The rain glistens on grassland that has not been overgrazed.

In Higgins, just before the Oklahoma border, a marker salutes Will Rogers, who moved here from Oklahoma in 1898 when threatened with discipline for pranks in high school. He worked as a cowboy on a nearby ranch, learning the rope tricks that would become his trademark. He died in 1935, the marker says, "during a globe-circling pioneer flight with aviator Wiley Post." Post, my father's cousin, was four years old in 1902, the same year Dad was born, when his family moved from northeast Texas to Taylor County, just south of Haskell. In 1907, Wiley's family moved to Oklahoma before the two cousins knew each other well.

When Jeanie and I registered at a Virginia motel about thirty years ago, the owner saw my name and asked, "Are you any kin to Wiley Post ... you know ... the great pilot who died in that airplane crash in Alaska with his friend ... uh ... what's his name?"

I said I was and the friend was Will Rogers and it happened during the Great Depression. She gave Jeanie a recipe for pokeweed salad.

A reference on another marker to a deadly tornado that killed forty-five townspeople in 1947 reminds me that I'm entering Tornado Alley. But the rain has stopped, and the air doesn't feel right for storms. Across the Oklahoma line, U.S. 60 veers due east, away from the railroad's diagonal toward Kansas. To the south, I make out the Antelope Hills beyond the Canadian River. Like many features of the Western landscape, this one marks tragedy that is invisible to the casual eye. On the Washita River beyond those hills, Black Kettle established a village for his band of Southern Cheyenne four years after the Sand Creek massacre of 1864 in Colorado. He was determined not to let white soldiers surprise them again, but Lieutenant Colonel George Armstrong Custer did so in November 1868. Custer's cavalry marched south from Camp Supply that had just been established on the North Canadian as the base for General Philip Sheridan's winter campaign against tribes of the Southern Plains. To Sheridan's delight, Custer's men killed Black Kettle and his wife on the Washita.

The anfractuous Canadian River has carved deep into the plains of western Oklahoma. With prose more ornate than the landscape but typical of road books in his time, Josiah Gregg marveled at such "magnificent sights" in his journal:

> Here rose a perpendicular cliff, in all the majesty and sublimity of its desolation; there another sprang forward as in the very act of losing its balance and about to precipitate itself upon the vale below. A little further on a pillar with crevices and cornices so curiously formed as easily to be mistaken for

the work of art; while a thousand other objects grotesquely and fantastically arranged; and all shaded in the sky-bound perspective by the blue ridge-like brow of the mesa far beyond the Canadian, constituted a kind of chaotic space where nature seemed to have indulged in her wildest caprices (Gregg 1844).

According to my rough guess, the Western Trail crossing comes sooner than Seiling, so I begin looking for landmarks that my grandfather may have seen, such as rock outcroppings, creeks, and bends in the Canadian. There is still enough open country for me to understand why cowboys moved herds slowly and let them spread out on the mixed grass prairie.

I stop for lunch on the east side of Arnett, home of the Lady Wildcats, the state's Class B basketball champions. The whole town must be at the Circle G Café for its Memorial Day buffet, from kids to great-grandparents. Three boys sip sodas on a bench near the entrance. I pause and nod toward the Bug.

"Have you ever seen a car like that?" I ask.

"Yeah, my dad's got one," says the biggest.

"How old is it?" I ask.

"I dunno, but it's a Baja Buggy," he says.

I ask if they know where the Western Trail comes through. They have no idea what that is.

Inside, the place bustles. I sit at the counter; order a burger, fries, and iced tea; and read the morning edition of the *Daily Oklahoman*. The headline story covers yesterday's disaster in eastern Oklahoma. On the Arkansas River, a few miles upstream from its junction with the Canadian, spans of the I-40 bridge collapsed when a barge hit their supports. Several people died, and traffic has been diverted. On the editorial pages, every essay, summary of editorials from other papers, and letter to the editor is conservative. There isn't a single exception. There are no hints of other points of view except to ridicule them, on subjects like taxation, President Bush, universities, defense policy, business, immigration, and health care. This paper prides itself on being "Oklahoma's state newspaper since 1907." It's far more biased than any paper called "liberal."

The patrons of the Circle G are upright and hard-working. If I needed help, they would give it generously. But what if I told them I'm a liberal Democrat committed to racial equality and social justice? I would stir up more than conservatism, a point of view with which I can argue. I cannot debate the bitter and conspiratorial passion of those conservatives, from farmers to so-called public intellectuals, who would label me disloyal as soon as I breathed the word "liberal."

More than fifty years after Joe McCarthy accused Democrats of treason and more than ten years after the fall of the Soviet Union, an alarming number of Americans call many of their countrymen "un-American," blaming them for every conceivable pain in the body politic. Why do we fear and hate ourselves so?

The waitresses work full tilt. Mine is the least overweight of the crew and has a friendly smile. When she takes my order, I ask, "Can you tell me where the old Western Trail crosses the highway?"

"Yessir, 'bout twenty miles east," she replies. "There's a marker by the highway."

After my first ten or fifteen minutes at the counter, the other customers stop looking me over. I talk funny, sit alone at the counter, and don't belong here, but I'm not going to hurt anyone. The deluxe hamburger is excellent. The lean meat is molded in-house. The trimmings are generous, and the bun is toasted on the grill. The mayo and yellow mustard are right for tradition. There is no burger better than the old-fashioned kind in Oklahoma and Texas.

I continue east in high spirits. What did these meadowlarks call from before there were fences and telephone lines? What are those blue wildflowers clustered along the roadside?

The large stone and brick monument appears on the south side of the highway about four miles west of the village of Vici. The sign reads, "Great Western Trail." To the left of a relief carving of cattle, cowboys, and chuck wagon is this text:

> In 1874, the cattle ranchers of the San Antonio, Texas area began blazing a trail with their large herds of longhorn cattle through western Indian Territory to the railhead at Dodge City, Kansas and to markets beyond into Canada and the Northwest Territories of America. It's estimated that over 11,000,000 head of longhorns passed over this trail on which you now stand. The trail's wake is marked only by a long sequence of depressions worn into the land by the millions of hooves that traveled it. An instance of one of these depressions is visible just to the back of this marker as a long 'U' shaped notch running through the rounded sandy ridge. The Cherokee Strip (located just over one mile north) opened to homesteading in 1893, imposing a barrier that meant the end of the cattle drives.

The text probably exaggerates the number of head, and by 1880 they weren't all longhorns. And the monument does not tell us why the Western Trail replaced trails to the east. As Kansas settlements spread westward, so did the state legislature's quarantine line prohibiting Texas longhorns because of the fever spread by ticks they carried. Texas longhorns were hardy enough to survive it, but northern cattle were not. The Santa Fe Railroad's progress up the Arkansas River reached Dodge in 1872.

Western Trail marker, near Vici, Oklahoma

The song of meadowlark, bobwhite, and field sparrow accentuate the quiet. Herefords stare at me from the notch behind the marker. Beyond them on horseback are my maternal great-grandfather, Walter ("Wat") Fitzgerald; my grandfather, Henry Post; and my great-uncle, Tom Ballard. Wat trailed cattle from south Texas to Kansas until he married in 1878. In 1884, he moved his family north to the good grazing he had found near Rice Springs. I see Henry and Tom more clearly. I sat on their laps. I have a copy of the photo handed down, Henry with a ramrod back and Tom with one leg crooked over the saddle horn. It's right before a drive. I shiver. Lives once lived are still alive. I see a part of myself that is buried.

Aged nineteen and twenty, Henry and Tom rode this way in 1885 and 1886. The best of friends, each married one of the other's younger sisters years later. They either joined or began drives just east of Haskell in Throckmorton County, and they may have called this the Fort Griffin or Dodge City Trail. It had already crossed the Clear Fork of the Brazos River north of Albany at the old Butterfield

Stage crossing near Fort Griffin. The friends headed north about a hundred straight-line miles to Doan's crossing on the Prairie Dog Town Fork of the Red River, north of present-day Vernon. They traveled another one hundred twenty miles due north to this spot, fording the North Fork of the Red River and the Washita River along the way. From here, they continued north and slightly west, fording the North Canadian and the Cimarron before reaching the Arkansas River and Dodge City, roughly another one hundred twenty-five miles.

In all likelihood, the size of the herd was no more than two thousand head. The trail crew numbered at least eleven, with two "point" men leading the herd, two riding "swing" behind them, two at "flank," and two riding "drag" in the rear. Additionally, the crew had a boss, a horse wrangler, and a cook. By the mid-1880s, the chuck wagon had been invented. Some outfits carried tents for rough weather. Dress varied, but the norm was a high-crowned hat (Tom's was black and higher than Henry's), a white cotton shirt with pockets, a dark vest with more pockets, and a multi-purpose bandanna. Heavy black or gray pants, maybe striped "California" pants, were tucked into high-top boots with stitching to decorate and reinforce the tops. Cowboys wore bullhide chaps, or leggings, and drop-shank spurs with rowels that were smaller and blunter than those of the 1870s. They tied their slickers behind the cantle and kept extra clothing, along with other possessions, inside their bedrolls. The bedroll, consisting of a water-proofed outer tarp, quilts or "soogans," and blankets, was stored in the wagon.

Like most drovers, Tom and Henry carried Colt six-shooters and Winchester rifles and rarely used them. They never shot at humans, but they may have had arguments with Kansans who had worn blue in the Civil War. They saw a few pistol-whippings, but no gunfights. They did not fire upon the Kiowa and Cher-okee whose land they traversed in Indian Territory, but they were prepared to offer beef or money for passage. I doubt they needed Army escorts from what had become Fort Supply.

Henry and Tom sang to calm the cattle and pass the time, songs learned or made up on the trail. By 1885, "Bury Me Not on the Lone Prairie (The Dying Cowboy)" had become so common that cowboys rarely sang it. Anything like the "Ogallaly song" (for Ogallala on the South Platte) was always popular because you could change verse and tune as you went along, telling the story of your own drive and its particular characters with whatever came into your head.

In Dodge, the cowboys collected their earnings, about a dollar a day. If the drive averaged ten miles per day for, say six hundred miles, they collected sixty dollars, or ten cents a mile. That money could go in a hurry, especially for young and single cowboys on their first drive who wanted to live up to the campfire stories of older drovers. The usual first purchase was a bath, shave, and haircut, about fifty cents at the barbershop. Some cowboys then bought new clothes. A hat went for twelve dollars, and so did a good pair of pants. Custom-made boots cost between twelve and twenty dollars. Many men went to dance halls or "sporting houses" for a certain kind of woman. All were bashful around "decent" ones. I don't know if Henry and Tom paid for women, but they certainly drank a few whiskeys and replenished their makings for cigarettes.

I don't want to leave this place. I walk up to the fence behind the marker. A couple of heifers approach, probably looking for a handout of cottonseed cake. I talk to them as Henry and Tom would have, softly but with a point to make.

"Hello, ladies," I say. "You lost or lazy? You got some catchin' up to do."

Returning to the Bug, I hear Henry say to Tom, "That boy sure takes good care of his horse."

I have always wished I could have ridden with them.

Many of the stores in Vici are vacant. One of the few signs of youth is a little girl in a long dress, carrying flowers while following her mother to the car they will drive to Sunnyside Cemetery east of town where others have already gathered around flag-bearing graves. Some of those buried here belonged to the unit memorialized by this stretch of Highway 60, the 42nd Rainbow Infantry Division, which defeated the Germans at Saint-Mihiel in 1918 and liberated Dachau concentration camp in 1945.

Those of us who served in the Cold War without firing at the enemy will neither expect nor have flags over our graves. A bitter Vietnam veteran from the baby boomer generation recently told me that my niche group did not deserve any recognition. If we wanted recognition we should be taken out and shot at.

The flags in Vici make his point without insult. Still, age and distance have heightened my awareness of the ironies of the Cold War. Millions of young Americans, whom no one promised that the shooting wouldn't start, helped win America's longest war peacefully. President Bush neglects that lesson in his haste to prove worthy of the generation that fought World War II. If the president makes war on the Axis of Evil, the Cold War is all the more likely to be forgotten, along with my Silent Generation.

The soil here is a darker shade of red than around Miami and Canadian. The area has had more rain than eastern New Mexico or the Texas Panhandle. Near Seiling, the highway takes successive ninety-degree turns, behavior learned when road construction on the Great Plains conformed to the rectangles of farms and townships.

When I cross the North Canadian River, my thoughts wander back to the notch left by herds on the Western Trail. Then I recall still-older depressions, including the Natchez Trace where my brother and I walked southwest of Nashville and the stairs of European cathedrals worn by knees as well as feet.

A few miles before Fairview, the highway drops amid red bluffs and gullies into the valley of the Cimarron River, a descent of eleven hundred feet in the ninety miles since Arnett (at an elevation of twenty-four hundred feet), about twenty-three hundred feet since Amarillo. That's not a dramatic change, but I'm suddenly aware I have left the High Plains. Somewhere this afternoon, I crossed the line, roughly along the hundredth meridian, that divides the Great Plains according to altitude, rainfall, and vegetation. Based on tanking up back in Seiling, I credit the declivity for increasing the Bug's efficiency to thirty-two miles per gallon.

Like the Red and the Canadian, the Cimarron has a wide and sandy bed. The slow current takes several shallow channels. The Cimarron should have paired up with the North Canadian by now. They rise in the northeast corner of New Mexico and come within ten miles of each other in the Oklahoma Panhandle. But the Cimarron holds its own all the way to the Arkansas River, joining it near Tulsa. Red, Washita, Canadian, North Canadian, and Cimarron. That's a lot of crossings going north from Texas, but if Wat, Henry, and Tom had any idea how much territory these rivers drained, they would rather have crossed five than fewer.

I register at a motel in Enid around three thirty. It's too late for Memorial Day ceremonies at Vance Air Force Base. But an American Legion baseball game is in progress on the other side of town, and I see the last five innings of Enid versus Claremore.

The new David Allen Memorial Ballpark is nicely done, user-friendly for both players and spectators. Among these, I do not see any Indian, black, or Hispanic faces. The ballpark is built right over the Chisholm Trail. During the trail's peak years from 1869 to 1875, Texas ranchers moved several million cattle north to railheads on the Kansas Pacific line (Abilene, Salina, Ellsworth, and others) and the Santa Fe (Newton and Great Bend). Inside the stadium, a plaque commemorates the trail, one of numerous markers placed along its Oklahoma course by a local hobbyist. A bunt down the third base line will roll toward Abilene.

Enid loses by only a run, despite seven errors. Will Rogers, a native of Claremore, would have found the right words to amuse both teams. The man seated to my left, who is about my age, warms to me as we talk about the weather, including the five inches of rain this month that broke more than a yearlong drought.

We also talk about baseball, my trip, local schools, and his grandson, who singles sharply to right. He tells me David Allen was a popular Enid high school student and excellent ballplayer who died in an automobile accident at the age of sixteen. The whole town pitched in to fund the stadium.

"Nice talking with you," I say as we get up to leave after the last out.

"You have a safe journey, you hear?" he says.

He means it, and his accent is thick Oklahoma-Texas.

I poke around town on the way back to the motel. Enid was founded in the 1890s when the Cherokee Strip (or Outlet) was opened to homesteading. Some of the largest houses look like oil money in the 1920s. People are friendly. They obey speed limits. Gas costs thirty cents less per gallon than in southern California. The Railroad Museum of Oklahoma is closed on the holiday, and it won't open before I leave tomorrow. I pass a small theater called "The Gaslight." Its marquee reads, "Free Shakespeare." Good idea, I think, do it!

Back in my room, I shuffle notes and fold maps. Since leaving Claremont, I have compiled a list of what is new on the road compared to 1963 when I drove my first Bug across America. Here is what I have jotted down: containers on trains and semis; outlet malls; wind turbines to generate electricity; desert suburbs with hulking houses; SUVs and colossal RVs; Japanese and Korean cars; cell phones; unleaded gas; seatbelts required; cat's eyes; "no problem," "you got it," and "like"; giant feedlots; interstate highways in need of repair; water-saving shower heads; espresso, al dente pasta, Dijon mustard, and sushi; shopping malls and gangs of fast-food joints on the outskirts of towns; satellite dishes; and no hitchhikers. "Burma Shave" signs have vanished and so have cabooses (except in Socorro). Only a few cafés still have signs with the simple commandment, "Eat."

After supper, the Weather Channel reports hail up to the size of tennis balls in the Texas Panhandle. I call Jeanie and tell her the storms haven't hit me, that everything is going well, and that the Bug's fine. I had a great time at Toad Hall and watched a baseball game on the Chisholm Trail. I describe finding the Western Trail.

I say, "It's spine-tingling stuff, and I still feel it."

"I can hear it in your voice," she replies. "You sound happy."

"I am. I miss you, but I'm glad I'm doing this."

"I know."

In truth, I haven't thought much about Jeanie all day or about the reunion ahead in Wisconsin. I have been carried away by trails: the Santa Fe, Marcy, Canadian River, Western, and Chisholm. The feeling surprises me, and it doesn't go away with the day's driving. Singly, historical markers have always taken me to other times. Rivers, like railroad crossings, have sent me in both directions to other places. But today's trails and rivers have opened the West as I have never seen it before. It is a whole made up of spaces, lines, places, and movement. The parts are often at odds, but nothing is random or isolated. Divides between drainages have purpose. Rivers and trails have good reasons to be where they are, as do we to remember them. They are pathways connecting everything: land, history, and us.

The title of Bruce Chatwin's *The Songlines* refers to the tracks that Australian Aborigines inherited from legendary ancestors:

> who had wandered over the continent in the Dreamtime, singing out the name of everything that crossed their path—birds, animals, plants, rocks, waterholes—and so singing the world into existence.

Aborigines "could not imagine territory as a block of land hemmed in by frontiers: but rather as an interlocking network of 'lines' or 'ways through'" (Chatwin 1987).

For several days, I have been singing out names as I drove an old Bug slowly over America with windows open and no radio. Today, rivers came alive. An aboriginal path along one of them turned into a major artery of Euro-American discovery. A generation of cowboys crossed the open range in the brief interval between opening and fencing. I can see the Great Plains under a sequence of historical transparencies. The land is hunted and explored in dotted lines from every direction before solid thoroughfares of emigration cross and fill it from the east. Trails follow and ford streams, deflect up and down the eastern front of the Rockies, locate headwaters and divides, and take short cuts and diagonals. They fan out, turn into wagon roads, provide routes for railroads and highways, and eventually interlace the West. Many natural features still exist that the Native Americans or Europeans named to mark the lines they walked. People are leaving and returning, discovering and retracing, trading and fighting, and homesteading and moving through. I'm free to stop at any overlay and imagine myself on the plains at that moment, alone or with company.

I stopped for the longest time today in 1885 on the Western Trail. That is family. But more than inheritance and history is working on me. As a boy in Madison, I sought distant neighborhoods and open country, on foot or bike. I was either with friends for the fun of exploring or alone after embarrassments at school or when I missed my mother badly and kept it inside. The boy's impulses grew into the man's enjoyment of wildflowers, wilderness, getting away, and peace of mind. The need has remained the same. It is the freedom to leave the everyday clamor behind, to wander and mend.

This is a rare and fragile kind of freedom. It lets you lose yourself while reading the country. It requires some degree of uncertainty, the possibility of not knowing where you are or what path to take. This freedom is threatened by indifference, cell phones, global positioning technology, and loss of open space. Tonight, I understand how John Muir felt after "another glorious Sierra day" in June 1869:

> Life seems neither long nor short, and we take no more heed to save time or make haste than do the trees and stars. This is true freedom, a good practical sort of immortality … (Muir 1911).

CHAPTER 3

▼

ARROW ROCK

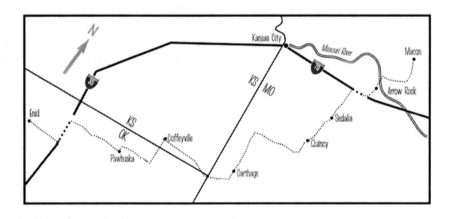

Tuesday, May 28

As I load for departure, a guy my age parks his Mercedes next to me and asks about the Bug's age and horsepower.

"I had a '61," he says. "Loved it. I'd like to buy a zippy car for my granddaughter, but I don't think old Bugs are zippy enough for freeways."

"You may be right," I admit. "It's been scary on the interstates, but you might have a look at what VW calls the New Beetle."

"I'll do that," he says.

The Weather Channel forecasts heavy thunderstorms for northeastern Oklahoma and southwestern Missouri. I take U.S. 64 and aim for Ponca City. I'll decide there whether to turn north along the Arkansas River or continue east to Pawhuska to see the Osage tribal capital and museum. The vastness of America, which normally hits me as I drive west from the Mississippi River, strikes this morning on my way east into the heartland. The look and feel of the large fields of green is Midwest, not High Plains, yet it's still a long way to the Mississippi. Insects splatter my windshield more in an hour here than in a day in New Mexico, suggesting the usefulness of a bug-splat guide to America. Size, number, and color will tell you location, rainfall, and soil.

Turning north onto I-35, I think its way south to Austin, where we could hear its noise from our house if the wind was wrong. A New Beetle overtakes me. The young man driving it gives no greeting. He has no sense of history, no class. After crossing the Salt Fork of the Arkansas River, I head east, again on U.S. 60. A sign points to the town of Tonkawa, named after the Indians who helped whites settle Haskell and neighboring counties in Texas before the tribe's small remnant of less than a hundred was relocated to Indian Territory. A marker off the highway notes that Chief Joseph and his band of Nez Perce were moved to this area in 1879, two years after their surrender at Bear Paws, Montana. They tried, unhappily and unsuccessfully, to become self-sufficient through agriculture. In 1885, the federal government finally shipped them to northern Washington; Joseph had requested his tribe's homeland in Idaho.

One look at the huge oil refinery near Ponca City is enough to discourage me from stopping there. After running into Chief Joseph, I don't want to visit another town made overnight by the land rush into the outlet that the Cherokee Nation, having suffered through the Trail of Tears in the 1830s, owned in perpetuity for hunting. Cherokee from Georgia, Nez Perce from the Snake River country, Ponca from the Niobrara River in northern Nebraska, and Tonkawa from Texas, I'm in the land of exile for tribes from all over America. The policy that put them here was variously called removal, relocation, resettlement, and rescue. The government's ostensible goal was to preserve and civilize Indians, but its underlying purpose, pushed especially by frontier states and by squatters beyond state borders, was to take land for a population on the move. Among the beneficiaries were my ancestors who made their way west from Kentucky, Virginia, North Carolina, and Georgia, and the southern families who gave their Anglo-Saxon names to the counties around Amarillo. That history decides me on Pawhuska. I need the Osage museum for what it meant to be compelled, betrayed, and civilized.

The Arkansas River is full and swift southeast of Ponca City, even though I'm only a few miles downstream from the dam that holds Kaw Lake. The land is still quite flat, having changed from crops to large pastures of even brighter green. Most of the oil wells scattered about are not pumping. It starts to rain, evoking mixed memories of loneliness and companionship under the tapping on homes, cars, and tents. I can't separate the rain from the memory or the mood. Looking at the map cheers me up. The Tallgrass Prairie Preserve north of Pawhuska sounds like my kind of conservation.

Damn! The Bug stalls about ten miles west of Pawhuska. The gas gauge shows nearly a quarter of a tank on hand, but I gamble on its having gone wrong. Rather than flag anyone down on a road that feels deserted all of a sudden, I grab my plastic, one-gallon gas container and start walking back to the white frame house I passed minutes ago. It looks like it's about a mile. The rain is warm, but I turn my face away from the southerly wind. Over my shoulder, the Bug grows smaller and more vulnerable. Ahead, a car doesn't slow down, and I don't signal. I hope the driver blames me, not the Bug, for the caricature of what can happen when you drive an old foreign car in rural mid-America. Contingencies come to mind, running the gamut from a slight delay to the Bug's long confinement while I bus or fly to Wisconsin. It doesn't occur to me that I should own a cell phone. The single-stroke clunk of an oil well pump sounds like the motor of the small Greek fishing boat that two Oxford friends and I hired to see Mount Athos forty years ago. The boatman had a thick black moustache. His name was Euripides.

The white house shows no sign of life until a dog barks furiously from the back porch. A man of about fifty comes out. Unshaven and yawning, he's wearing work pants and an undershirt. He quiets his dog and reckons I'm not dangerous.

"What can I do for ya?" he asks.

Soon, we are talking in front of his shed while he fills my container.

"I thought we got smarter as we got older," I say, my summation of running out of gas.

He laughs. "I'm the same way. Worked with horses all my life. Used to be able to do just about anything with 'em. Now, well, ya know, not gettin' any younger."

He says Pawhuska is an interesting town, but he doesn't add anything complimentary about the Osage.

"You prob'ly know Ben Johnson came from here," he says. "Well, there's a lotta cowboy actors did. The old 101 Ranch near Ponca City sent a Wild West show all around the country and a lotta their cowboys and Indians wound up in the movies. Tom Mix worked at the 101 for a while. Hollywood needed cowboys in those early days. Real ones, boys who knew what they were doin' with horses and cattle."

"Why did so many come from this part of Oklahoma?" I ask.

"I'll tell ya why. 'Cause this is bluestem grass country. From here on up into Kansas and Nebraska. Wonderful grass for cattle. And for cowboys."

I recount my grandmother Ada Fitzgerald Rike's story about the grasses she saw as a little girl when her family arrived in Haskell County. "High enough to brush a horse's belly," she'd say.

The rain has let up, and I want to move on. "What do I owe you?" I ask.

"Nothing. I figure you'd do the same for me," he replies.

I insist, and he accepts two bucks.

"But this ain't for the gas, okay?"

"That's right," I reply.

We shake hands on it.

Partway back to the Bug, I hitch a ride from a highway patrolman, a kindly sort who waits while I funnel the gallon into the tank with a rolled-up tourist brochure from Enid. The engine starts, but the patrolman offers to follow me to Pawhuska just in case the fuel gauge isn't the real culprit. As we approach town, I motion him around and hit the horn. He waves.

"Welcome to Pawhuska, The Heart of the Tallgrass Prairie," reads the sign at the western edge of town.

The deciduous foliage tells me I'm now in the eastern, wettest zone of the grasslands that stretch from the Rockies to the Ozarks. I fill the tank at the first service station. A pickup hauling a long horse trailer pulls in. The rain has let up, but fresh mud streaks the truck and trailer down low. The horse inside the trailer is a pretty brown, alert, ears pointed forward. The driver looks like the late Ben Johnson, the most authentic cowboy actor I ever saw. He comes over, and we begin talking about Bugs. He and a buddy owned one.

"We rolled it back in the seventies," he says. "Musta been a '69 or '70 'cause we rolled it in '73 or '74." He shakes his head and chuckles. "Boy, your Bug is the nicest one I've seen in a long time. You drivin' it all the way to Wisconsin?" he asks.

"Yeah, plan to."

"Well, you just stick to that plan. I like that," he says.

"What sort of town is Pawhuska?"

"Oh, it's awright. That Osage museum's pretty interestin'. Worth a look. But I don't think you'll be spendin' a lotta time in Pawhuska."

His smile and drawl are Ben Johnson, too. Must be the bluestem grass, I guess. He excuses himself to go into the station. "Be seein' ya," he says, just like Johnson to Alan Ladd in *Shane*.

I top off the tank for the first time since leaving Claremont. Until now, I have settled for what I presumed was almost full when the pump shut off automatically. That was the source of my mistake, compounded by my casual habit of ignoring the gauge when in doubt of its accuracy and computing the remainder according to my estimate of miles per gallon since the last fill-up. When I thought I had ten gallons after filling up, I actually had between eight and nine. I draw several conclusions. For the old, wide neck of the Bug's tank, I can't trust the shutoff point of new pumps that are designed for unleaded gas and environmental regulations. My average between Amarillo and Enid was not thirty-two miles per gallon. It was more like twenty-eight. I should have bought gas in Ponca City. Since my average for the whole trip is less than thirty, the new engine is either too rich or has intestinal trouble. Finally, I screwed up.

I turn opposite the stone city hall, formerly the Osage Tribe Council, and drive uphill to a cluster of buildings, including the Osage Tribal Museum, Bureau of Indian Affairs' Osage Agency Building, and Pawhuska Indian Health Center. Cardinals call "what-cheer" from trees on the hill, a particular sound of many summers spent in Madison and Austin. A marker outside the museum commemorates the site of the "million-dollar elm." In the shade of that tree, oil barons like Getty, Sinclair, and Phillips bid for Osage leases in the early twentieth century.

The museum building, constructed of Oklahoma sandstone in 1874, originally housed a school, chapel, and dormitory. Opened in 1938 and remodeled twice since then, the museum has galleries and a gift shop. The artifacts and photographs include other tribes from the former Indian Territory. I wander into the large, adjacent room that contains a library and archives. Stopping at a desk to inquire about the Tallgrass Prairie Preserve leads to a two-hour conversation with Pauline Jones.

Her tribal name is Sacred Eagle Woman. She is Osage with a Jones dash of Welsh. A plump and graying seventy-one, she has six children, thirteen grandchildren, and eight nieces and nephews from a sister who was her only family left before she died in 1985. To my surprise, Pauline frowns on the prairie preserve.

"I don't like the way they moved in and did that," she says. "It's a silly idea. They won't be able to connect all the grassland they want to from Nebraska down to Texas and let those animals go back and forth. Just too many towns and farms now. It's the idea of coast people. Coast people feel stuck out there, so they come here and tell us what to do. Besides, I'll bet most of the really tall grass is Johnson grass."

She gives me a short course on the Osage. This is not officially a reservation. Anyone can buy and sell the land in Osage County, but the mineral rights belong to the Osage themselves. The tribe's origins are unclear, but tradition places them along the Ohio and Wabash Rivers before the time of Columbus. They migrated slowly west into Kansas and Missouri. By the seventeenth century, they occupied a large area between the Missouri and Arkansas Rivers.

"We policed a lot of territory," she says.

In the eighteenth and early nineteenth centuries, the Osage let whites travel through their lands so long as they kept moving. If the intruders started clearing brush and showing other signs of setting up permanent camp, "some ended up dead." The Osage shifted southwest in the nineteenth century through a series of treaties and capitulations. They finally arrived here around 1870. The tribe made money off the sale of lands as they moved, and they have profited from oil royalties since the twenties. She argues that's a major reason why other tribes dislike the Osage.

"We want to get along," she asserts, "but, wherever we go, the others just don't like us. I guess I don't blame them. We're the wealthiest tribe in the United States. We have been lucky, blessed, just by accident, with land, mineral rights, oil, and so on."

"Didn't some tribes resent the Osage for providing scouts to the army?" I ask.

"Well, yes, that's true," she replies.

Pauline corroborates evidence in the museum and gift shop that whites came in droves after the discovery of oil. Many exploited the Osage, even to the extreme of marrying into Indian families and then murdering them to acquire sole ownership of the oil income. Other schemes included pumping oil for longer than the prescribed periods and not reporting the surplus.

She continues, "Now white developers want to build more lakes up here. They don't consider water a mineral, so we don't have the rights to it like we do to what's more than two or three feet below the surface of the land. If we could figure out a way to have water declared a mineral, we could tax their use of it."

She throws me a shrewd look with a twinkle in her eye.

Pauline regrets that so many Native American tribes have died out.

"Congress can decide whether to create a tribe or end one." She snaps her fingers. "Technically, no matter how long we have been around, Congress could, just like that [*snap*], decide to end our tribal status. They're only a few thousand of us left. But we're doing more and more to teach our language to our children in school, something I wasn't allowed when I was a girl."

She faults whites for double standards and misguided paternalism in the old days.

"They did nothing if one Indian killed another," she says. "They stalled if a white killed an Indian, but yelled 'law and order!' if an Indian killed a white."

Whites prohibited tribal forms of religious worship and took Indian children away for what they regarded as proper schooling. She's glad she had to learn English, but she wishes she spoke fluent Osage.

"I would," she says with an edge in her voice, "if educational policy for Indians then had been as generous as it is now for Spanish-speaking students."

Wistfully, she says some of her grandchildren don't look Indian at all. "The only way I can tell they are part Osage is they call me Grandma," she says.

She's sad that young Indians have so few job opportunities here and lose touch with the tribe if they leave for work elsewhere.

"If you are an Osage working in Oklahoma City," I ask, "could you call a local tribal office to ask for help?"

"Unfortunately, no," she replies. "But Osage do get together wherever they live. There's a group in northern California and another in southern California. They stay in touch and meet at least once a year. But, as far as I know, there's no office or central telephone number."

Pauline was on her own after having her fourth child.

"I went back to college then," she says. "It was tough, but my kids and I made it. I don't believe in all this complaining about things being tough. If something's tough and you don't think you can do it, well, just decide you can and go ahead, and if you run into obstacles then find a way to get around them."

As a child, Pauline read everything she could get her hands on. She would hide when her sister wanted to play. "We had a two-story house over there," she says. "It wasn't hard to find a place to read by myself."

"I studied art and history," she says. "And I've done a little teaching. I think it's awful when teachers lord it over their students and tell them they're dumb and can't learn. A lot of our kids are smart."

I tell her I'm a retired history professor.

"Sometimes, I thought I would like to be a professor," she says.

"Well, I think it's overrated," I reply. "Good teachers in grade schools, high schools, and community colleges are more important for the country than college professors."

Sacred Eagle Woman, Pawhuska, Oklahoma

Pauline says nothing, but I can tell that she agrees with me. She has a warm smile and quick mind. I like her way of storytelling with purpose, detail, and wit.

"You know, I'm proud of our culture," she says. "It's a great culture, just as great as the Incas or Aztecs. But we pass it down differently. We don't have big temples and carvings. We pass ours down with stories, dances, and ceremonies. You can't understand our culture unless you get inside the Indian mind. Very few white people can do that. The Western way of thinking is different. Take colors, for example. I'm all mixed up about colors because I learned in white schools from white teachers. I learned that certain colors don't go together. That's Western. But we Osage have a wonderful way of looking at colors. You can mix anything you want, and it works. You don't have to worry about what's compatible."

She tells me that there are two groups of Osage: the sky people and the earth people. They don't intermarry.

"Isn't it wonderful that you can go way back and find the same thing in older civilizations? In fact, cannibals in Borneo knew they should avoid intermarriage with blood kin. What nationality are you?" she asks.

"Well, American."

"No, no, I mean what's your bloodline?" she explains.

"A mixture of things from Europe: mainly English, Scottish, Irish, German. But I don't think of that as bloodline."

"Well, it is."

Some of the comments that whites make while visiting the museum amuse Pauline.

"They ask 'Where are the pots?' and 'Why don't the Osage make pots?' I say, 'We stopped making them long ago because we preferred the pots we got from French and English and American traders.' One woman asked, 'What do you wear when you dance?' I said, 'What dance do you want me to do?' She dropped the subject. Another woman, a cosmetologist, saw pictures of Indian women a hundred years ago and said, 'Their skin is so wrinkled. They didn't take care of it.' I wanted to be angry at her, but I didn't. It wouldn't have been right. But you have to understand that it was different back then. When people say 'smelly Indian,' they should know that Indians covered themselves with grease, usually bear grease, to ward off mosquitoes and other bugs."

She describes how Osage men used to bathe in creeks, no matter what the weather. Families taught children to tolerate icy water so boys could prepare themselves for the manly custom. She had heard about a man called "Bear Legs" who walked to the creek clad only in his leather G-string. He'd hang it on a bush while he bathed. Some white boys began regular snooping. One day they grabbed his G-string from the bush and stretched it all out of shape.

"You could do that with leather, you know," she says. "Well, the story got around and amused the Osage as much as the whites." She grins.

Someone begins playing a rag tune loudly on the piano over in the corner. We move to a bench at the front entrance of the museum. Soon, one of Pauline's many cousins greets us as he walks in.

"I just dropped by in case you need any more relics for that case over there," he says to another cousin, who runs the museum.

Pauline apologizes and says she has business to attend to. I thank her for her kindness and ask if I may take her picture. She consents, but, as soon as I aim my camera, her expression turns somber. It's probably just camera shyness because the warmth returns as we say good-bye.

I point toward the street and say, "That's my Bug."

"Yes, I see that," Pauline replies.

She looks at me, smiles, tilts her head ever so slightly, and then looks again at the Bug and back at me. As I walk to the car, I wish I knew what Sacred Eagle Woman saw. It's her tribal name in my wish. I know she's looking beyond my résumé.

The center of Pawhuska has been designated on the National Historic Register. It's sad that so many of the old brick buildings are boarded-up and crumbling. The Bluestem Restaurant advertises biscuits and gravy for two dollars, but I decide to skip lunch and snack in the car. Two guys at the museum said they had just come from the prairie preserve. They were disappointed that the grass is not so tall.

"Maybe it's still too early in the growing season," they guessed.

I decide to move on and make some distance before it rains again. I drive northeast through rolling country of hardwood and lush grass. I left home with some dried apricots, but they have begun to ferment. The new chemistry causes me to sneeze. I don't stop in Bartlesville, Phillips Petroleum's town, to take a close look at the green and copper high-rise that one doesn't expect to find in northeastern Oklahoma. It's Price Tower, which Frank Lloyd Wright designed in 1929. It was constructed in 1956 as oil headquarters for H. C. Price Company, which was later sold to Phillips Petroleum. Now it's about to become a fancy hotel.

Having taken U.S. 60 most of the way since Phoenix, I feel disloyal turning north on U.S. 75, but I want to visit towns in southeast Kansas that preceded Abilene as railheads for Texas cattle.

"Leaving Cherokee Nation." The sign north of Bartlesville jars me.

I know so little about the Cherokee, their sovereignty and constitution, their removal to concentration camps (in all but name), their desperate trek to Indian Territory, their punishment for supporting slavery and the Confederacy, and the treaties forcing them to open their lands to other tribes after the Civil War. Theirs is perhaps the saddest of all the forced migrations of Native Americans. Last night's enthusiasm about freedom now seems foolish. Sacred Eagle Woman has given me not only good bearings for the Osage, but also a good measure of my ignorance.

Across into Kansas, I turn east on U.S. 166 and stop in Coffeyville, the westernmost terminus of the Shawnee Trail, also known as the Kansas Trail and Osage Trace. As early as the 1840s, Texans drove small herds of cattle northeast to St. Louis along or near established trails that settlers had followed southwest from Missouri and Arkansas. By the 1850s, the main trail forded the Red River near today's Preston (north of Sherman), entered Choctaw and Chickasaw lands, crossed the Canadian and Arkansas Rivers, passed near Fort Gibson, and followed the Spring and Neosho (or Grand) Rivers into southeastern Kansas.

One of the most notable of the early trail bosses was not Texan. Thomas Candy Ponting, son of an English farmer, had migrated to Illinois and driven cattle north for sale to Wisconsin settlers. In 1853, with that market drying up, Ponting and his partner rode to Texas, bought cattle, and trailed them back to Illinois. Not satisfied with the sale of most of their herd in the spring of 1854, they continued east with over a hundred head. After a pioneering drive on land and on railroad cars not meant for livestock, they sold their cattle at the Hundred Street Market in New York. We owe one of our best Western tales to an Englishman who trailed Texas cattle to Manhattan.

Later in 1854, Texas herds were moving north along the eastern edge of the Kansas Territory to the Kansas City area. The stream of emigrants embarking on the Santa Fe and Oregon (California) Trails needed cattle, and Missouri farmers along the Kansas border had begun turning back Texas longhorns that carried "Texas fever." The drives became shorter when railroads building south from eastern Kansas reached Baxter Springs, Chetopa, and Coffeyville around 1870. These were new towns of the post-Civil War boom that competed for cattle as well as trade with Indian Territory. But by this time, the Shawnee Trail was already losing traffic to the Chisholm Trail further west.

Coffeyville is most famous for the Dalton Raid of October 1892 when three Dalton brothers and two associates attempted to rob two banks simultaneously. Their plan miscarried. Eight people died in the ensuing gun battle, including four of the outlaws. One of the two banks, the Condon, is the centerpiece of historical preservation that tempts me to hang around, but Joplin has planted itself in my afternoon mind as day's end.

East of Coffeyville, I cross the Verdigris River, a major tributary in the Arkansas River's watershed that extends into southeastern Kansas and southwestern Missouri. The size and arrangement of farms suggests Iowa and Wisconsin.

In 1870, weeks after coming into being, the Missouri, Kansas & Texas Railroad built a line through Chetopa and hit the Indian Territory border a few miles south of town, thus winning the race to capture sole right-of-way through the Cherokee Nation. The Katy laid track over or near the Shawnee Trail all the way to Texas. U.S. 69 now follows the same route.

The Neosho River east of Chetopa is full, swift, and about a hundred yards wide. A half hour later, I enter Baxter Springs, where John Baxter settled in 1855, sold staples to Texas cowboys, built corrals, expanded his cabin into a tavern, and died in 1859 before there was a town to name after him. Rebel guerillas under the notorious William Quantrill attacked the Union garrison here in 1863 on their way south after raids that included the massacre of more than one hundred fifty citizens of Lawrence, a staunchly abolitionist town. The bitter conflict over Kansas statehood had already bloodied the Kansas-Missouri border country before the Civil War.

I cross the Spring River and veer southeast into heavy rain, having decided to bypass Joplin on I-44 and to spend the night in Carthage. Both cities were on Dad's usual route between Madison and Haskell. We would drive south from Iowa through central or western Missouri; hit U.S. 66 at Rolla, Springfield, or Carthage; and take that road into Oklahoma. In those days before interstates, car travel introduced you to the towns in which you dined and slept. For entertainment, we had parks and movie theaters as well as train stations. I remember having breakfast in the coffee shop of a redbrick hotel on a rainy morning in Joplin. Right now, rain pelts the Bug. The wipers can't keep up when semis add thick fountains of spray.

Just before I exit on U.S. 71, a sign promotes "Precious Moments" in Carthage. "Visit the Precious Moments Super Store!" it exhorts. Now what is that all about? There's more on U.S. 71, where a sign reads, "Tour Victorian Wedding Island at Precious Moments, 2 miles."

I duck into a modest motel on the south side of Carthage, managed by a Pakistani who once lived in the San Francisco Bay area and misses his former home. He recommends the Ranch House Restaurant, where I find the barbecued ribs good and the bonhomie more contagious than at eateries in Oklahoma. I exchange smiles with apparent regulars at neighboring tables who know I'm not one of them. They look confident that drinking wine or beer with dinner will not send them to hell. They confirm my hunch that each state has a personality that shows as soon as you cross the border.

I telephone Jeanie before hitting the sack. She laughs at my running out of gas. "So unlike you," she says.

She likes the sound of Sacred Eagle Woman.

"Yeah, but I missed you today," I say. "Must be the rain, pud."

"I love you, mud," she replies.

We courted in the rain at Stanford, and we weren't always mindful of the puddles. The nicknames have been dormant for many years.

Wednesday, May 29

The morning is overcast and humid, but the rain has stopped. An SUV in the next parking space dwarfs my Bug and carries a sign saying, "Jesus, don't leave Earth without Him." Or without your SUV, I pray.

Over coffee and donuts in the motel lobby, the manager's nephew recommends Precious Moments Chapel as the most interesting thing around Carthage. I guess I'll have a look. Sounds kitsch, but what the hell, it's America.

The brochure he hands me changes my mind: "Fountain of Angels Show! Cubby Bear's RV Park, Grandpa's Island, and the inspirational illustrations of Samuel J. Butcher, the creator of Precious Moments art and figurines." The art is sloe eye and corn syrup. No! I can't do it! I drive into Carthage.

There are spectacular Victorian mansions on South Main and Grand Avenue, some of them constructed of local gray stone. They reflect the town's recovery after the Civil War, thanks largely to lead and zinc mining. The styles are eclectic: Italianate; Romanesque; Chateauesque; Queen Anne; Georgian; Victorian Vernacular (I like the alliteration), one called the "Dr. Post House"; and Classical Revival.

I park in the Jasper County Courthouse Square. The massive, turreted courthouse was built of Carthage stone in Romanesque style in the mid-1890s. Many of the buildings around the square date from the same decade and have ornamental facades. It's a most attractive ensemble.

As I look for a good camera angle, a car honks, and the driver waves. He parks, joins me on the sidewalk, and introduces himself.

"Hi, I'm Dick Ferguson," he says. "Saw your camera."

He is eighty-two, slim, and a little under six feet tall. He wears glasses, and his hair is gray. Judging from his facial lines, he seems affable by nature. A small emblem on his jacket identifies him as a veteran of Pearl Harbor. He was in the coastal artillery there and lost several buddies.

"Those damned Japs," he blurts. "I'm sorry, but I still carry that with me. It seems like it happened yesterday. I have given talks about it. When my generation dies, there'll be nobody left to tell about it."

He looks pleased when I tell him that my boyhood admiration for his GI Generation led to my serving in the artillery in the Cold War.

I explain why I'm here, and Dick leads me down the sidewalk to the office of the Carthage Chamber of Commerce, which he once presided over. Inside, he grabs a few brochures and introduces me as "a man from Wisconsin who's on an odyssey." I'm grateful no one asks me what he means because I'm not sure what I'm on.

Dick has led tours of Carthage since retirement, including eleven Belgian doctors who were driving Route 66 on Harleys. When he bragged about the age of the courthouse, one of the Belgians laughed and said he lived in a three-hundred-year-old apartment. Dick moved here about fifty years ago.

"I'm not a native, but I sure feel like one," he says when we are back outside.

Then he switches into guide mode. Behind us is the site of the hotel and bar owned by the father of Belle Starr, who grew up in Carthage before the Civil War made her a Confederate spy and outlaw. Leggett and Platt, Inc., invented the coil bedspring in Carthage, and bedsprings are still made here.

"We have a cheese factory with home base in your Wisconsin," he says. "Makes a lot for the fast-food business. Mostly mozzarella, I think. We also have a Butterball turkey factory. Oh, and there's a Vietnamese preacher here, and one day every summer, fifty thousand Vietnamese come to Carthage for a religious retreat. You can never tell about these small towns."

When I mention driving through Carthage on Highway 66 with my father in the forties, Dick says, "Well, you would have been a couple of blocks over that way. There's an old motel over there you should see, Boots Motel. Clark Gable stayed there when he came through Carthage back in the late thirties and early forties. I wish I could tell you that's where he composed the line, 'Frankly, my dear, I don't give a damn.'"

I thank him for his help and compliment him on looking so fit. "You and your fellow veterans are redefining what it means to be in your eighties," I say.

"Well, thanks," he replies. "You know, the time is going too fast."

We shake hands. I know that I'll not see Dick or Sacred Eagle Woman again. Road trips cheat you that way.

Wednesday is market day at the curb around the courthouse, but only a few farmers have set up tables. The father of an Amish family explains there has been too much rain for vegetables. A plaque on the courthouse lawn recalls the Osage War of 1837 when state militia forced the Indians from this region. Another tablet commemorates the Battle of Carthage on July 5, 1861. It salutes the Missouri State Guard for pushing the Union forces out of town. In the small museum inside the courthouse, I admire a German mine-thrower (*Minenwerfer*) from World War I. A security guard comes over to chat, and I reveal my interest in Germany.

"Did you know," he asks, "that Hitler called General Motors during the Second World War and placed an order for fifty tanks? Said 'Don't bother to send 'em. I'll be over to pick 'em up sometime soon.'"

I have heard many myths while teaching German history for thirty years, but that's a new one.

I find the Boots Motel on old Route 66 three blocks west of the square. I can see Dad, John, and me driving past the place in the cream-colored Chevy. I don't remember staying at Boots, but we stopped at many like it.

The sun pokes through as I arrive at the Battle of Carthage State Historic Site, a small park. I'm the only one here, apart from cardinals, chickadees, robins, blue jays, and Carolina wrens. This first significant land battle of the Civil War began in the morning several miles north of Carthage, swept through town in house-to-house fighting, and ended in the evening with both sides claiming victory. The park's displays emphasize Missouri's conditional unionism as a border state. Although slavery was legal, the majority of citizens, especially the large German American population of St. Louis, opposed both slavery and secession. But the secessionist minority, which included the state militia as well as pro-slavery border ruffians who had already fought against free-soil Kansans, was large enough to guarantee a Missouri civil war within the national one.

My great-grandfather, William Curtis Ballard, belonged to the minority. He and his younger brother, Gaines, the surname of their paternal grandmother's Virginia family, were born on a farm near Cape Girardeau in the mid-1830s. They were sons of James Ballard, who migrated west from Kentucky after service in the War of 1812, and Rachel Hitt of Cape Girardeau County. William married Artamissa Boyd in 1856. They had eight children: two before the Civil War, one during the war, and five after the war, including my great-uncles, Tom (1866) and John (1872), and my grandmother, Rachel Post (1874).

During the war, William rose to the rank of major in General John Sappington Marmaduke's cavalry division, part of General Sterling Price's Missouri militia. A portion of Ballard's Civil War journal, printed in a Ballard family genealogy, covers Price's 1864 expedition into Missouri from Arkansas, where Missouri's Confederate governor and legislature had set up a government in exile after the Battle of Carthage. Price admired—and coordinated his movements with—Missouri guerillas like Quantrill, the James brothers, the Youngers, and "Bloody Bill" Anderson. They encouraged him to believe that Union forces in Missouri were weak and the state was ripe for Confederate picking. Ballard's entry for August 30 begins, "Started on the great raid to Missouri."

But the optimism was misplaced. Missourians did not flock to Price's cause, and Union troops fought better than Price expected them to. On October 25, after four days of constant fighting on the retreat south from the Kansas City area, Ballard wrote the following about what became known as the Battle of Mine Creek (Kansas):

> We was soon surrounded and had to seek safety in flight. About this time the artillery was limbered up and all started toward the branch [Mine Creek] in wild confusion. At the time the scene was the worst could be imagined. There was Rebels, Yankees, men afoot, and men running back and artillery all mixed up together and fleeing in the wildest state of excitement, the enemy had possession of nearly all the crossings. After we got across the branch there was a great many officers trying to rally the men but few could be rallied. We fell back about 3 miles. We lost our artillery and a great many prisoners. At 3 o'clock they again came up with our rear but we held them in check until sundown. Then we stopped one hour to get something to eat, packed and burnt our train and started at 2 o'clock A.M.

On October 26, Ballard wrote, "We camped on Spring River near Carthage, that distance this day was 63 miles" (Draper 1979).

Marmaduke had been captured at Mine Creek. Price continued the retreat to Arkansas. Confederate regulars never again threatened Missouri.

Like many Confederate veterans, William Curtis Ballard migrated to Texas and brought the creed of the lost cause with him. So did my great-grandfather Post, who told my father that corn popping in the fireplace sounded like muskets at Shiloh. A lithograph of Lee and his generals hung over Granddad Post's oak bureau in Haskell. My great-uncle, "Bud" Rike, gave me his books on the Civil War when I was in high school. Among them were the memoirs of Lee and Longstreet, Jefferson Davis' *Rise and Fall of the Confederate Government* (1881), E. A. Pollard's *Southern History of the War* (1866), and a flattering account of Quantrill by one of his guerrillas who, during the First World War, wished the old gang could reassemble and gallop on to Berlin.

During boyhood summers in West Texas, I never heard a kind word for Yankees or a critical one for Rebels. Although my brother and I were loved and relatives did not call us anything worse than Yankees, we knew we were "blue bellies." We were the first in the history of either side of the family since the Rikes moved from Pennsylvania to the Moravian community of Salem, North Carolina, in the 1770s. I got hooked on the Civil War in Haskell, but I always felt relieved to return to Madison, where the war was over. It was also where I learned about the black-hatted Iron Brigade, which both sides considered the bravest out-fit in the Army of the Potomac from Second Manassas (Bull Run) to Appomat-tox. Three of its five regiments were Wisconsin Volunteers: the 2nd, 6th, and 7th Wisconsin Infantry. The Iron Brigade suffered over 60 percent casualties at Get-tysburg. The final tally for the war gave the 2nd Wisconsin the highest casualty rate of all Union regiments. Those "blue bellies" could fight. I'm still conflicted about that war. Every battlefield I visit brings out both sides. So does being in Missouri.

Preoccupied with this duality as I fill the tank before leaving Carthage, I'm startled by a young man who has walked over from his pickup.

"Didja drive that Bug all the way from California or haul it?" he asks.

"Drove it," I laugh.

I tell him about my trip. He approves, adding that the '66 was the best Bug ever. He and his father collect old Bug parts.

"Whole cars?" I ask.

"Oh no," he replies. "My wife wouldn't let me do that. Just parts. Not many people around here drive old Bugs anyway. If they do, they're jazzed up. You know, dune buggies and such."

"How much do you think I could sell mine for?"

"Better to sell it in California. Wouldn't be surprised if you got over ten thou-sand dollars for a car in that shape and you're the original owner. Around here, you'd be lucky to get twelve hundred."

"Well, I'm not going to sell anywhere," I say.

"I sure understand," he says. "Well, good to talk with you. Have a safe trip."

He rejoins his companion in the pickup and gestures toward the Bug. It's good to have strangers talk about my car and me. It's good to know that he will pass this encounter on to his father.

I drive north on U.S. 71 to pay my respects to Harry Truman in Lamar. I don't know where to go after that. My AAA guide lists the Bushwhacker Museum in Nevada, a center for raids against Kansas Jayhawkers. There's an old courthouse in Warrensburg, railroad history in Sedalia, and a museum in Ver-sailles.

But first things first. President Truman was born on May 8, 1884, in a small frame house in Lamar, where the state now maintains a modest historic site. According to a sign about local tradition, his father "planted an Austrian pine near the corner of the house and nailed a mule shoe above the front door in observance of his son's birth."

Good old Harry. I grew up with him. I was seven years old when he became president and fifteen when he left office. It was a time when I chose my political heroes with the help of a gut feeling about adults I would want to live on West Lawn Avenue. Truman was the right choice. Joseph McCarthy was the archvillain because he accused my president, my neighbor, of treason.

The atmosphere in the Blue Top Café at the Lamar turnoff on Highway 71 is similar to last night's dinner at the Ranch House Restaurant. It's friendly, open, and welcoming. After a good hamburger, I return to the Bug. Two bulbous SUVs flank my car, reminding me of childhood picture books with plucky little houses or tugboats surrounded by heartless skyscrapers or tankers. I have always rooted for the underdog.

I stand by the Bug's door, reach inside for my map of Missouri, and open it. An old guy parks his pickup to the right of the café and smiles at the Bug. When he catches my eye, I know we will talk. We bought our vehicles just months apart. His is a '65 Chevy with a vintage, low-profile Airstream canopy over the cargo bed. He made the canopy from a kit, and he treats its wooden interior framework like antique furniture. He's on his way from home in Fort Smith to his hometown near Lincoln, Nebraska, to attend his high school reunion. Ten of the eleven members of his class are alive, and they get together every year. He served in the Korean War as an aviation mechanic.

"The minute I got outta high school, I joined the Marines," he says.

His Korean wife sits in the cab while we talk. Though slightly stooped, he's a good six feet tall. His fair skin is dappled red. He makes no attempt to cover his baldness with side tufts of white. Pale blue eyes look straight at me through horn-rimmed glasses. He walks with some difficulty.

"I jus' love this truck," he exclaims as we walk around it.

He has attached a sign on the back end that says, "If your foreign truck has gone over six hundred thousand miles and is in as good shape as this, then you've got something."

He shows me the engine. Most of it is quite new. He rattles off parts as fast as only mechanics can, valves, cams, rods, hoses, plugs, carburetor, coil, pulleys, and so on. I nod as if I understand.

"When we were fixin' to leave Fort Smith," he says, "I jus' thought I'd check her over, even though I take good care of her and knew everything was okay. Now, we're Christian, and God is awesome, and I found all kind of things wrong. Some bearings were shot, and the brakes were shot. And that was God tellin' me to check the truck before we left."

He admires the Bug. "Awful nice little car you got there," he says. "That engine sure is tiny, but it's a good one."

"Sorry, I don't have six hundred thousand on it," I say.

"Well, that's okay. That's a good little car. Ya know, I've seen a few around. They get dinged pretty bad on the fenders and lights. Yours, she's in beautiful shape."

People going to and from the café notice us adoring our vehicles. I'm jealous that they look longer at his. Depends on the part of the country, I suspect. I tell him I was nervous driving the Bug across the California desert and the Southwest with a lot of miles between towns.

"Well, shoot," he replies. "Out there, you should be nervous. But here, all ya gotta do is get out and wave and people stop and help. In fact, ya oughtta move back here. I lived in California after Korea, and movin' to Fort Smith was the smartest move I ever made. We're real happy there. Got a third of an acre and flowers, and my little Korean wife is a great gardener. She raises vegetables. I got my own workshop, still work every day with engines. We're blessed."

He agrees with me that Korean War veterans have been overlooked far too often, particularly during the recent spate of movies and books about World War II.

"Ya know," he says, "I had a lotta trouble with the VA about benefits until a few years ago."

We wish each other well and shake hands. He opens the pickup door for his wife and waves as they disappear into the Blue Top Café.

"God is awesome," he said.

I check the oil. It's only a little low, but I add a quart.

I continue north on U.S. 71 and decide to spend the night in Sedalia because the old Marine said it was an interesting town where a cattle trail ended. In April 1954, during spring vacation, my brother, two friends from West High, and I drove this highway on our return to Madison from visiting relatives in Haskell and San Antonio. Back trouble prevented Dad from going with us, but he trusted us with his new Dodge. One of the friends, John Keene, mispronounced Fort Smith as we drove through it. "Smort Fith" has been the name of our spoonerism hall of fame ever since.

The other friend, John Brueckner, recently sent me a copy of his diary entries: "82 cents—ham dinner (good) at Hello Café in Carthage"; "26 cents—3 pancakes in Bethany."

Some time between those two meals, we slept off the highway. The trip became legend before it was over.

For the first time since leaving Claremont, I feel Wisconsin pulling on me. Last night, I telephoned John and Andy from the motel in Carthage. They said we faced a major existential question: what should we have for dinner on Saturday night, steak or shrimp? Andy would do the cooking, so I left the choice to him. I'd buy red and white wine on the way in. But it's not just the reunion that attracts or the memory of boyhood trips to Texas with my father and friends. If you draw a line from Haskell to Madison, Carthage lies slightly east of the halfway point. I'm on the Yankee side of my history, a Wisconsin boy going home.

I turn east on U.S. 54 without stopping at the museum in Nevada. The weather has cleared to the east and south, but the humidity remains high. Between Lamar and Nevada, I left the south-flowing watershed of the Arkansas River and entered the northeasterly drainage of the Osage River, which joins the Missouri near Jefferson City.

Dodging a small terrapin in the middle of the road, I shout encouragement, "Come on, buddy! You can make it."

I have been singing in the Bug since the first day of the trip, but when did I start talking aloud? Probably on the second day when I was in eastern Arizona or western New Mexico. But I simply haven't noticed. Freshly picked flowers adorn a small roadside cross, as if to say good-bye in the last split second. A corpulent woman under a wide straw hat straddles a barely visible mower and waves from her front lawn. In the village of Weaubleau, fine latticework clings to the sagging front porch of a dilapidated white house like a forgotten piece of lace.

Instead of continuing east until I hit U.S. 65 for Sedalia, I turn north on State 83, a byway with no shoulders and scarcely another car. There are small farms on either side. I have been disappointed by the lack of roadside markers since leaving Texas. However, I find this gem in the placid hamlet of Quincy across the street from an abandoned filling station with a lonely Skelly sign out front: "Butterfield Overland Mail in Missouri, 1858–1861. Quincy in Hickory County, 76 miles from the Tipton terminus, was a relay station."

In the 1850s, while Congress debated the question of a transcontinental railroad, Californians pressed for improved overland mail service. In 1857, the postmaster general requested bids for an "oxbow route" from St. Louis to San Francisco, bending south of the Rockies to avoid winter snow and appease Southern states that lobbied for railroads at their latitudes. John Butterfield's bid won. He placed eastern terminals at St. Louis and Memphis. By the time his line was ready in September 1858, the Pacific Railroad of Missouri, which was reorganized in 1876 as the Missouri Pacific, had built from St. Louis to Tipton, about thirty-five miles west of Jefferson City.

On September 16, Butterfield's Overland Mail began service from Tipton. San Francisco was about twenty-seven hundred miles distant at a passenger fare of two hundred dollars. The first mail, with postage of ten cents per half-ounce, reached San Francisco on October 10, several days before it would have arrived by steamship. The average distance between stations was about twenty miles. The more numerous "swing" stations provided fresh horses or mules, in teams of four or six to a coach. "Home" stations charged fifty cents or more for dinner, usually bacon, eggs, and biscuits or dried beef, beans, and hard tack.

The Overland Mail (or Butterfield Stage) went south from Tipton to Springfield and Fort Smith, where it merged with the Memphis branch. It crossed the Red River by ferry near the Shawnee Trail's ford. From the Red River to El Paso, which was called Franklin then, the road followed most of the trail that Captain Marcy had blazed in 1849 on his return from Santa Fe to Fort Smith. Captain Marcy camped in what would become Haskell County, not far from where Wat Fitzgerald would build the family dugout into the bank of California Creek and where his daughter, Ada, would play in the high grass, about halfway between Rice Springs and the Clear Fork of the Brazos. Between El Paso and Fort Yuma, the Butterfield Mail took established trails and wagon roads, including the ancient Gila Trail from Tucson to the Colorado River. Texans also used these roads to drive herds to the lucrative California market in the early 1850s. The Southern Pacific Railroad later shadowed this route across southern New Mexico and Arizona, as Interstates 10 and 8 do today.

Just as I was thinking North, the Butterfield marker throws me abruptly back to the Southwest. In 1860, I could have boarded the stage here and hopped off about eight days later at the Clear Fork of the Brazos station. It was a time when buffalo and Comanche still watered at Rice Springs. If I had continued all the way to San Francisco, I would have approached Los Angeles through the San Gabriel Valley, where this real trip began.

The Butterfield Overland Mail is not news to me, but I'm stunned to chance upon it in this remote place that choosing Sedalia a short while ago placed in my path. It's far from any guided tour or visitor center. Quincy-Haskell-Claremont, that oxbow joins my life to larger designs across land and time. I need that kind of reassurance. Then, as suddenly as I find it, I don't need it. I am without ego, purpose, past, or future. This is a moment of absolute contentment. It begins to slip away as soon as I grasp it.

North of Quincy, farmland gives way to hills and hardwood forests. I cross the Pomme de Terre River, where it has become an arm of Truman Lake, which was formed by damming the Osage just upstream from Warsaw. Around here, rivers don't have the space to meander in long parallels as they do in Oklahoma. These are too busy dodging hills, connecting valleys, and coming together as they drain the Ozark Plateau and aim for the Missouri. This was good country for trapping. French and Spanish fur traders had already established good relations with the Osage when Lieutenant Zebulon Pike followed the Osage River in 1806 on his way to the Rockies, leading one of the many expeditions that President Jefferson authorized to explore the recently acquired Louisiana Territory.

Warsaw was named in honor of Polish-born patriots who fought for the colonies in the Revolutionary War. The town's markers make for good reading. The first settlers of the county, named for Senator Thomas Hart Benton, were French, German, and English, with surnames like Pensineau, Hogle, and Williams. They coexisted with Osage villages that remained after the tribe had ceded this area in 1808. Warsaw itself grew up in the 1830s at an Osage River ferry crossing on the road from Boonville (Missouri River) to Springfield. The Butterfield Mail's Warsaw station was fifty-five miles from Tipton. Riders could find accommodations in the Lemon House and sustenance at Nichols Tavern. Rebel guerillas and state militia ruined the town in the Civil War. Even before the raids, the beginning of the war in the spring of 1861 forced the Butterfield Company to abandon its oxbow route for the central overland road from Independence through Wyoming.

I continue north on U.S. 65 toward Sedalia. An attractive young woman in a bright red sports car overtakes me. She neither tailgates nor sprints past. The words "low key" are on her license plate. That might have been interesting in my twenties.

Occasional signs point to prairies that are out of sight to the east and west. I gratefully infer that Missouri is setting aside land for native grasses. I begin humming. I don't recognize the tune. It's road impromptu.

I enter Sedalia on Broadway, the business route of U.S. 50, the highway that connects Jefferson City and Kansas City. After several shady blocks of Victorian houses, I turn into the Downtown Sedalia Historic Business District. Among the oldest buildings is an 1886 Romanesque in stone. It's across the street from the Hotel Bothwell. The hotel, seven stories in light brick, opened in 1927. It has been tastefully restored to what its current owners aptly call "an elevated standard of service." I ask the young woman at the registration desk for a small room at their lowest rate. She puts me in one of the original single rooms, warning the double bed leaves little space to navigate.

In the lobby, I discover an old menu and a picture of Harry Truman. On August 30, 1946, the Bothwell Coffee Shop offered several choices for lunch, all priced between sixty-five and seventy-five cents. There were broiled filet of perch, ham and boiled cabbage, braised veal, and stuffed green mangoes. Dinners included short-cut steak with mushroom sauce at a dollar seventy-five, prime rib au jus at a dollar sixty-five, chicken wings with gumbo noodles at a dollar twenty-five, and homemade layer cake at fifteen cents. The wine options were "Sauterne, Rhine, Sherry, Claret, Burgundy (bottle)."

At the bottom of the menu is this declaration, which was characteristic for the time, "Our ceiling prices are in conformance with the provisions of the Emergency Price Control Act of 1946."

Price controls, one of Truman's major dilemmas as America returned to a peacetime economy, would cost his party in the November elections. The Republicans regained control of the House and Senate for the first time since before the Great Depression.

The narrative beneath Truman's picture states, "In early May 1934, Harry S. Truman learned that he had been selected as Tom Pendergast's candidate for the U.S. Senate."

Truman had been summoned to the Bothwell from a meeting in Warsaw by the Kansas City political boss, who had come to believe, remarkably for him, that a man as honest as Truman could succeed in politics. David McCullough's splendid biography confirms my sentiment that Truman was America's finest president of the twentieth century. The fact that Truman trained as an artillery lieutenant at Fort Sill, Oklahoma, where I followed forty-two years later, adds fraternal weight to my judgment.

Several blocks east of the Bothwell, the 1896 Katy depot has been nicely restored. Sedalia dates from 1860, when you could start a town and name it for your kid. The Pacific Railroad had begun laying track west from St. Louis in 1852, but the going was slow. It did not reach Sedalia until 1860. It had been courted by George S. Smith, who renamed the town that he had called Sedville after his daughter Sarah, affectionately know as "Sed." Briefly before and after the Civil War, this was the closest railhead for Texas cattle bound for northern and eastern markets. More than seven hundred fifty thousand head were trailed to Sedalia in 1866 as Texas ranching and long drives recovered from the Civil War. One branch of the Shawnee Trail proceeded northeast from the Red River Crossing to Fort Smith. Then it bore slightly east of north to Sedalia, avoiding farmers west of that route who took offense at Texas longhorns.

Katy officials came to Sedalia in 1870. They were determined to build their railroad along an arc, not exactly a diagonal, from St. Louis to Texas. In March 1871, work was completed between Sedalia and Parsons, Kansas. There, it joined the line being built from eastern Kansas south through Indian Territory. Soon, the Katy had laid or acquired track from Sedalia to St. Louis. The railroad had its headquarters in Sedalia from 1873 to 1881. The repair and car building shops built in the 1890s were still in use after the Second World War.

Not far from the depot is the western end of the Katy Trail for hikers and bikers. It was completed in 1996 and covers more than two hundred miles of old right-of-way east to St. Charles. This is the country's longest such example of rails-to-trails conversion. I would call it a reversion.

I circle back to the hotel by way of Main Street, where Scott Joplin played his "Maple Leaf Rag" at the Maple Leaf Club when he lived here in the 1890s. Two blocks west of the hotel, the neoclassical Sedalia Public Library of 1899 made of Carthage stone was the first library in Missouri built on one of Andrew Carnegie's well-targeted grants.

The Bothwell's old coffee shop has gone Italian. It's now the Del Amici restaurant. The service and food are good. The décor is from the twenties. The wallpaper is new, but the original floor is inlaid with geometric designs. The Muzak fills the dining room with today's style of harsh wailing from tormented throats, completely wrong for this otherwise hospitable anachronism of a hotel. Gershwin or Cole Porter would be more like it.

Thursday, May 30

I breakfast on coffee and a danish off one corner of the lobby in what was once the barbershop but is now the "Excellent Coffee Shop and Bakery." The local newspaper, the *Sedalia Democrat*, is moderate Democrat, judging from its editorials and letters, which contain none of the conspiratorial obsessions of the *Daily Oklahoman*. A middle-aged man walks in from his rusty pickup. Wearing a faded baseball cap and dirty overalls, he orders a double espresso. Life is good.

Soon, I begin my departure ritual. I clean the windshield, secure books and papers, and place maps, tape recorder, and writing pad within reach. On my first sunny morning since New Mexico, my destination is Arrow Rock, where the Santa Fe Trail crossed the Missouri River. I head north on U.S. 65 and jog a few miles east on I-70, which was formerly U.S. 40, a story in itself. From Maryland to Kansas City, Highway 40 followed the route of the National Old Trails Road, whose association of boosters was energized by the Daughters of the American Revolution and headed in the twenties by Judge Harry S. Truman of Kansas City. This transcontinental honor roll of pioneer trails included General Braddock's Road to Cumberland, Maryland, built in the 1750s; the National, or Cumberland, Road from Cumberland to Vandalia, Illinois, completed in the

1830s; and the Boone's Lick Road from St. Louis to Franklin, which is near Arrow Rock, constructed in the early 1800s.

If a Missouri River boatman from the 1820s came back to life and saw I-70, he would think us mad. I gladly escape onto a side road near the simple white-frame Peninsula Baptist Church built in 1873 and its small cemetery.

In the village of Blackwater, the U.S. Army has funded a small obelisk dedicated to "all veterans, past, present and future." A plaque near a wooden carving of an Indian chief reads:

> The Osage Indians thought so much of the French explorer, [Jean] Pierre Chouteau, as a fur trader, that on March 19, 1792, they gave him land along the Lamine River, including what is now Blackwater township.

The bridge over the Blackwater River is out, damaged by spring floods in central Missouri. I stop near a restored brick building to check my maps, but they show few county roads. A frail old man approaches. He's made of a few thin lines here and there like a Japanese drawing. He limps up to the passenger window and asks if he can help.

"Lemme come 'round to your side of the car. I'm harda hearin'."

White blotches cover his arms, and his few remaining teeth are darkly stained.

"Well," he says, "there's a coupla ways ya can do this, but ya prob'ly don' wanna go on the back roads in that little car, so ya oughtta go west on 70 and north on J and that runs into H. Then ya go east and then ya come out on this hill just across the river here, where the bridge is down. Then go north on this road and hit 41 and turn left."

"Much obliged," I say, as confidently as I can.

He tips his cap.

After turning north on J, I follow my nose toward Arrow Rock on gravel roads. Crossing the Blackwater River, a muddy brown, I see signs of flooding. The soil is a rich brown-black color. Nothing else about the landscape tells me that one of North America's greatest rivers lies only a few miles to the northeast. I ask new directions from a road repair crew in an orange truck.

The driver says, "Well, ya go up here and take a left on the double A and then a right on the TT and that'll take you right on in."

Sappington Negro Cemetery soon appears on my left, a small field of headstones with no farms in sight. I park the Bug off the road and walk over to read the marker:

> Oral tradition says that prior to 1856 Dr. John Sappington, pioneer Arrow Rock physician, gave approximately two acres of land to Emmanuel Banks, a long-time and highly regarded servant, to be used as a cemetery. Since the mid-nineteenth century, over 350 Arrow Rock citizens of African-American descent and their descendants have been interred in this cemetery ... They helped to build the historic community of Arrow Rock and made major contributions to the history of this area.

This quiet place moves me deeply. Some of my forebears held slaves. One owned Hayes plantation in Edenton, North Carolina. He opposed secession and freed his slaves after the Civil War began, thereby estranging his nephew, namesake, and heir, James Cathcart Johnston, who took his family to south Texas after the war, where his daughter Kate married Wat Fitzgerald.

Shortly after the end of the Third Reich, the philosopher Karl Jaspers asked his fellow Germans to confront honestly the question of guilt for Nazi crimes. Many Germans did not commit crimes, but he argued that all of them bore collective responsibility for the way in which they were governed.

"A people answers for its polity," he stated. All Germans were liable for the actions of their state, including horrible deeds that violated "the highest demands made on [them] by the best of [their] ancestors." They were responsible not only for their present but also for their past, "the links of tradition" (Jaspers 1961).

I believe I bear the collective historical responsibility for slavery in America. I am not criminally or morally guilty for acts I did not personally commit, but slavery was policy. It violated the highest demands of our best. It will always be our history. Its legacy of inequality stays with us. Owning slaves is in my history, in what Sacred Eagle woman calls my "bloodline." I disagree with those who say affirmative action just encourages the politics of special pleading and victimization. It is the right policy.

It is right to linger in the warm sun with those who rest here.

Minutes after leaving, I stand in front of Prairie Park. Nestled in tall trees behind a white picket fence, the two-story, redbrick mansion has four graceful Ionian columns on the small front porch. Above these are four columns like them, outside French doors on the second floor.

According to the plaque:

> Prairie Park was built between 1845 and 1849 by William Breathitt Sappington and his wife, Mary ... It is one of the finest surviving examples of nineteenth-century Greek Revival architecture in rural Missouri, and was a center of early social and political life in the Boone's Lick area.

William's father, the physician John, had made a fortune manufacturing anti-malarial pills. William sided with the Confederacy. His brother-in-law, Governor Claiborne Fox Jackson, tried unsuccessfully to withdraw Missouri from the Union in 1861. William's nephew was Confederate General John Sappington Marmaduke, whose election as governor in 1885, the plaque tells us, "signaled that hatreds created by the war were at an end."

I question that last statement. The plaque makes no direct reference to slavery, the Missouri Compromise, prewar hatreds that produced guerilla warfare, or Marmaduke's raids into Missouri.

Prairie Park, near Arrow Rock, Missouri

In Arrow Rock, I park in the shade, away from the tourists on Main Street who are splayed over shop porches and benches near their enormous bus. As I drive by them, I notice a boy sitting in front of the general store. He's eating an ice cream cone and shouts, "Hey, lookit the Bug! Lookit the Bug!"

The museum inside the State Historic Site Visitor Center is a treasure. I have rarely seen so many cultures meet in so small a place, Native American, French, Hispanic, Anglo, and African American. French explorers encountered the Osage in Missouri in the 1680s and called them "Ouazhaghi," mispronouncing the name of one of the tribal clans. Osage men, who shaved their heads and faces, called Frenchmen "heavy eyebrows." In the early eighteenth century, French explorers named the bluffs at this point on the Missouri River as *"pierre à flèche."*

Indians made arrowheads here long before Europeans and Americans traveled the river. Among the Europeans and Americans, some going downstream, were the Mallet brothers in 1739, Don Pedro (Pierre) Vial in 1792, and several French and British traders in the 1790s and early 1800s. Meriwether Lewis and William Clark were here in 1804 and 1806, Manuel Lisa in 1807, members of John Jacob Astor's Pacific Fur Company between 1811 and 1813, and Major Stephen Long in 1819. In 1822, Jedediah Smith came here with William Ashley and Andrew Henry, who had just started the Rocky Mountain Fur Company. In 1830, Smith returned this way after eight years in the West. In 1831, restless several months after buying a house in St. Louis, Smith passed Arrow Rock for the last time, on his way to Santa Fe. A group of Comanche killed him on the Cimarron cutoff. Finally, Francis Parkman came through in 1846. The ferry established at the ford here in 1811 served William Becknell, whose trading trip to Santa Fe in 1821, weeks after Missouri became a slave state and months after Mexico won its independence from Spain, traditionally marks the founding of the famous trail, though most of it already existed.

France ceded its Louisiana territories west of the Mississippi to Spain in 1773 but took them back by secret treaty in 1800. During the interval, the Spanish had little control over this vast region, even though they commissioned Vial's expedition of 1792 from Santa Fe to St. Louis, encouraged the French to establish trading posts among the Osage, and offered Missouri land to American settlers. Among French traders, the Chouteau family of New Orleans was the most famous. The post established in 1764 by René Auguste Chouteau and his stepfather, Pierre Laclède, became St. Louis. René Auguste's half-brother, Jean Pierre, was appointed U.S. agent for the Osage in 1804, a year after the Louisiana Purchase. He later co-founded the Missouri Fur Company. Pierre's sons, Auguste and Pierre (Jr.), stayed in the business, the latter eventually reorganizing the American Fur Company and expanding its reach to the Rockies and Minnesota.

In 1805, Daniel Boone's sons became part-owners of a salt lick across the river from here. Their name stuck, and this whole area was soon known as "Boone's Lick." The salt operation shipped about thirty bushels daily to St. Louis by keelboat. It took four pounds of salt to cure twenty hams, fifteen pounds for a hundred pounds of beef, and up to one-third of the weight of a buffalo hide to tan it. Sac and Fox Indians, along with the Miami and Iowa tribes, sided with the British in the War of 1812 and attacked American settlements around Boone's Lick. After the war, emigrants from Kentucky, Tennessee, Virginia, and North Carolina came up the Boone's Lick Trail from St. Charles and settled this area, some of them bringing slaves. The community of Arrow Rock became a town in 1829. It was briefly and loftily called New Philadelphia. Traders and emigrants outfitted here, and the town bustled until railroads streaming west after the Civil War reduced traffic by boat and wagon. The trail from St. Charles to Arrow Rock continued west to Fort Osage on the Missouri River. Farther upstream, Independence, along with Westport Landing in what is now Kansas City, replaced Franklin as the Santa Fe Trail's main eastern terminus in the 1830s. From there, the Oregon Trail later followed the Santa Fe Trail for about fifty miles before turning right.

I walk down to the spring where Becknell and other parties filled their water barrels, having crossed to the south bank of the Missouri after leaving Franklin a few miles downstream. They would then climb uphill past the tavern and take a shortcut west while the river doglegged north. Since then, the river has changed course. Now, it's about a mile east of the channel that took it beneath the bluff overlooking the ferry. Lewis and Clark passed under the bluff on June 9, 1804, just before they almost capsized. Clark recorded:

> We had like to have Stove our boat in going round a Snag her Stern Struck a log under Water & She Swung round on the Snag, with her broad Side to the Current exp[ose]d to the Drifting timber (Moulton 1986).

The historical preservation of the village has been well done, even though it allows buses, coughing fumes, to park in front of the old tavern. Some of the houses date back to the 1830s, such as the redbrick home of the artist, George Caleb Bingham. John P. Sites opened his gunsmith business in 1844, advertising:

> GUNS. PISTOLS. BOWIE KNIVES! POWDER, SHOT, LEAD, SPORTSMEN'S APPARATUS & FISHING TACKLE. All of which I offer to sell as low as any house above St. Louis.

The tavern, which Joseph Huston built in 1834, is now "the oldest continuous operating restaurant west of the Mississippi." Waiting for the fried chicken special, I thumb through one of my purchases at the museum bookstore, the reminiscences of T. C. Rainey, who arrived in Saline County in 1865. He came "in search of something to do." Having failed to purchase a drugstore in Columbia, he chose the merchandise trade. He only knew:

> red-top boots, yarn socks, hats, pocket knives, and had come in contact with a few ready-made shirts with enormously starched 'bosoms,' bullet-proof until after the first washing. However, I was young and hopeful.

Among Rainey's engaging stories and character sketches, I discover that Major Long came up the Missouri in 1819 "in the first steamboat which ever ascended as far as Arrow Rock" and William Becknell's brother, Henry, was the ferryman here in 1821 when William began his journey to Santa Fe (Rainey 1971).

Rainey mentions the Sappingtons and Marmadukes, prominent settlers of this area, but not John Sappington Marmaduke's return during General Price's raid of 1864. According to my great-grandfather's journal, Marmaduke's cavalry arrived here on October 14: "Marched 16 miles to Arrow Rock. Crossing the Missouri River took until midnight to get across" (Draper 1979).

After lunch, I scout the camping area. I am pleasantly surprised to find a section back in the trees that is reserved for tents. I packed gear with every intention of camping out often enough to say I can still do this forty years after I couldn't afford motels. So far, I have yielded to the comforts of a warm shower and good bed after entire days on the road. This will be an appropriate place to toughen up.

On the way back to the museum for a second look, I park in front of the small log cabin that served as Saline County's courthouse in 1839. The sixty-ish-year-old man who has just finished mowing the lawn comes over.

"Boy, that's sure a nice car," he says. "But it's a long way from home."

I explain my trip.

"Well, that's just great. Just a great idea," he says, smiling.

I point to his lawnmower and ask, "Why don't you drive that to California?"

He slaps his leg and replies, "Well, I hadn't thought of that. Might take me a good while."

Soon, he wishes me well, lowers the American flag from the pole in front of the cabin, folds it, climbs on his mower, and chugs away. I suddenly recall the 1999 movie, *The Straight Story*. I'm surprised I haven't already thought of it on the road. In the film, Richard Farnsworth, who knew horses as well as Ben Johnson did, rides a lawnmower across northern Iowa to see his brother in Wisconsin. Many of the anecdotes along the way begin with, "What in the world are you driving that thing for?" Farnsworth's Alvin Straight says little about why, but he speaks volumes with his eyes. That prompted me to call my brother right after seeing the film. Farnsworth received nominations for the Golden Globe and

Academy Award for best actor, but he won neither. I hoped he would. I did not read his eyes correctly when I watched the Academy Awards ceremony on television in March 2000. He had terminal cancer. His suicide seven months later still saddens me.

Saline County Courthouse for 1839, Arrow Rock, Missouri

Back inside the visitor center, I converse with its director, who is writing a new history of Arrow Rock, and a young woman on his staff who has just drafted essays for a college take-home exam in German history. I offer a few suggestions for her account of the Nazi policy of genocide, emphasizing the racial and mystical connotations of the word, *Volk*. For example, Hitler wanted a people's car for the Third Reich, and the Volkswagen fulfilled his dream of Aryan German families driving about on holiday in small, inexpensive, streamlined cars. The young woman scribbles.

The director tells another colleague, "I was just telling her something about German history and here this guy comes along who has done it for a living."

"Sure," I reply, "but now I'm trying to learn that." I point into the museum.

I return to displays that connect the Missouri River to Wisconsin. Henry Dodge, a Missourian known as "Honest Harry," fought in the War of 1812. In the summer of 1814, he commanded a militia force that defended Boone's Lick settlements against hostile Indians. Dodge crossed the Missouri at Arrow Rock and attacked a camp of Miami upstream. After they surrendered, he ensured their safe passage away from the area, preventing acts of revenge that local whites threatened. Dodge's fame grew during the Black Hawk War of 1832, when he commanded a battalion of militia. He then became the first governor of the Wisconsin Territory from 1836 to 1841.

Black Hawk, the great Sac leader, had resented American expansion ever since the Treaty of 1804. By its terms, which the Sac and Fox representatives did not understand, they ceded all of their lands east of the Mississippi River, that is, in Illinois and Wisconsin, and a portion in northeastern Missouri to the United States in return for an annuity of a thousand dollars.

Dictating his autobiography in 1833, Black Hawk called this treaty "the origin of all our difficulties." He remembered debating whether to join the British or remain neutral in 1812:

> I had not discovered one good trait in the character of the Americans that had come to the country. They made fair promises but never fulfilled them. While the British made but few, but we could always rely upon their word (Black Hawk 1964).

He soon joined the British, whom he trusted to return his tribal lands. After the American victory, his persistent refusal to accept the government's interpretation of the 1804 treaty eventually led to the war named after him.

The Osage and other tribes of the region preferred the French to the Americans and English. French trappers and traders were more inclined to learn the customs and take Indian wives. Jean Pierre Chouteau, for example, lived with the Osage in western Missouri as a young man. He soon spoke the language fluently. It was good for business, of course. But the French attitude toward Indians was less racist than that of most Anglo Americans, who looked down on the French for socializing with so-called "coloreds" and producing "half-breeds."

On the island of Mykonos in 1962, I met a tall, young Frenchman with wavy, black hair who wished he had been a trapper "*avec une femme rouge* (with a red wife)."

French Catholic missionaries had a reputation among Indians for unpreachy benevolence. Sister Rose Philippine Duchesne came to America in 1818. Inspired since childhood by Jesuits who told stories of the Indians, she established schools for the Society of the Sacred Heart in and around St. Louis. In 1841, Father Pierre Jean de Smet encouraged her to open a school for the Potawatomie tribe in northeast Kansas. They loved her, naming her "the woman who always prays." Her niece, six generations later, is Marie-Christine Gray, who is married to my English friend, Robert, an Anglican. Sister Philippine was canonized in 1988.

At the general audience with Pope John Paul II following the ceremony, Robert heard cries of "*Priez pour la France* (Pray for France)!"

He interjected, "*Et pour l'Angleterre aussi* (And for England also)!"

Leaving the visitor center around four o'clock, I decide to hit the road rather than the campground. I had not expected this local history to be so large or personal. I welcome the familiar confines and motion of the Bug. It's good for pondering. In *Travels with a Donkey in the Cévennes*, Robert Louis Stevenson wrote that he traveled "not to go anywhere, but to go. I travel for travel's sake. The great affair is to move" (Stevenson 1996).

At the age of twenty-seven, at the same age when Stevenson made his trip in southern France, I might have agreed with him. Now I don't. I'm traveling with a Bug for my sake. The great affair is to be moved.

Upstream and north of Arrow Rock, I take State 240 across the Missouri on an old, steel bridge in Glasgow. The river is high, wide, fast, and brown. Indians called it "muddy water" or "big muddy," the latter name borrowed by many Anglo Americans and capitalized on their maps. In 1673, the French explorers, Louis Joliet and Father Jacques Marquette, traveling down the Mississippi from the Wisconsin River, saw the mouth of the Missouri at full flood. Subsequent French expeditions on the Mississippi promised a colonial empire from the Gulf of Mexico to the Great Lakes and east to the St. Lawrence and the Atlantic. But the French also looked west after the Indians told them the big muddy led to other great rivers and finally to the sea.

Long after I cross the Missouri, my mind stays in Arrow Rock. The village is deceptively tranquil. A potent energy surrounds it, both magnetic and centrifugal. I have never felt anything like this energy elsewhere in America or anything more essentially American.

Missouri attracted all sorts, from both sides of the Mason-Dixon Line, for purposes that ran the alphabet from adventure to zoology. It threw some north and south, but many more west along latitudes, diagonals, and oxbows on land, water, and rails. Slaves did not come by choice. The same can be said for the Indians, who were pressed across the Mississippi and eventually beyond Missouri. The unwilling and the West itself capitulated to Euro-American cravings for exploration, freedom, commerce, property, wealth, and empire. But I sense a power at work here over which even masters had no control. Its most visible manifestation is the Big Muddy.

The Missouri River made the state central and symbolic. It's a border state linking North and South, the greatest gateway to the West, a nexus for millions of lives. All and each, we are capable of fratricide, we dream of new beginnings, and we cross paths. I met my family's southern past in Sappington Negro Cemetery and my great-grandfather's crossing of the Missouri below Arrow Rock while dressed in Confederate gray:

> Behold the silvery river, in it the splashing horses loitering stop to drink,
> Behold the brown-faced men, each group, each person a picture ... (Whitman 1969).

In Arrow Rock, the old Santa Fe Trail carried me to Dodge City and payday for Wat Fitzgerald, Henry Post, and Tom Ballard. Maps of exploration took me to what the Indians called "shining mountains," where I have backpacked upstream from trappers' rendezvous. Following Jedediah Smith beyond the Rockies, I walked through Cajon Pass into the San Gabriel Valley. The Oregon Trail led me back twelve years to moving cattle along its ruts on Two Creek Ranch in Wyoming. Henry Dodge pointed north to Wisconsin, home.

I did not chance upon Arrow Rock as I did the Butterfield Overland Mail at Quincy. I would have come here just for the Santa Fe Trail that lay over my left horizon as I drove east. But something else also drew me, a power that is deeper than the river and greater than history. It's of the land, but the eye for landscape cannot see it and cannot name it as a feature of the many pathways that go through here. The power whirls around like a vortex. It pulls you in with no interest in where you have been. It pushes you out with no concern for how you will find your way. Under this power, no destiny is manifest.

CHAPTER 4

▼

GOING HOME

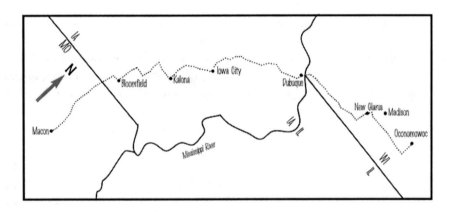

Friday, May 31

I spent last night in Macon, Missouri, almost exactly two thousand miles from Claremont. I had driven north on U.S. 63 through the most fertile farmland so far, passing the General Omar Bradley Memorial Airport in Moberly. (He was born in the nearby village of Clark.) A drive-in theater on the south side of Macon still screens films on weekends.

In the motel parking lot this morning, as I read maps in the Bug with the door open, a man in shorts stops to say hello.

"I used to drive one of those," he says.

"What year?" I ask.

"It was a '60."

"Good year. This is a '66. I had to convert it to twelve volts about ten years ago."

"Wish I had done that with mine," he says. "Wish I hadn't sold it."

We exchange stories about aging electrical systems run by six-volt batteries. What do you do if it's raining at night, you are about to make a turn, and a road hog is threatening your life? Before signaling the turn or honking, consider first what might happen if you turn off the headlights or the windshield wipers to get the necessary juice. You can increase the available current by shifting to neutral or engaging the clutch and revving the engine, but no one who has not driven an old Bug will expect this trick or reward its creativity. We remember yelling instead of honking, turning off wipers and leaning out the window, relying on parking lights for a few seconds, honking while coasting in neutral and stepping on the gas, and several other permutations. Those were the tough choices and quick decisions that separated us from the ordinary.

While paying my bill, I ask, "Is there an electronics store in town? I need tapes for my cassette recorder."

"Oh, you wanna Wal-Mart," says a geezer in coveralls who overheard me.

He's apparently a local who hits the motel's free coffee every morning before work. He offers directions. He looks from my trim, black Teva sandals to his scuffed, brown boots. Then he looks at my Tevas again.

"What the hell can you do in those things?" reads the look on his face.

Missouri is "The Show Me State."

North of Macon, U.S. 63 follows an imperceptible and narrow divide between tributaries of the Missouri and the Mississippi, coming within fifty miles of the latter's long bend that defines Illinois' western bay window. The land looks more and more like Iowa. If state lines are fuzzy, must I revise my thesis that each state has a distinctive personality? Then I recall taking the train home for Christmas during my first year at Cornell. A cheer went up between Chicago and Madison.

"We're home!" everyone yelled.

Many passengers crowded over to the windows. I asked one man how he knew we had entered Wisconsin.

"Look at the farms!" he replied. "The barns are red and the houses are white and they don't need paint!"

On trips with Dad, the farther we left Wisconsin behind, the more enthusiastically John and I waved at cars bearing "America's Dairyland" license plates. We sometimes drove this highway. We took U.S. 151 from Madison to Dubuque, Cedar Rapids, Amana, and Ottumwa, and U.S. 63 from Ottumwa to Jefferson

City. I can hear Dad saying "Ottumwa" with a long A. In an instant, I'm back on the road with him and John, reading Burma Shave jingles aloud, playing games of white horse, naming state capitals, hearing lectures on geology, finding railroad stations, and tossing the softball. We stayed in motel rooms where the bed vibrated for a quarter. If I was lucky, a small radio gave me faint baseball scores. None of the motels had television, but neither did my family back in Madison. Sometimes Dad took us to a movie. I had nightmares after seeing *Rocketship X-M* in Grand Island, Nebraska, on our way to Wyoming and Colorado in the summer of 1950. Lloyd Bridges and his crew, having narrowly escaped barbarians on Mars, could not prevent their ship from crashing back into Earth. My Cold War anxieties had already been giving me nightmares for some time. The Soviet Union had atomic bombs, the Korean War had just begun, and Joseph McCarthy, my senator, saw Reds under beds everywhere.

Passing a survey crew, I remember that my brother operated a theodolite for the Wisconsin State Highway Department in the summer of 1956 after his sophomore year at Harvard. One evening at the dinner table, he said and ate nothing. Mom eased it out of him. His crew had witnessed a grisly accident with two fatalities, and he had assisted the injured before police and medics arrived. Dad began to commiserate, but John shook his head.

"You don't understand," he said, weeping. "You don't understand."

He left the table and slammed the front door. Dad looked perplexed.

"Leave him alone," Mom said softly. "He'll be all right."

I knew I could believe her.

South of Kirksville, Sydenstricker Farm and Garden Equipment prepares me for German names on into Wisconsin. Two un-Californian novelties strike me at a busy Phillips 66 station in town. There are no SUVs, and the pumps don't take credit cards or require prepayment of cash. The good people of Kirksville do not feign utility or presume dishonesty.

A pickup stops at the next island, and the driver walks over to admire the Bug. He's in his thirties and wears glasses, a gray-flecked beard, overalls, and a cap with a farm equipment company's insignia on it. His wife and son pile out and join him. They are as curious as he is and have none of the signs of spousal subordination or adolescent sulkiness one often sees in households encountering strangers. They are the friendliest, merriest family I have met all trip.

"What year?" the man asks.

"It's a '66," I reply. "Did you ever own one?"

"No, but my older sister dated a guy who had one," he says. "When they went off in her car, he let me drive his Bug. Boy, I really loved it. It was the kind with that handle down below the dash for your fuel reserve. No gas gauge."

"My first Bug was like that. It was a '60 that I bought in Germany," I say. "What year model was the one you drove?"

"Don't know."

"What about the rear window? Was it this shape?" I ask, pointing to mine. "Or was it the small oval?"

"It was smaller than yours. Yeah, yeah, that's right. Oval."

"Then it was a Bug from the fifties. Who knows? Maybe it was one of the first to hit Kirksville."

"Well, I'll be durned," he says. "Boy, that ol' car was sure good on snow an' ice. I just went right through that stuff when everyone else was slidin' around."

"Yeah, weight over the rear wheels. See many around here now?" I ask.

"No, haven't seen one in a long time," he replies.

"How many were there back in the sixties?"

"Oh, lots of 'em. Lotta people drove 'em. Kids, mainly. You know, teenagers and college kids."

"What did old people think about that?"

"Oh, they thought it was crazy. You know, just like kids."

I look at his son, who must be in his early teens.

"Just like old people today, huh?" I say, winking.

The boy laughs and looks down for a second and then back up at me with disarming recognition. We connected.

His father asks how fast I drive.

"Cruise at fifty-five or sixty," I reply.

"Well, that's just great!"

"I could go faster, but I'm taking my time," I say.

"No, don't. That's just fine."

"I hate the freeways. Those trucks and vans and SUVs eat me for breakfast."

"I'll bet they come right up on your bumper," he says.

"They sure do."

Back on the road, I'm grateful for the kind of conversation I had hoped to have more often. My car would pry open the fifties and sixties. Back then, driving Bugs was an act of protest, no matter what your political leanings. I would ask people if they saw anything comparable to the Bug today, something every generation recognized instantly as a symbol of youth and nonconformity. I think there isn't. America needs one. Do the father and his boy agree?

Maybe I should be more forward when opportunities like this arise. On the other hand, the trip is introducing me to people who remember the Bug as nothing more than a good car at a younger age. If it also stands for something in the American consciousness that needs reviving or is best forgotten, they haven't told me. Why shoehorn their memory into my seminar topic? I'm retired!

This morning, Arrow Rock and its Confederate associations seem far away. Wisconsin seems close, but the father's accent had southern shading. It was more than I expected for northern Missouri. A brochure back in the Macon motel indicated that most of the pioneers who settled the town before the middle of the nineteenth century came from slave-owning states. In the 1860 national election, the majority of voters in northern Missouri cast ballots for two candidates who would not oppose the expansion of slavery into western territories: Stephen Douglas, who was in the northern camp of the divided Democratic Party, and John Bell, a member of the Constitutional Union Party. Douglas also outpolled Lincoln in a number of counties in southern Iowa as well as most of southern Illinois, part of what became Copperhead country during the Civil War.

Just where does the South stop and the North begin? That's still hard to say from Missouri on up the Ohio River Valley, where Southern and Northern cultures have overlapped since the early stages of migration west of the Alleghenies.

I see numerous fireworks stores from Lancaster to the Iowa border. There are none across the state line in Amish country.

A sign cautions, "Watch for Horse-drawn Vehicles!"

Minutes later, in the southbound lane, a lanky man with long beard and dark glasses drives a pair of fine, black horses pulling a wagon. Maybe he owns the farm I soon pass, where an abundant pasture holds twenty-five or thirty horses, most of them palominos, all of them sleek and frisky. The Amish take good care of their animals.

Where the highway doglegs east, joined briefly by State 2, a sign commemorates the Mormon Pioneer Route across Iowa. Early in 1846, Brigham Young's Mormons came this way from Nauvoo, Illinois, on their trek to the Missouri River and the Emigrant Trail beyond. But I do not find a marker for the cattle drive that launched Clint Eastwood's career.

In 1866, George C. Duffield and his partner, Harvey Ray, both of Burlington, Iowa, rode to Texas and purchased a thousand longhorns in the hill country west of Austin. While Ray returned to Iowa separately, Duffield hired cowboys and started north on the Shawnee Trail, reaching Baxter Springs three months later. They looped to the west because of inhospitable Kansans. Then they headed northeast to Nebraska, swam the Missouri River at Nebraska City, crossed southern Iowa to Burlington, and shipped the cattle from there to Chicago. Duffield's diary of this seven-month drive became a major historical source for the television series, *Rawhide*, which ran from 1959 to 1966. Eastwood played Rowdy Yates. The trail boss, Gil Favor, played by Eric Flemming, was based on Duffield himself. Uncle John Rike considered *Rawhide* the most credible depiction of cowboys in the many television Westerns of its time. He didn't know Gil Favor came from Iowa.

West of Bloomfield, a new house hulks alone in a treeless pasture. The ponderous stacking of rooms and roofs, utterly out of tune with this land, is certainly not Amish. The courthouse in Bloomfield brings me to a stop. I ask an old-timer loading groceries into his car to tell me something about the building.

"Let's go look at some signs," he says. "Got nothin' else to do."

We walk over to a plaque for Davis County Courthouse:

> Built in 1877 at a cost of $45,201 … an outstanding example of Second Empire architecture with its distinctive Mansard roof and dormer windows … and walls made of red brick covered by a sandstone veneer. Surmounted by a statue of the 'Lady of Justice,' the belfry tower raises the total height to over 123 feet. The tower houses the original 1876 Seth Thomas Clock and an immense 1878 Kimberley Bell that was also rung in the early days as a fire alarm. The design was the work of architect P.J. Tolan of Indiana, considered at the time to be the most successful in this style of courthouse. In continuous use since its construction, the large courtroom seats nearly 300 people on the original walnut chairs and benches. The basement still contains the cells that were the county and city jail until 1973 … One of the most unusual visitors to view the building was a human fly, who succeeded in scaling the outside walls in the early 1930s.

At a large headstone commemorating veterans of this area, the old man says, "My brother put that up. Used to sell gravestones."

On the west lawn is a small replica of the Statue of Liberty, dedicated in 1950 by the Boy Scouts of America "as a pledge of everlasting fidelity and loyalty" during their fortieth anniversary "crusade to strengthen the arm of liberty." I keep the echo to myself. The dedication occurred not long after my brother and I, who had been Cub Scouts, decided we would not join the Boy Scouts because they were too regimented and used air mattresses. We wanted to be free and tough.

Walking the man back to his car, I compliment the pretty square.

"Well, yeah," he replies. "It's nice. But ya know, business has really gone downhill on the east side."

"Is that because of the highway?" I ask. Highway 63 takes the east side of the square through town.

"Prob'ly is. My wife and I were sittin' on that bench over yonder one evenin' and we started countin' trucks. In fifteen minutes, musta been forty of 'em went by. Where you headin' today?" he asks.

"Iowa City," I reply.

"Well, you should see some of the Amish communities on your way. Nice people. Not many of 'em here in Bloomfield," he says.

I walk around the square before returning to the courthouse. The second stories of old brick shops form an eclectic layer of graceful moldings, window trim, and decorations attached like barnacles to walls and cornices. Inside the courthouse, there is no museum or visitor desk. It's just the functional, with treasurer, recorder, clerk of the district court, auditor, elevator, assessor, restrooms, and so on.

Davis County Courthouse, Bloomfield, Iowa

The exterior must have guaranteed the building's place on the National Register of Historic Places. I think of catchier titles for the sign on the lawn, something like "Second Empire Hits Southern Iowa!" Bloomfield, like Carthage, illustrates European influences on American architecture in the late nineteenth century. But the Second Empire of this courthouse outdoes anything I have seen in France for exuberant entablatures and wedding cake towers.

What got into P. J. Tolan? It may have been Iowa for I have accorded rare powers to this countryside since discovering how it got to A. Dvořák. Antonin Dvořák composed his String Quartet No. 12 (*The American*) in Spillville, a Czech community in northeast Iowa, in June 1893. Some say this piece contains hints of the black spirituals and Native American music that captivated the Czech composer during his three years in the United States. I sometimes hear the beat of Indian drums in the fourth movement. I always hear Midwestern farmland in the first, at the end of which Dvořák left a note about the beautiful sunshine. I'm partial to music that evokes landscape.

Dvořák's quartet started the memorial concert for Sir Edgar Williams in Oxford in November 1995. "Bill" Williams was secretary of the Rhodes Trust and warden of Rhodes House at Oxford from 1952 to 1980. A brilliant young history don, he left Oxford soon after the outbreak of the Second World War to join an armored regiment. He became Field Marshal Montgomery's chief of intelligence in North Africa. I arrived at Oxford after army service in Germany, just after the Berlin Crisis of August 1961 had nearly dashed my hopes of taking up my Rhodes scholarship. Bill, as I began calling him many years later, and I easily conversed about military history. I drank in his stories and lessons.

Vanity, he stated, is the enemy of military intelligence. Following the historian's careful rules of evidence is its ally. He dropped no hint of another ally, ULTRA, the code name for British intelligence decrypted from Germany's Enigma cipher machines, a top-secret program that was not made public until the 1970s. Now, I wonder how Bill would assess America's War on Terror for vanity, evidence, and secrecy.

Bill's affection for America in the war carried over to his mentoring American Rhodes scholars in postwar Oxford. When I greeted his widow, Gill, before the memorial concert in 1995, she said, "We start off with *The American* quartet. That's for you."

The Davis County Courthouse didn't stick when I drove past it as a boy. Now it stitches boyhood to the Midwest, France, Dvořák, the Berlin Crisis, Oxford, El Alamein, and the Grand Alliance.

Spillville is too far north for tomorrow's final leg into southern Wisconsin. But I begin to whistle and hum Dvořák after leaving Bloomfield, fragments from the quartet, Symphony No. 9 (*From the New World*), and "O Silver Moon" from his opera, *Rusalka*. I cross the Des Moines River and pass the John Deere factory in Ottumwa, elevation 650 feet, the same as Glasgow on the Missouri yesterday afternoon. The wind has shifted to the northwest, but the low clouds ahead don't mean rain. Soon, U.S. 63 bears northwest. I continue north on Iowa 149, which

I presume was part of old U.S. 151 but was demoted because of the many ninety-degree turns that survived the upgrading of federal highways. My speed of fifty miles per hour is too fast for some of the angles, but it's a good road with little traffic. I hope I'll never see another interstate.

The Amish either found or made this land serene. I slow down opposite a fragrant field of freshly cut hay. I want my ashes to replenish the soil. Now where did that thought come from? Dvořák and Bill Williams? The small country cemetery on a rise overlooking a valley a few miles back? The quiet? The reunion?

Large fields, small towns, and the carefully mowed lawns around orderly farms have me thinking again of *The Straight Story*. Tomorrow, I'll meet John and Andy. We'll see Stan when possible. The reunion is the start of saying good-bye, especially to Stan, though none of us will say so, least of all Stan.

South of Sigourney, I cross the south and north forks of the Skunk River. They soon get together and head southeast to join the Mississippi near Burlington. Sigourney's fine shade trees arching over small houses and narrow streets remind me of Wisconsin towns. After about ten miles, I turn east on State 22 and drive through the decaying village of Kinross, where a large Victorian house and brick school building lie deserted.

I stop for lunch in Kalona. With a population of nearly two thousand, it's the largest Amish settlement west of the Mississippi. It's a modest community with small frame houses, a handsome brick public library, and a central shopping district that inoffensively caters to tourists. The Kalona Bakery has a horse-drawn buggy on its sign and features "Grandma's Old-Fashioned Cinnamon Rolls."

I step inside, purchase two packages of homemade egg noodles, and order a sandwich. On the wall near my table is a signed photograph that reads, "To our neighbors at the Kalona Bakery from Mr. McCready. Speedy delivery!"

The two young Amish women waiting tables are dressed conservatively in jeans and dark shirts. One has light brown hair and a round face. The other is darker and has longer features. Both have slight German accents, handed down through generations of speaking Pennsylvania Dutch in the home and learning "Deitch" in elementary school. I'm startled to see "New! Taco Wrap!" advertised at a counter. After lunch, I write to Jeanie about Kalona from a shady bench down the street from the bakery.

I close the letter with, "*Je t'aime.*"

Most of the Amish in Kalona belong to the Old Order, the most conservative of the various Mennonite groups that descended from the Anabaptists of the Protestant Reformation. Although there are Mennonite churches in the area, the Old Order Amish worship in homes, in congregations of about three hundred members each. They oppose education beyond junior high because this violates their convictions and does not prepare the young for the Amish way of life. In 1972, the United States Supreme Court upheld this position as a matter of religious freedom, finding against the State of Wisconsin's argument that Amish children must attend high school.

Unlike many Christians, the Amish do not judge people outside their own faith. I thank the Amish for that as I leave Kalona. Driving this old Bug alone, I thank them also for subscribing to a particular biblical injunction, "Be ye not conformed to the world."

A girl in Amish dress stands at a table under an awning where the driveway of her farmhouse meets State Highway 1 north of Kalona. Her sign reads, "Bake Sale."

Half an hour later, I'm in Iowa City. I would not be here but for "Sprie." I have never met Duane Spriestersbach, but I like him just from our correspondence since the publication of my memoir two years ago by the University of Iowa Press, which he had helped get off the ground in the sixties. Our first meeting will probably be our last. He must be pushing eighty, and I don't foresee driving through the Midwest again in the near future. It's never too late to make new friends, but late is getting shorter for both of us. We will start with clean slates. My memoir has already introduced him to my ghosts, so I don't have to silence or mention them.

I ask directions to the University of Iowa's Memorial Union from a goateed youngster in dark glasses behind the wheel of a bright yellow, souped-up pickup.

"Just turn right at the next light and cross the bridge over the Iowa River," he replies, nodding approval at the Bug. "Very nice. Very nice."

My cherried-up Bug has that effect on young hotdogs. Several weeks before leaving Claremont, I was waiting for a green light when a car pulled up next to me with stereo thundering.

"Hey, mister!" I heard through the din.

I looked over, prepared to disdain the hooligan.

"Nice Bug! Nice Bug!" he yelled.

"Thanks!" I shouted to the fine young man.

Nothing compares to the campus of a great Midwestern university in a small city. A heterogeneous multitude of buildings spreads out from Old Main or its equivalent. Literature rubs against engineering; theory against practice. Stadiums compete with intramural fields. Tuition is affordable for most, and budgets are tied to politics. Gown and town overlap, both physically and intellectually. The entire organism lives on debate and interdependence. It works because the people are willing, sensible, and accommodating. Iowa City feels like Madison.

Sprie picks me up at the hotel in the Memorial Union around three thirty. He shows me around the university and town and takes me to dinner. All the while, we exchange stories about backgrounds, careers, and families. He grew up on a small dairy farm in Minnesota, the oldest child and only boy in the family. He assumed he would become a farmer like his dad and inherit the place.

"Boy, that's not what I wanted to do with my life," he admits.

He studied speech pathology at the University of Iowa but was drafted in 1941 before Pearl Harbor. He reported to Fort Riley for basic training at a time when military experts still disagreed over the relative merits of tanks and horse-mounted cavalry. Assigned to the horse cavalry, he found classes on the "nomenclature of the horse" ridiculous because he had grown up around animals. He had his own pony by the age of five. He was a member of a group of GIs who accompanied a Methodist minister from Fort Riley on visits to churches in the area to provide music, readings, and even sermons. Sprie did readings. On December 7, they were returning to the camp when the program on the car radio was interrupted for the news about Pearl Harbor. One of the GIs was Japanese American.

"I didn't know what to say," Sprie recalls. "I wanted to reach over and tell the Japanese kid that everything was going to be okay and I loved him, but I couldn't say anything."

"What happened?" I ask.

"Nothing," he says. "Everyone was quiet. All the way to Fort Riley."

After Officer Candidate School, Sprie was assigned to the personnel section of division headquarters, Thirteenth Armored Division, in California. He assumed the Thirteenth would become part of the Third Army in time for D-Day because the commander knew General Patton well, but the division did not arrive in Normandy until January 1945 … without horses. They had their first taste of combat in the Ruhr pocket, a skirmish in which they sustained few casualties. Riding in a half-track one day with several others of the staff, Sprie was surprised to see his name on a street sign, "*Spriestersbachstrasse*." On leave in Paris after V-E Day, he and a buddy could not find a hotel with vacancies. A French couple sitting behind them on a boulevard bench offered their spare room, gave the two soldiers a key to the apartment, and refused any payment.

"Your memoir's chapters on Paris took me back," he says. "I envy your facility with the language and people. I'd love to go back with you as guide. Let's do it!"

I suspect he'd find the bench and toast the couple.

Sprie's division soon received orders to take thirty days' furlough, report to California, and prepare for combat in Japan. Hiroshima and Nagasaki changed everything.

"On the way to California to join the division," he says, "I listened to a radio broadcast of the formal surrender ceremony on the battleship *Missouri*." He pauses and swallows. "Then they played Beethoven's Fifth Symphony." He hesitates again. "There are times when you don't need words," he says of that moment and this memory of it. I wait a good while for him to break the silence.

Sprie found my memoir very moving. He contacted me because of the photo taken of me in the mess hall in Germany on Sunday, August 20, 1961, a week after the East Germans started building the infamous wall. Rumors of war had been increasing even before this provocative act, and now the tension was palpable. My artillery battalion was on standby alert while an American battle group drove across East Germany to West Berlin. No one could be certain how the East German and Soviet armies would react.

"There's something compelling about that picture," Sprie says. "It's very suggestive. There's something haunting about it."

"Was it the uniform and the tense moment of the Cold War?" I ask.

"Yeah, that's part of it, but it was more than that. I was interested in your face and the look on it."

"Well, I'm glad the picture brought us together."

"So am I," he says.

We concur on politics, especially the country's need for a good, solid Midwestern president for a change. Not one has been elected since Eisenhower in 1956. Sprie likes my suggestion that, for the next twelve years, Congress require that all presidential nominees be Midwesterners, ideally from Wisconsin, Minnesota, or Iowa.

"But what about Texas?" he asks. "I thought you liked Texas."

"Not Texas politics, certainly not today," I say. "Not with the likes of Dick Armey and Tom DeLay. And if Bush is a Texan, which is questionable, he's nowhere near the kind of president this country requires."

Sprie sees a similar decline in the quality of academic leadership. He served as graduate dean and vice president under several presidents at the University of Iowa, among whom he admired Howard Bowen a great deal. Sprie himself was acting president for seven months before the arrival of James Freedman in April 1982. He has recounted these experiences in *The Way It Was: The University of Iowa, 1964-1989* (1999). He gives me a signed copy at dinner. He sees a nationwide trend toward university presidents who boost themselves at least as much as their institutions.

"Like major-league ballplayers?" I ask.

"Exactly," he says.

"You're right, Sprie. But I could accept it more easily if presidents were intellectual leaders as well as fundraisers. We have almost lost the tradition of deans and presidents coming from the ranks of the best scholars and teachers, most of whom are too wise to enter administration these days or too bruised to last very long. The ideal of an intellectual community suffers on the inside. And on the outside, critics with no teaching experience distort selective evidence into false generalizations about our profession. My dean skin was too thin for the politics of a college that divided sharply along ideological lines. I thought some of the fund-raising amounted to doing anything for a buck. Sorry, I'm sounding defensive, probably trying to find excuses for not making it to a college presidency."

"Don't worry," Sprie says. "Few make it who should. Besides, you wouldn't have had time to write your memoir."

"Thanks for that, Sprie. Or time for this trip."

In fact, though I don't say this to Sprie, both the memoir and trip are symptoms of withdrawal, the antithesis of administration. I'm not sure how long solitude and introspection sparred with ambition, probably since boyhood, but they won.

On our way back to the Memorial Union after dinner, he invites me to breakfast at his home tomorrow.

"Eggs or pancakes?" he asks.

"You choose," I reply.

"Okay. My wife is a bit disabled, so I'll be doing the cooking."

"Any advice on caring for an invalid spouse" I ask. I had told him about Jeanie at dinner. "I'm afraid I might not be good at it."

"I understand that feeling," he says, "but you seem the type that will do what's right. That's all we can do. All anyone who faces adversity can do. Do what's right."

I call Jeanie from my room and describe my time with Sprie, omitting the part about caregiving. Even after thirty-three years of marriage, I hold things back. I have never shown Jeanie as much love as I feel for her. Now, expressing my fears about what lies ahead might tell her I don't know what's right. If I do know, I might not do it. I'm afraid of the words.

Sprie saw something haunting in my face in that photo of 1961. An old Madison friend said my memoir helped explain what he saw in my eyes in high school. The parents of one of Dad's graduate students invited us to dinner in their New York apartment in September 1951 before Dad, John, and I sailed to France and a reunion with my mother.

As we left the apartment, the student's father said to me, "I can tell that, when you grow up, you will sometimes be very happy and sometimes very unhappy."

Later, I asked Dad what that meant.

He said, "Don't worry about it. The man didn't know you."

I still worry about it, about what people read on the outside. What's inside?

Saturday, June 1

Sprie and Bette live in a hillside neighborhood on the northern edge of town. Their house reminds me of what Jeanie and I called our "tree house" in Austin, surrounded by trunks marching downhill, foliage at eye-level, and birdsong. Also trained in speech pathology, Bette taught before their children were born and after they began high school. She changed the spelling of her name from "Betty" to "Bette" as a girl.

"I adored Bette Davis," she explains.

"So did my mother," I reply.

Bette is kind and bright. She doesn't complain about having to use a cane or wheelchair. They have a portable wheelchair for trips, and they recommend I get one like it for Jeanie. Sprie shows me his copy of the history of the Thirteenth Armored Division. In pictures, he looks like a college student. He and Bette married after the war.

"What was it like marrying a veteran?" I ask her.

"Well, what do I have to compare it to?" she replies with a chuckle.

At breakfast, they describe the Amana communities west of here. These were established in 1855 by German Pietists who had immigrated first to western New York in the 1840s. Sprie and Bette brag about the fresh produce from farms in Amana and closer to Iowa City. They freeze a lot of it. Sprie's pancakes contain last year's blueberries. They are delicious with maple syrup. I compliment him on his cooking.

I ask, "Why do you keep referring to me as 'young man'?"

"Because you are," he says.

"Well, how old are you?" I ask.

"Eighty-five."

"My gosh, I would have said seventy-eight. Maybe eighty at the outside. "Okay, you can call me 'young' if you want. It's a moving target, isn't it?"

"Yes," says Sprie. "Yes, it is."

We say good-bye as if we will meet again. As I leave Iowa City, I hold onto that remote prospect like a good book. They are wonderful people, witty, informed, ethical, tolerant, unpretentious, and rock-solid. They don't fit today's bloated conceptions of success and importance. Just look at their lives. Sprie: active duty and the reserves, teaching, writing, and administration at the University of Iowa, which he helped through an expansive and difficult period for higher education. Bette: teaching and advising in speech pathology, mothering two children. Our society doesn't recognize people like them who show up every day and are honest, dependable, and effective.

Perhaps universities ought to announce major fund-raising campaigns with something like, "We want to raise X million dollars to honor all of those who have made this a great institution." No buildings would be named for wealthy donors or recent presidents. The money raised would be a general tribute to the lifeblood of education, a reminder that we aspire to be a republic.

When I was a boy, my parents had friends and colleagues like the Spriestersbachs. The goodwill of dinner parties floated upstairs. I missed it while my mother was away.

The morning is clear and bright, but I don't put on my dark glasses. I want to see the colors of this country as they are. I travel northeast on State 1, the route of the military and stage road from Iowa City to Dubuque in the 1840s. If I were a Republican, I would detour ten miles east of Iowa City to visit Herbert Hoover's birthplace in West Branch.

In the town of Solon, a sign welcomes me to "Spartan Country." Why Spartans? Because they won? This Solon was the son of the town's founder, but the original's legal reforms in the early sixth century BC helped Athens become the democracy that eventually fought autocratic Sparta and lost. According to Herodotus, Solon visited Croesus late in life. The wealthy king of Lydia asked Solon whom he considered the happiest men he had met in all his years of politics and travel. When Solon did not mention him, Croesus demanded to know why. The wealthy man may be fortunate, Solon replied, but no one is happy before death, and even then happy only if dying peaceably.

I will see John and Andy in about five hours. They both left home yesterday morning. John is coming from Nashville and Andy from Dallas. They would stay in motels last night and spend this morning driving through southern Wisconsin and Madison. As we corresponded about this reunion, we began calling ourselves "Fellows of West Lawn" after our boyhood street in Madison, or FOWLs for short. The street and the memories have always brought us together, but this would be our first meeting as aging, self-described FOWLs. I wonder how it will go. I hope to savor the event and not worry about consequence. But living for the moment has always eluded me. How can you disengage moment from expectation or remembrance?

I'll probably revert to the status of younger brother. I often defer to John, as I did when we were kids. It's no longer a question of size, age, or confidence. But it's still Pavlovian, like classmates at high school reunions minding old hierarchies. How much private ground will each of us open up? I'd like to know their joys and regrets and tell them mine. It's still hard for me to talk about Mom's illness and absence, even with John and Andy. It's harder for John. What about Andy? In an e-mail message a couple of months ago, he said that, before he died, he wanted to understand Gustav Mahler and Ezra Pound. Andy has always had an ecumenical curiosity about literature and music. He has sold himself short as an interpreter or critic and as a teacher of English at two private schools. Modesty often accompanies an open mind. In his case, like my mother's, low self-confidence foreshadowed breakdown and never fully recovered.

We'll drive over to Milwaukee to see Stan. I can't imagine him with Parkinson's disease. I can only see him with hay fever. He would come out onto his front porch, open the screen door, haul out a blue bandana, and rock the neighborhood. He threw the door open one Friday evening the summer after my freshman year in college, just as I returned home from a hot day's work on a section gang for the Chicago & North Western Railroad.

I braced myself for the blast, but Stan shouted, "Hey, Gaines! Wanna go to Duluth?"

We left an hour later and drove all night. Stan took early morning photos of the huge Mallets that pulled long trains of iron ore from the Mesabi Range to the docks on Lake Superior.

Meadowlarks sing from both sides of the bridge over the Cedar River, south of Mount Vernon and Cornell College. Soon, I turn northeast on U.S. 151, which has been widened and straightened since the late 1940s. Two monstrous new houses squat on a hillside, overstacked like the one near Bloomfield yesterday morning. Even pastoral Iowa has caught this grotesque architectural virus. I have been searching for a name for the style. Now I have it. With apologies to the animal, I'll call it "buffalo hump."

On the way to the Mississippi, I encounter two rivers sounding like Wisconsin and Minnesota, the Wapsipinicon and the Maquoketa. I see rolling farmland with dark soil and red barns on stone foundation walls. I see signs for "Ski Sundown Mountain, Dubuque, Five Lifts!" and "Dubuque Field Archers Range."

Julien Dubuque, a French Canadian trapper and trader, so impressed the Fox that they granted him land here in the 1770s along with sole permission to mine the lead ores it contained. I bear east in his town and cross the Mississippi.

The river dwarfs everything but the sky. The bridge is a Tinkertoy. Weekend pleasure boats leave petty wakes. Barges moving fast against the current make slow headway against the shore. My generation of Madison schoolchildren could easily point to the Mississippi on the large rolled maps that our teachers pulled down like shades to open up the world. We were proud that Marquette and Joliet had to cross our state to find the river. We knew about Tom Sawyer and Huck Finn and paddle wheelers. We knew what Tom and Huck meant by the river's "June rise" because rivers near Madison flooded in June. We didn't know the meaning of the Michissipi or Mesi sipi ("big river") to the Indians, before and after whites began to settle the upper Midwest. We didn't know about the first French explorers' belief that the river flowed to the Pacific. We didn't know about the decline in steamboat shipments of grain from Minnesota and Iowa south to the Gulf as railroads and steel bridges opened faster routes across Wisconsin and Illinois to eastern cities. We didn't know the astounding size of the river and the territory it drains from the Rockies to the Alleghenies, which is about 42 percent of the area of the lower forty-eight states. We knew nothing of such things.

Growing up only ninety miles east of the Mississippi, I thought of the great river as out there. Beyond it were only two of the Big Nine (later Big Ten) universities whose teams marked the center of my universe. Out there beyond Minnesota and Iowa was the West. Way out there was California, where you could play football on New Year's Day without mittens. To the east, Lake Michigan was over there. Ted Williams hit home runs, and Dad got his PhD back there in Boston. The North Woods were up there. Texas was down there. It was also a little out there because of cowboys, but Haskell County looked nothing like the Westerns of Hollywood, which, to this day, will put mountains around Dodge City.

Attending graduate school at Stanford in 1963 was my Louisiana Purchase. Since then, I have resided west of the Mississippi, hiked the Rockies and Sierra Nevada, roamed the Great Basin, trailed cattle in Wyoming, and read Wallace Stegner, Ivan Doig, John McPhee, Larry McMurtry, Dee Brown, Ian Frazier, William Least Heat-Moon, Rick Bass, Dan O' Brien, Barry Lopez, and Scott Momaday. After forty years, I believe I am a Westerner, at least by adoption. But a funny thing happened several years ago when I picked up Hamlin Garland's *A Son of the Middle Border* for the first time since college.

He begins, "All of this universe known to me in the year 1864 was bounded by the wooded hills of a little Wisconsin coulee" (Garland 1927).

The Garlands moved to Minnesota in 1868, and then to Iowa and South Dakota, pursuing the father's dream of farming wheat on virgin soil as the frontier moved west. As I accompanied them this time, my eagerness to explore their next place changed to regret that they left Wisconsin.

The Midwest is a moving target. To American colonists, the West meant beyond the Alleghenies. Later, the Founding Fathers referred to the land north of the Ohio River and east of the Mississippi as the Northwest Territory. As European Americans migrated west, they hung onto the word as they pushed the idea beyond the homestead. After the Mississippi changed from national boundary to gateway, the Union Army's Iron Brigade, with regiments from Indiana and Michigan as well as Wisconsin, was a western unit in the Army of the Potomac. The Northwest became Midwest, not Midlands or Middle East. Now, the Midwest extends from Ohio to the Dakotas, Nebraska, and Kansas. Except for paradoxical Indiana, the Midwestern states derive their names from the languages of woodland Native Americans. White settlers hung onto the names while humbling the Indians and pushing most of them beyond the Mississippi onto the Great Plains and into stereotypes of the West. Six of the names denote lakes and rivers: big (Michigan), cloudy (Minnesota), muddy (Missouri), broad or flat (Nebraska, the Platte), fine (Ohio), and place of the beaver (Wisconsin).

This enormous midsection measures eleven hundred miles from Cleveland to Scottsbluff, eight hundred miles from Joplin to International Falls. Two-thirds of it lies in seven states west of the Mississippi. Only those who live in the Midwest know that their portion is not like the others. Eastern classmates at Cornell believed I came from "out near Montana." And Lady Something-or-Other at a black-tie dinner in Oxford forty years ago exclaimed, "Oh, yes! Where they grow all that wheat!"

"No, no," I corrected her. "Dairies and lakes and woods. Not wheat and Missouri River and Great Plains. Upper Midwest. East of the Mississippi. I come from Wisconsin."

I angle north on Illinois 35, where a sign indicates the way to Wisconsin, not Prairie du Chien or Platteville or Monroe, just Wisconsin. The youthful thrill of returning has aged and I no longer have kin there, but the very name still sounds like home. I like the W sound, the symmetry of three syllables of equal length with vowels in the middle, the repetition of the I and N sounds. The associations still run deep. They crowd to the surface as I approach the state line: boyhood, university, "On Wisconsin," Camp Manitowish and canoe trips, camping, wayside parks, Devil's Lake, Ingraham hill, Madison's lakes, the combined high school choirs singing carols in the capitol, the sound of Dad stoking the furnace on winter mornings, WHA radio, hospitals, and West Lawn Avenue.

Illinois 35 becomes Wisconsin 11. The pavement improves, and I pass Fairplay Road. The state highway sign has the shape and design of old. The first barn is red; the farmhouse is white. Neither needs paint.

"Hooray!" I cheer.

For the moment, I have no need for ancestors or trails. Sacred Eagle Woman, my bloodline is irrelevant. Jed Smith, the West is all yours. Gaines, the purpose of your trip is simple. Driving the Bug is incidental. This is your place. You're home.

One thing has changed. There are no elms. Large stumps are all that remain of the once standard shade tree for Wisconsin farms and towns. But even the stumps are trim, as if to accentuate the harmony of the tableau. I'm in hilly country with steeper valleys and fewer lakes than elsewhere in the state. Southwestern Wisconsin is part of the Driftless Area that escaped glacial grinding during the last stage (Wisconsinan) of the Ice Age. Altitudes reach over twice that of the Mississippi. The elevation is about six hundred feet at Dubuque, twelve hundred fifty feet in Dodgeville, and thirteen hundred feet at Blue Mounds, the twin hills west of Madison that Indians once used as a landmark.

The Fox, Sac, and Winnebago valued the region's lead ores for trade. Surface mining began to attract Americans to northwestern Illinois and southwestern Wisconsin after the War of 1812 secured American control over its own Northwest Territory. The British had promised the Northwest to Tecumseh's revived Indian confederacy in return for their alliance. The American victory doomed the French-Indian culture that had prevailed in Wisconsin since the seventeenth century.

The majority in the first wave of Americans to hit Wisconsin, then part of the Michigan Territory, hailed from states south of the Ohio River. So did most of the emigrants on the move from both sides of the Appalachians after the peace of 1815. It was a restless time for Anglo-American Southerners and Westerners. The defeat of Tecumseh and the federal policy of removing Indians beyond the Mississippi unless they agreed to become civilized farmers opened up land. Some of it was given to veterans as bounties for enlisting. Among the most restless Americans were those who had fought for the expansionist aims of Washington War Hawks like Henry Clay from Kentucky and John Calhoun from South Carolina. Many of these emigrants made their way northwest, but more kept to familiar latitudes, as did war veterans on both sides of my family who crossed the Mississippi. The Ballards moved from Kentucky to Missouri in the 1820s. The Fitzgeralds moved from Georgia to Texas in the 1830s. Shortly after marrying in July 1935, my parents defied tradition in both families by moving north when the University of Wisconsin offered Dad a steady job during the Great Depression.

Henry Dodge entered Wisconsin's history in the 1820s when he came up the Mississippi from Missouri to open a lead mine near what became Dodgeville. Although called "Honest Harry" in Missouri, he was a squatter in Wisconsin. He was like others who settled on Indian land without permission or on public land before it had been surveyed and put up for sale. But squatting and government acquiescence became common long before the Preemption Act of 1841 legitimated the practice. With military support from Forts Crawford (Prairie du Chien) and Howard (Green Bay), Dodge and others compelled Indian tribes to continue giving up their rights to the land. When Black Hawk refused, Colonel Dodge's volunteers played a major role in the war that followed.

Black Hawk's defeat in 1832 opened the floodgates of settlement just as the Erie Canal and steamboats on the Great Lakes were transforming patterns of migration. Hitherto, most emigrants bound for the Northwest, where slavery was prohibited, traveled through the Ohio and Mississippi Valleys, natural routes for yeomen from Kentucky, Tennessee, western North Carolina, and Virginia. But transportation by canals and lakes changed the axis of settlement. Wisconsin's population grew from about twelve thousand in 1836 when the Wisconsin Territory was established to thirty-one thousand in 1840. Two years after statehood, in 1850, the population was a little over three hundred thousand. In 1860, it was nearly eight hundred thousand.

In 1854, when the Republican Party was founded at Ripon, settlers from north of the 40th parallel—Pennsylvania, New York, New England, Canada, and Europe—far outnumbered those from south of it. The rapid growth of railroads in the 1850s, which expedited trade with the East through Milwaukee and Chicago, strengthened economic and political ties between northwestern and northeastern America. In 1856, Abraham Lincoln won a lawsuit against the steamship company whose boat rammed the Rock Island Railroad's new bridge across the Mississippi. He argued that Americans have as much right to travel east-west as north-south. In 1860, Wisconsin was firmly Yankee and voted for Lincoln.

During the mining boom that began in the 1820s, many of the miners lived like badgers in the holes they dug with shovels, picks, gads, hand drills, and blasting powder. Most of their excavations and mounds have grown over since settlements like New Diggings and Lead Mine turned into ghost towns. Here, unlike the arid Southwest, nature has hidden the wounds from view. A roadside marker near Benton pays tribute to Father Samuel Mazzuchelli, a Dominican missionary who came to this region in 1835 and began to establish schools and train teachers. Irish miners called him Father "Mathew Kelly."

When I stop in Benton to photograph an old Methodist church, a van parks behind me. A large family climbs out. Parents and kids look at my Bug, California plates, and Teva sandals, but no one comes over to strike up a conversation. I read both disinterest and suspicion in their faces, and I hate to see either in Wisconsin.

More markers appear from Benton to Schullsburg, which was founded in 1827 and is now the home of the Badger Mine Museum. Wisconsin and Texas have at least one thing in common. They offer a lot of history on the road, more than the other states I have driven through. Informative signs are clearly placed and easily accessible. If you can measure the degree of a state's historical self-consciousness by its roadside markers, then I owe even more to both states than I thought.

A sign reads, "Wayside, 1 mile." Wisconsin prides itself in what most other states call "roadsides." The typical Wisconsin wayside is green, clean, and wooded with picnic tables. There's an occasional fireplace, and fresh water is sometimes drawn from an old hand pump.

I slow down to let a car pass. The driver makes an "O" sign with thumb and forefinger so I can see it through his rear window. I return the sign. A red-winged blackbird hovers to a landing on a bush off the right shoulder. Nearing Monroe, I pull over and glance at my map. I see names long forgotten but instantly familiar, such as Monticello, New Glarus, Brodhead, Janesville, Beloit, Belleville, Evansville, Paoli, Mt. Horeb, Verona, Edgerton, Stoughton, and Footville. I'm tempted to continue east to Footville, where our Chicago & North Western crew rebuilt a grade crossing in the summer of 1956. The oldest gandy dancer, a shell-shocked World War II artilleryman, showed me how to shovel asphalt. But the track has probably been torn up by now. In any case, I want to stop in New Glarus for a Swiss-German slice of America's Dairyland. I follow the bypass around Monroe and turn north on State 69 near the Alphorn Motel.

In Monticello, a sign points to the Zwingli church and a marker honors Nickolaus Gerber. Born in Switzerland, Gerber came to America and established New York's first Limburger cheese factory. He moved to this part of Wisconsin in the 1860s, started cheese factories on several farms, launched the cooperative farmer factory system, and co-founded Green County Cheese Days. North of town, I pass "Voegele Farm—Brown Swiss Cows." America's Dairyland indeed.

The ranger at the entrance to New Glarus Woods State Park is unimpressed by my story of returning more than fifty years after picnicking there with my family.

I ask, "May I look around briefly and use the men's room?"

He says, "Sure. For three dollars. Entrance fee."

But I'm old now and stubborn, and the Bug reminds me of being young and broke. So I circle his kiosk and leave.

New Glarus teems with activity. Swiss Historical Village always draws weekend crowds, but there is also a large public party in the center of town today. Switzerland prevails. There are flags, chalets, cuckoo clocks, cowbells, streets with Swiss-German names, and the bright redbrick Swiss United Church of Christ (*Schweizerisch Reformierte Kirche, gebaut AD 1900*).

In front of the church, a monument to the first settlers of the Swiss colony of New Glarus, August 16, 1845, includes names like Baebler, Becker, Duerst, Hoesly, and Aebli. You can still hear the Swiss-German dialect in shops and on sidewalks. On a block of First Street closed to traffic, a large, red-white striped marquee shades a dance floor, an oompa band with accordion, and hundreds of revelers seated at long tables drinking beer. They celebrate the First Annual Roger Bright Polkafest. Bright is the "goodwill ambassador of New Glarus." The music takes me back to Uncle Julius' band playing the "Too Fat Polka" on the radio in Madison in the 1940s.

In Deininger's Restaurant, an old house on a slope two blocks above the party, I lunch on Thuringer sausage, sauerkraut, fried potatoes with onions, and a nutty pilsner from the New Glarus Brewing Company: excellent. The proprietress is too young to tell me where I ate Swiss steak in this town as a boy, but I remember a stone building and basement dining room. Dad had taken John and me to Schiller's *William Tell* in a field outside of town. The woman says the play is still performed every Labor Day weekend, twice in English and once in German.

"We also have Heidi Days," she says eagerly.

"Not when I was a boy," I reply.

I catch myself before adding that I cannot imagine any red-blooded Wisconsin boy at Heidi Days ever.

North of New Glarus, small dairy farms nestle into vest-pocket valleys below wooded knolls. From a hill just after entering Dane County, I see more tilled fields than anywhere else on the trip, and more silos rising above the treetops. This is some of America's richest, most beautiful farmland. The scale has remained small. The valleys and farmhouses are inviting, self-contained, and comforting. Someone has been cutting hay.

People obey speed limits here, even the bikers ahead of me who have just slowed to twenty-five miles per hour for Belleville. The standard limit in Wisconsin towns is twenty-five, sometimes twenty. The Californian in me wonders what the hell's wrong with the guy in front and wants to ride his bumper. Relax, another voice tells me. You're in Wisconsin. Drive accordingly and enjoy.

North of Belleville, I take County A east, cross the old Illinois Central tracks that ran from Freeport to Madison, and remember the IC freight trains rumbling two hundred yards from my house. I'll bet I'm the first person to drive County A in a '66 Bug with California plates. If I'm not the first, then I'll surely be the last. My dad knew every side road in these parts, pursuing wildflowers, autumn color, tracks of the Wisconsin Glacier, and long stretches where our dog Barbos could run alongside the car. County A, paved since Dad and I drove it together when most of these roads were gravel, takes a series of ninety-degree turns around fields. Madison, about fifteen miles north, has crept down this way. There is more traffic on the larger north-south roads. Homes here and there have a commuter feel, but at least they aren't built in the buffalo hump style. In Stoughton, along the main street, Norwegian flags alternate with American. I pass the Viking Laundry. A young man in a new American car flashes me thumbs up.

About thirty Holsteins have gathered for afternoon tea in a pasture near the Jefferson County line, where my road changes from A to C. The land has flattened out and settled since lunch. Somewhere north of New Glarus, Dad would have shown me where I left the Driftless Area, crossed the southwestern limit of the last glaciation, and began slowly to descend into the broad basin left by the retreating ice ten to fifteen thousand years ago. The soil grows lighter brown as I approach Fort Atkinson, elevation about eight hundred feet. The fort was named after the general who built a stockade there during the Black Hawk War. I turn north on State 26 to Jefferson, where I buy two bottles of California wine, one red and one white. The wine, egg noodles from Kalona, and remains of a bottle of Scotch will be my first contributions to the reunion larder. I take U.S. 18 east, avoiding Interstate 94. I skirt Golden Lake and crisscross the Bark River, both of which look good for leisurely canoeing.

Around four o'clock, I cross I-94 and reach the resort outside Oconomowoc where Andy has rented a condo for the week. It's about halfway between West Lawn and Stan. Andy and John planned to arrive by three o'clock. I'm sure they have staked claims to the two bedrooms, leaving me the sitting room couch. I'm the youngest FOWL.

I park, get out, and stretch. I made it, twenty-four hundred miles. John and Andy questioned my sanity when I told them I would do it in the old Bug. I showed 'em. My last call to either of them was from Carthage, three days ago. Keep 'em in suspense.

I rap on the door of the condo. No answer. I try again. Still no answer. Did I get the wrong number? Have they gone shopping? I put my ear to the door and hear scrambling and low voices. I knock again, firmly and impatiently. The door opens. There's no one in sight. What the hell's going on?

The short hallway is dark. The sitting room is faintly visible beyond. Music suddenly blasts down the hallway. It's Wagner's "The Ride of the Valkyries."

CHAPTER 5

▼

FELLOWS OF WEST LAWN

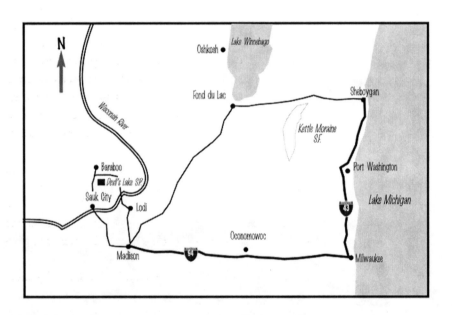

In some ways, the reunion of FOWLs became what I would have expected if I had flown to Wisconsin. Old companions, we engaged in long, episodic streams of consciousness from beginnings to retirement, Second World War to War on Terror, horseplay to depression, love to heartbreak, and dreams to deeds. As is my nature, I would have tried later to find meaning in all of this. Maybe I would have sent John and Andy a long letter for their comments. But the reunion turned out to be the middle of the story, not a narrative in itself. Eight days of driving alone in the Bug was not incidental. By the time I arrived in Wisconsin, I was ready to explore the origins of my deep feelings about the land, the early use I had made of it for enjoyment, seclusion, and recovery.

"Just like the relationship between Adams and Jefferson," Andy says over steaks and Kalona noodles on Saturday night.

Andy and John had indeed claimed the upstairs bedrooms, so I stowed my gear in the downstairs closet. I'll sleep on the sofa bed. Halfway through the CDs that Andy has loaded into his portable player, Mahler's First Symphony has just finished. Prokofiev's *Romeo and Juliet* now fills the sitting/dining room.

"They were necessary to each other," Andy continues. "Otherwise, things would have fallen flat. That's why you guys are so dear to me."

"As you are to us," John replies. "And it's more than a guy thing. There's a long history."

The friendship between Post and Mailer brothers began in Madison in May 1942. The Mailers had moved from Galesburg, Illinois, to the dark brown house with white trim across the street, number 2310. The father was off at war. The mother wanted to be near her family in Madison. We were boys then. Andy was eleven, Stan seven, John five, and I four. Sixty years later, our parents are gone, and our children look ahead. Andy has snow-white hair and too many pounds. John has a bad back and a weak Achilles tendon. I take pills to lower my cholesterol. We have become "keepers of the tablets," as Andy puts it. We are custodians of family history, tellers of stories, and retirees who will soon replace GIs as the oldest generation.

Over the next seven days, conversations and outings return us to old haunts. Stan will join us on the two days when we can persuade him that he's well enough to leave his rented room. Madison, Devil's Lake and the Baraboo Hills, the North Woods, farmland, side roads, and moraines. Wisconsin's landscape helped us locate ourselves early on. That grounding experience is essential to the story.

We fought the Second World War on the 2300 block of West Lawn Avenue. Tall elm trees arched over our battlefield. They were planted when the houses were built about twenty years earlier. No two houses were alike. No fences surrounded them. Houses on the southeast side of the street, like the Posts' house at 2313, occupied slightly higher ground. Their front lawns and driveways sloped upward. A stone wall supported our upper terrace. The driveway burrowed into the garage under Dad's study. Mom had a small wildflower garden outside the kitchen window, with trillium, lily of the valley, and jack-in-the-pulpit. Everyone on our block was white. There were probably more Catholics than Protestants because we lived near parochial schools. There were two or three Jewish families.

Madison's rich lived elsewhere in places like University Heights, Shorewood, and Maple Bluff. West Lawn housed the middle class from postal workers to doctors. Several families still used iceboxes, which delighted us when we climbed into the back of the delivery truck to gather cold shavings on hot summer days. Dogs followed us, sat with us on front porches when we read comics, and watched us play touch football in the street.

The Post brothers (author on the right) at home, Madison, Wisconsin

In June 2002, the houses seem not only smaller and closer together, but also a few rungs lower on the middle-class ladder. No dwelling has been demolished to make way for upscale bulk. Not much has changed on the surface, save the disappearance of ice trucks; the absence of kids and dogs playing outside; the addition of a porch here and there, including 2313; the colors of some sidings; and the substitution of other hardwoods for trees lost to Dutch elm disease. I want to race around back after football late on a fall afternoon, open the kitchen door, have my glasses steam up, and ask Mom or Dad what's for supper.

"It's not our West Lawn anymore," John says.

He puts his hands on his hips as we stand in the middle of the quiet street. Andy and I grunt in agreement. We shall always dress up the street for that other time and long to be young there, free to try again. If we dig around the nostalgia to find who we were then on our only try, it's still our street. We dig all week during this first reunion of FOWLs. We do not long for everything we find. And we can't separate then from now.

"Remember that tree on our terrace?" I remark. "About five feet up from the wall? Right about where that squirrel is. It had twin trunks branching off low down. In one of my last nightmares about animals, a lion was chasing me across the terrace. I jumped through that V-shaped trunk and stopped on the other side and looked around. I laughed at the lion as it jumped after me. The lion vanished, and that was that."

"I read about an African tribe," Andy says. "When the child has a frightening dream about an animal, the parents tell the child to go back and dream the dream again. The child must make a friend of the animal. Seems to work. We've lost that wisdom."

"Nobody gave me that advice," I recall. "I had lots of bad dreams during the war. In the summer, I'd go to bed while it was still light. I'd hear robins chirp on the lawn, 'Cheer up! Cheer up!' is how Mom described their song. I hoped I wouldn't dream about bombs falling on the house or Nazis coming through the door. Hey, look at that retaining wall in front of our house and the Stevens'. Natural rock, like the old one we had. But this one's got cleaner lines and less moss in the cracks."

Andy was an older kid, which excluded him from our war games by mutual agreement. Every older kid was a potential enemy, but Andy didn't join the gang of junior high bullies in our part of town. The Hitler who lived next door to him led the gang. After Andy punched Hitler for taunting him, Adolf left us alone when Andy was near. I looked up to Andy from then on, but I wasn't immediately aware that he had taught me the central moral lesson of the war.

Stan specialized in explosives, model airplanes, and sound effects. John and I mastered laying down smoke screens and building snow forts with clear fields of fire. We bartered after school for insignias, C rations, medals, and anything with powder in it. We rehearsed tactics in case German or Japanese soldiers came through the Mailers' screen porch or over the Posts' stone wall. On the way home from Dudgeon School, we sabotaged German trains on the Illinois Central tracks or rooted out Japanese machine gun nests in the woods on the shore of Lake Wingra. In a few years, we had to be ready to fight alongside our GI heroes.

Stan and Andy did not talk about their father during the war. He was away in the Army. That's all John and I knew about him then. He had fought in France in the First World War, when he was in the field artillery and wounded twice.

"I have a picture of him in uniform in Scotland after World War I," Andy tells us in front of 2310. "Very heroic. He came back and got through the University of Wisconsin and med school. Then he went down to Chicago, Cook County Hospital, to train in orthopedics and abdominal surgery. He operated on one of the Genna brothers. It was like trying to sew up a sieve, and the guy died on the operating table. A few days later, my father's getting a shave near the hospital. It's a rough section of town and the barber's using a straight razor. He says, 'So you're the doc operated on Tony Genna, huh?' My father thought his time had come."

Members of the North Side Gang shot Tony Genna eight times in the back on July 8, 1925. He was the third Genna brother to die in forty-five days. The remaining three brothers soon left Chicago, where the North Side bunch continued to fight Al Capone for gangland supremacy.

Dr. Mailer showed no fondness for Andy or Stan, but he wept over the death of former comrades-in-arms. He joined the Illinois National Guard in the mid-thirties and gladly left the family for active duty shortly after Pearl Harbor.

"He handed everything off to my mother," Andy says, as if he were testifying against him in court. "You know, 'I'm off to the wars, dear.'"

"Well," I interject, "I don't like saying this, but my dad let a whole lot of stuff accumulate on Mom's shoulders. He just assumed the wife should hold the home front while he did his teaching and research."

"That's the way it was done in those days," John adds. "Very hard on women."

"Yeah," Andy agrees. "And they got stronger and stronger lifting all that weight."

"Not all of them," I say. "Not Mom."

Dr. Mailer commanded a medical unit in the China-Burma-India Theater. He came back as a full colonel. Andy and his mother met him at the Milwaukee Road station in the fall of 1945.

"He was in uniform," Andy says. "He weighed about one sixty-five and looked great. His chest was full of ribbons with silver eagles up here. Things soon went downhill from there."

Andy's mother was a Hanks, one of Madison's oldest and most distinguished families. She was distantly related to Abraham Lincoln's mother, Nancy Hanks. In the late 1850s, Andy's great-grandfather, Lucien Stanley Hanks, shared a bed one night with Lincoln in Janesville, Wisconsin, in a house that was short on beds.

Lincoln asked the young man, "Lucien, do you kick?"

"No, sir," he replied.

"Well, I do, so move a little further over," Lincoln said.

Soon after the transcontinental railroad opened in May 1869, banker L. S. Hanks joined a party of Wisconsin businessmen and politicians to travel from Madison to San Francisco. They dined on buffalo and antelope in Nebraska and attended a performance of Bellini's *La Somnambula* at the Laramie Opera. At Sherman Summit just east of Laramie, the highest point on the line, they unfurled the Wisconsin state flag and gave three cheers for the flag and the rail-road. In Salt Lake City, Brigham Young assured them that faith made it easy to manage many wives for women gladly gave up trifles and vanities for religion.

"Think of it," Andy exclaims. "These guys are gentlemen at the top of the social scale, and they hop on a train to see what's going on out West, way beyond the frontier. Just think of it. They saw virgin land. They were privileged. They had a sense of history and legacy."

"I don't see much of that among today's youth," I reply. "It's hard to chart rates of change, but I think our society has changed more since we were kids than it did between our grandfathers and our childhood. Whether we felt blessed or saddled by ancestry, we knew it was inside us. John and I could always hold on to Haskell, especially after Mom left. Haskell meant the ranch, relatives and friends 'visiting,' as they called it, on porches and under shade trees, and stories about the old days. People thought Mom was the prettiest tomboy in the county and Dad was the smartest kid with no sense at all. That sort of historical bequest is price-less. It helps you steer. But after Jeanie and I go, I doubt that our kids will have much interest in what came before us. For one thing, they don't feel part of what Sacred Eagle Woman, the Osage I met a few days ago, calls my bloodline. Even if they were our biological kids, they'd probably not look closely at legacy as some-thing about character that we inherit and pass on. That's Sacred Eagle Woman's worry, too. Her grandchildren are losing their tribal memory. Maybe every older generation feels this and I've sounded the old fart theme of this reunion."

"But one of the positive differences between our grandfathers and our kids is attitudes toward women," John argues. "Also race. Night and day differences!"

"True," Andy admits, "but it's a shock to see things so radically altered in such a short time and so many people whom Arthur Koestler refers to in *Darkness at Noon* as those 'born without umbilical cords.'"

L. S. Hanks' son, Stanley, built one of the first houses in Maple Bluff in the mid-twenties on Lakewood Boulevard near the shore of Lake Mendota. Mrs. Mailer would often bring the boys up from Galesburg before the war to see her parents and her brother, Lucien.

"The big house at 315," Andy still calls it.

He shows us a photo of himself taken in 1947.

He says, "That's the shirt Uncle Lue gave me when he came back from the war. Right after the bomb, August of '45. He had been in air intelligence, stationed in Italy. He was single, a great support to my mother. He stored his old uniforms in our front closet for a while. I needed a father. Thank God, Uncle Lue was there."

Andy's father moved out of the house on West Lawn three years after the war. I noticed the change, and I was puzzled. Dr. Mailer liked my dad and treated me kindly when he took out my appendix in 1946 or 1947. Mrs. Mailer sued for divorce in 1952, and the brothers were not sorry. According to Andy, Stan had retreated before the war into "his private world of watching trains and building models." He was unhappy to see his father return in 1945. Andy had everything his father admired, including excellent grades in high school, extraordinarily good looks, athletic prowess as a letterman in football and track, and a circle of close friends.

"But my father couldn't reach across the chasm between us," Andy says.

In December 1950, when Andy was about to be drafted, his father blew a fuse.

"'I'd rather see you dead than in the army!'" Andy remembers him yelling.

"That's strange coming from him," I observe.

"Well, he was coming apart. War was for him, not us. And he thought he had gone to war the second time so his sons would not have to. My mother and Uncle Lue had the presence of mind to have me look at options for service. Several friends and I picked the air force. It was a new branch that a lot of smart young guys were signing up for."

I envied Andy and Stan in those days for having relatives in Madison. I was thrilled when their uncle told John and me to call him Uncle Lue. Our kin were in Texas. That was good for summer adventures and reassuring memories, but it was too distant for hands-on guidance through our postwar bewilderment. But we had the father we needed. He was there for us when Mom was away, doing his best and loving us. We somehow knew this, despite his worries about career and his bashfulness around any show of affection.

I tell John and Andy that I telephoned Mrs. Rengstorff while in Madison in 2000 for my high school reunion. Spry and delightful company at ninety-two, she was the only person remaining on our block of West Lawn from our time when she and her husband owned a popular bookstore near the university.

"Now come pick me up. I'll take you to dinner and we'll tell stories," she rejoiced.

That's what we did.

"I really liked your mother," she said, "so effective with children. When we moved to West Lawn during the war, we found you, John, and a couple other kids roaming around inside the empty house. Your mother came over and just gently insisted you come home and let the new people move in. That impressed me, and I stayed impressed from then on."

Mrs. Rengstorff said that a woman down the street, who had lost a son in the war, came to her after Mom left and asked, "'What would you think if I asked Mr. Post if I could take in his boys?' I said, 'Absolutely not. No chance of that. I know Mr. Post and those boys.'"

"John, I got the impression from Stan back then," Andy recalls, "that you were tough to get along with. There was some kind of conflict going on between you and your dad. Stan said he saw your dad hit you."

"I was very unhappy and undisciplined, disturbed," John replies. "If it hadn't been for the family getting back together in Paris, God knows what would have happened to me. I had a lot of verbal fights with Dad. He hit me once when I called Gaines a 'little shit.' But he kept us going. I guess I would have survived as a mixed-up kid, but, if Mom hadn't come back, I don't know what else could have turned me around."

"We had no idea she would come back," I add. "I think, deep down we had given up. As I look back, I can see why Dad would be more anxious and upset by you than by me when Mom was gone. I tried hard to be liked. That meant being funny, cheerful, and helpful. It worked, and you resented that. I pretended to be happy, Andy. John didn't. Sort of like the difference between you and Stan. You tried to please. Stan said to hell with anything that interfered with his world of railroads. That's probably why John took to Stan and started his own model railroad. They were more honest than I in coping."

"Well, I was confused," John says.

His admission comes from the heart. But, as usual, John stops short of recounting the heartbreak. That would undo him too much for telling even us.

"But when a kid pretends the way I did, he's hurting," I say. "No one knew how I felt when pretending didn't work. I wanted to be alone, ride my bike, or hide somewhere. I'd go in the attic if it was raining. And that started during the war, before Mom first went to the hospital. John had his ways of dealing with the hurt. I had mine. That's still true."

It's late Sunday afternoon. We have spent all day at the condo talking.

"In the divorce proceedings," Andy says out of the blue, "my father accused my mother of having an affair with your dad."

"What!" I blurt.

"That's right," Andy replies. "His pride was wounded. He had to justify himself as being the wounded one, even though he had left us."

"Good God!" John cries. "That's the first I've heard that."

"I can imagine," Andy says.

After a moment of complete silence, we burst into laughter. The secret sex life of parents! And what else to do when there is an absent father on one side of the street and an absent mother on the other! But this was fiction. John and I knew our father saw a woman while our mother was away, but it wasn't Mrs. Mailer. After Mom came home with us from Paris in the summer of 1952, she and Mrs. Mailer became good friends, collaborating in the Madison Theater Guild, dancing the Charleston in Dad's study, and crossing the street for tea.

One afternoon, Mrs. Mailer was sitting on the Victorian couch in her living room.

"Just had it re-covered," she smiled, running her hand over the red silk fabric.

"Why, Julia," Mom said, "you old whore."

They laughed hard enough to bring tears. That scene alone gave the lie to Dr. Mailer's allegation.

We fall quiet for several minutes.

"Your mother was very dear to me," Andy says softly, as if to himself.

Only now, during the reunion, do I learn how long Andy had been hurting before his breakdown in December 1958 and what it was like to go over the edge. Soon after he was released from Mendota Hospital the following May, he came across the street to see Mom. John remembers seeing Andy come up the front steps.

"Mom seemed to be expecting you," John says. "She went to greet you at the door. She didn't wait for you to knock, just opened the door and said, 'Oh, Andy, come on in and let's compare scars.'"

"Yeah, those were her words," Andy says. "Never forgot them."

"She never showed me her scars," I reveal, "and I was too afraid to ask. Did you talk with her often?"

"No, didn't have to," Andy says. "It was enough just to know she was a soul mate, a survivor like me. She gave me a copy of *Nabokov's Dozen*. We talked about Paris. I thought that would be a nice place for me."

I see Mom start down the front steps, grasping a small suitcase. It's the spring of 1945. She's going to Wisconsin General Hospital.

"Just for a little while," Dad told us last night. "She needs rest."

She stops, turns, and looks back. For a second, I think she'll say, "I'll be home soon."

Mom's absence and Dad's reserve heightened my need for approval from younger men and older boys. A number of veterans on the GI Bill took Dad's courses. He sometimes held his graduate seminars at the house. He admired and envied those men, having himself been too young to fight in the first war and too old for the second.

"Best students I ever had," he often said.

"I remember sort of hanging around the edges of those seminars," John says as we brew more coffee after breakfast one morning. "I was just listening and, my God, I knew those men had seen combat. One time, Dad asked why a particular student was absent. Another veteran said, 'He's having bad dreams.' He was one of the two or three that Dad would ask to baby-sit us. You, too, Andy!"

"Bizarre that here we are in 2002 with our babysitter," I say.

"Corrupted you guys, did I?" Andy says, chuckling from the kitchen.

He rejoins us at the table for the story of his bringing over a movie projector and showing a 1930s black-and-white silent cartoon of *Felix the Cat* against the living room wall. Among Dad's "78" phonograph records, Andy found one for a soundtrack.

"I have never forgotten the piece," John says.

He hums it in his baritone. He's still solid, but a bit off-key, as we all are many years after singing in the West High choir.

"Shostakovich," Andy says, nodding. "The polka from *The Age of Gold*."

"That's it!" John affirms.

"Classical music on West Lawn," I add. "Parents and phonographs. And radio, of course. Rossini and Liszt on *The Lone Ranger*, Prokofiev on *The FBI in Peace and War*, and that theme on *Sergeant Preston of the Yukon*. And *The Bell Telephone Hour*. Was it an accident that night, Andy, or did you know Shostakovich would be perfect for Felix?"

"A bit of both, I guess," Andy says.

"Andy," I continue, "though I didn't realize it at the time, you were a Renaissance teenager. Music and literature as well as sports and camping and canoeing.

I could hear your piano-playing float across the street. I recognized the Chopin that Mom had played during the war. You skied in Colorado before it was trendy. In the late forties, your picture was in the paper as one of the most promising new members of the UW boxing team."

"Yeah," says Andy, "the guy coaching me was giving me all this stuff coaches do ... you know ... like 'You're gonna be somebody!' But when I'm in the ring the mind is saying, 'What the hell am I doing in here?'"

"But you combined two usually contradictory tendencies in American culture. One was athletic, male, macho ..." I reply.

"That's all a sham. You realize that, don't you?" he asks.

He looks somber without any hint of an ironic smile. I'm caught off guard.

"No, it's not a sham!" I protest. "Not in your case. And the other side is poetic and artistic. My God, Andy, you were my best role model, so incredibly versatile, and there wasn't anything sham about you. Still isn't."

"The two tendencies are not contradictory," John insists, "except in a specialized culture like America has become. If America had the Renaissance ideal, you were it, Andy. I grew up taking that ideal seriously myself. It's one reason I went into the army, took up climbing, and did a whole lot of stuff other than books. I wanted as much experience as I could get in as many things."

"Is that our generation?" I ask. "Or is it peculiar to us FOWLs?"

"Some of both, I think," John answers.

"Here's one big difference between our silent generation and the noisy younger ones of the last thirty years," I observe. "We didn't branch out in order to puff up our résumés. Today's kids do that all the time. You know, here's what you have to do to get into Stanford or be a Rhodes scholar. That's not Renaissance. That's vita creep."

"True," John agrees, "but let's not claim too much virtue by comparison. Major changes in the economy have put far more pressure on today's young people to get tracked so they can earn a decent living, if not climb the greasy pole."

"I grant you the economic argument," I say, "but the attitudes I have seen in college students and Kate's high school friends from fifteen years ago go well beyond economic security. They go into stratospheric yearnings to be famous, number one, and top dog and have trophy houses and a Lexus. That smacks of Hollywood married to Wall Street."

"But that's an old and deep theme in our culture," John says. "You know, Horatio Alger, get to the top. And it's but a step from there to thinking the top means being a celebrity, too."

"Look at our classes at West High," I continue. "Good school with great teachers in a high-class town. The postwar economy was pretty healthy, so many of us assumed we would become successful. But hardly anyone in my class, not even from the richest families, talked about glitz, mansions, five cars, and the whole fat-cat ball of wax. I can't think of a single classmate who defined success as ostentatious greed, à la Donald Trump. This may be partially a regional thing with fewer Trump-ettes per capita in Wisconsin than California, but I'm sure the main difference is generational."

"I'll pass," Andy says. "I just remember working hard at school because everyone did. It was expected of us because of the Depression and war. We felt we were there to do a job, not cut up. And that carried over after the war."

"There's a huge difference between that war and this so-called War on Terror," I go on. "And it's not only a question of generations. It's a question of how they use history. Notice how often Bush and company trot out the World War II analogy. You know how it goes. We fight not only terrorists but an 'Axis of Evil.' Bush is Churchill. Critics of his policy are appeasers. America and Britain are Anglo-Saxon pillars. Europe can't be trusted. That's straight from neoconservatives, particularly the deification of Churchill. And it plays right into the hands of someone like Bush, who wants to be worthy of his father's GI Generation after dodging Vietnam. Talk about dodgers! Look at Cheney and most of Bush's advisors on defense and virtually all the right-wing superpatriots in Congress, think tanks, talk shows, and you name it. They want war, but none of 'em ever dug a latrine. 'Whomper-jawed hypocrites,' Granddad Post would call 'em. They strut and sneer a lot. That's not what great generations are made of, and it's no way to keep this country unified after 9/11."

"This is a very different time and war and country and leader," John interjects.

"You bet it is. But these guys don't really know history. They abuse it. I attended a conference several years ago where a panel of neoconservatives idealized Churchill. Now, I think he's one of the truly great men of the last century, but I pointed out that he had advocated arms cuts while in the government in the late twenties. Later, no longer in the cabinet, he was ambivalent over Mussolini's invasion of Ethiopia in 1935. I knew the facts. I was writing a book on British defense policy in the thirties. But this young ideologue, all freshly scrubbed and smug and humorless, says, 'Aha! There are too many historians who denigrate heroism and just look for feet of clay.'"

"And there are many boxers who were at defeat of Clay," Andy quips.

"Ooh, Andy," John says, groaning. "You're stinkin' up the joint. Go to your room."

"The tragedy of 9/11," I continue, "gave Americans the opportunity to come together, and we did for a little while. But then the government says, 'We're in this together, folks, just like World War II, so spend more money at the malls.' Hell, as kids, we collected fat and scrap and saved our pennies for war bonds."

"There were real and widespread sacrifices," John says. "There was none of this business of government saying we can't upset the people because we want their vote. And taxes were raised on the wealthy, the idea being it would be unfair for them to profit too much from war production. It's quite the opposite of what Bush has done. We had a paper route on West Lawn, Keyes, Leonard, and Commonwealth. I saw silver and gold stars in the windows of some of the houses we delivered papers to, and I was awfully quiet when I went to their doors to collect money for the paper every month."

"Me, too," I add. "I wouldn't look at those flags if I was already sad about something. I wonder if they made it easier for us to decide later to serve instead of dodging the draft. You know, Cold War as an extension of the Second World War we were too young to fight. There's another difference between us and younger generations, at least since Vietnam. No draft."

Andy clears his throat the way he does when collecting his thoughts has reached an emotional point of no return.

He says quietly, "I had great friends, terrific guys and girls. I treasured that brotherly feeling. That helped a lot of us get through the war, and it helped me get through my father's inability to connect with me after the war. I was just crushed when one of the sweetest girls in our class hanged herself. It was at the end of the summer after we graduated from West High, the summer of '48. She had been one of the three little maids in *The Mikado* that spring, and her mother and mine took a bunch of us skiing near Wausau the Christmas before. I was at home thinking about her, shaking my head. I had a book of poetry open. My finger happened to fall on Byron's poem, 'She walks in beauty, like the night.' Her parents asked me to say a few words at the memorial service. I said what a delight she was. I wanted to read something by someone who could express our feelings better than we. And I read the Byron poem."

"Oh my God, Andy, that must have been shattering," I say, trying to commiserate. "I find it remarkable that a kid who has just graduated from high school takes a Byron poem …"

"Not unusual for me," he says.

"How about your generation?" I ask. "How many of your classmates read poetry?"

"Well, I was probably rare," he admits. "If any other boys read poetry, they did not let on. The Romantic poets spoke to me right away. I could see the stuff. I happen to be a very visual kind of guy."

"How did you have the guts to stand up there and read a poem?" I ask.

"I don't have a strong ego," Andy replies. "My mother was drawn to dramatic stuff and language. That resonated in me. It's something in me that comes from her."

That something caused Andy to take English courses at the university when he returned from four years in the air force during the Korean War to finish his undergraduate degree in business. In August 1957, he headed for Berkeley and graduate work in English. There, sixteen months later, he "went over the edge," his words.

The three of us drive from West Lawn to West High, Lake Mendota, and the university. There's no use watching for trains on the Illinois Central line at Commonwealth Avenue. The rails and ties have vanished and the old roadbed is now a hiking trail. Circling the redbrick high school, we compare notes about our respective classes.

"I figure I was conceived the night the stock market crashed," Andy says, laughing.

We fondly remember Coach Bob Harris, the harelipped, square-shooting, former Marine and Golden Glove boxing champion who meted out the same punishment to jocks as geeks for breaking the rules of the gym.

"Mr. Wilson, that'll be ten laps," he'd say.

"But, Coach, I didn't ..."

"Make that fifteen."

"But ..."

"Twenty! Start runnin'."

And a few days later, "Mr. Wilson, tell this young gentleman what happens when I'm not happy."

We used to chase gophers with Inkie in Forest Hill Cemetery west of the high school.

"I visited the Hanks burial plot there Saturday morning, before I met you guys," Andy says. "They're all there ... from my great-grandfather's generation to my mother's. There's a large, granite stone with the Hanks family motto, '*studio esse utilis*.' Translated, it's something like, 'Apply yourself to be useful.' It's a good motto. I've tried to follow it."

"We don't have a motto," I reflect. "Maybe it should be, 'Hang in there.' Has either of you thought about your epitaph?"

"No," Andy replies, "just the same as the rest ... name and dates and motto."

"I used to think of being buried in Haskell or Madison," John says, "but now they seem too far away in time. Maybe I'll have my ashes scattered in the Smokies and Rockies. Haven't given it much thought lately. I must be in denial. As for epitaph, how about, 'On the whole, I'd rather be in the mountains,' with apologies to W. C. Fields."

"Maybe ashes is the best way to go," I say. "I'd want some of mine next to Mom and Dad in Haskell, some in the Wind River Mountains, and some in Paris. Maybe the park across from our apartment on rue St. Julien le Pauvre or the Seine."

On the way to Lake Mendota, we pass the Unitarian Church that Frank Lloyd Wright designed. His personal life shocked many of Madison's faithful into loathing his architecture. Along the lakeshore and around campus, we regret the university's encroachment on the green fields and modest neighborhoods of our youth. One story follows another. We rode bikes to Picnic Point, swam at the Willows, and sang in the high school choir at the Stock Pavilion. Andy was a lifeguard at one of the dormitory piers and his tanned good looks attracted pretty girls, including Lilias, with whom he fell in love. Bascom Hill still has the university's carillon tower but lost its ski jump long ago. Dad's office was in Bascom Hall. The university radio station, WHA, called itself "the oldest station in the nation." We saw Laurence Olivier's film, *Henry V*, at the Memorial Union theater late in the war. John and I sneaked into Badger football games at Camp Randall Stadium and dined with Dad at the University Club. Rengstorff's Bookstore and the Brathaus bar and grill on State Street became favorite hangouts. Andy's best friends at UW, though five years younger than he, were Richard Lamm, the governor of Colorado; and the late Stephen Ambrose, the historian. Their egos were already much larger than Andy's.

At the foot of Bascom Hill, we pass a brick building named for Helen White, the distinguished professor of English whom Dad greatly admired as a colleague. I recount being invited to speak at UW in 1982 by the head of the Integrated Liberal Studies program that Dad helped launch after the war.

"The lecture was held in Helen White Hall," I say. "It was a clear winter afternoon. The room faced out on Lake Mendota, and there was ice on the lake. I sat near the lectern as people drifted in. I looked out the window and saw this solitary cross-country skier setting out across the lake, following his shadow. Some of Dad's old colleagues came, like Dean Mark Ingraham, who took me to dinner that night. There was also my high school English teacher, Joyce Steward; and Myron Stevens, our family lawyer back then. Afterward, Mr. Stevens came up and said, 'Well, Gaines, I really enjoyed that. I didn't understand much of what you said, but I really enjoyed it.'"

"You guys," I conclude when the laughter dies down, "that was a beautiful afternoon. Everything about it. Still gives me the shivers."

"A palimpsest," Andy nods. "Same when I walked around campus Saturday morning. That's what this whole reunion is, a palimpsest."

On State Street, I recall football nights at the University Club when the coach showed movies of the previous Saturdays' games. I remind Andy and John how "Ivy" Williamson turned the program around in the early fifties after the disastrous Stuhldreher years.

"Stuhldreher," Andy notes, "one of the Four Horsemen at Notre Dame in the twenties. Stuck with the box formation at Wisconsin. Didn't go over to the T."

"Then in came Williamson, Alan Ameche, and Harland Carl," I continue. "Ameche 'the Horse' and Carl 'the Colt.' Lots of faking in the backfield with great runs. That Ohio State game with our Ameche and Carl against their 'Hopalong' Cassady was the greatest football game I ever saw, even though we lost after missing a field goal with seconds left. Ivy's twin sons, Dave and Jack, were in my class at West. Really nice guys. We played on the same summer league baseball team. I went over to their place several times. Mr. Williamson was terrific. 'Oh, yeah,' he said once, 'your dad teaches history, doesn't he? Heard good things about him.' He was unassuming and inquisitive, valued the academic enterprise. In those days, coaches like Williamson knew what the university was for. But these days, no way."

Andy remembers Snowball, a large, black man who was mentally impaired and did odd jobs along State Street.

"He'd go up and down the street, washing windows and humming to himself," Andy says. "He saved fountain pens, had all these pens sticking out of his pockets. He wore bib overalls under his black overcoat. Everybody knew Snowball."

"My God, Andy," John declares, "our Uncle John had a black helper called Snowball. He was really nice to Gaines and me on the ranch. Helped us with chores and horses and so on. One time, we were taking a leak over near a mesquite tree. I hadn't finished yet when Snowball walked around in front of me. He looked and said, 'Oh, that's white, too.' He wasn't teasing me or anything like that. He was just making a discovery."

"Snowballs in Madison and Haskell," I point out. "Must have been gray hair. To think, that's about all the contact we had with blacks back then. And giving them nicknames like that."

We stop on Observatory Hill for a long look at Lake Mendota, the largest and bluest of Madison's four lakes. Far across the lake, we pick out the smokestacks of Mendota Hospital, now called Mendota Mental Health Institute.

"The judge pronounced sentence on me over there," Andy mutters.

"So you didn't go voluntarily," I say.

"Oh no, I was committed. Came home from Berkeley and lost it. I went off on this wild ride, and my mother didn't know what else to do. I had already lost it in Berkeley. I had a full-fledged panic attack over a twenty-page paper on Hemingway, couldn't think of anything except one word, 'Hemingway,' the only word in my head. Well, I finally wrote the paper. Friends advised me to see a psychiatrist, but he didn't tumble to the fact that I was seriously ill. Nobody did. I flew home, and Uncle Lue met me at Truax Field. Dear Uncle Lue. I told him I came home to straighten out things in the family. He did this double take. No wonder, 'cause I wasn't making any sense."

Andy takes a deep breath. I think he has dropped the subject, but he hasn't.

"After I don't know how many sleepless nights at 2310, I dreamt I was flying back through time. I was going around and around the world. I went back to ancient Greece and looked down at the Acropolis. I woke up feeling I was about to reach the end of the universe. I felt I had to control this or I'd blow up the whole universe. I turned on a cold shower and began punching my way up, like I was in the ring."

Andy clinches his fists and crouches. "Like this."

He punches, right and left.

"Up out of wherever my mind had taken me. An hour later, the police are there. In walks our family doctor, the one who had taken care of me when I had a bad fall in the big house at 315 when I was about three. He gives me a shot, and they take me to Mendota. I walked into the dayroom naked and asked for a bar of soap. They put me in a leather belt, chained to the bed."

"How long did they treat you like that?" I ask.

"Not too long. I settled down, and I guess I sort of got with the program. A few months later, I was well enough for them to let me out for the evening. One of my best friends came over and took me to the university field house to watch the boxing, one of the qualifying rounds for the '60 Olympics. He knew what that meant to me. Among the boxers that evening was one Cassius Clay from Louisville, Kentucky. Seventeen years old. Clay had no problem at all because he was such a beautiful mover and had such a length of arm and deftness. He was in the heavyweight class even though he weighed only one hundred seventy-eight pounds. Usually in these bouts, the heavyweights were very clumsy. They were often converted tackles from the football team, in the college ranks at any rate. So Clay went dancing right through this thing. Never had to punch hard. Just jab-jab-jab and lean back from the hips. The big guys could never get to him. Bup-bup-bup. And he wins. Just a kid in high school. God, what a beautiful mover."

"What was your illness?" I ask. "Manic depression?"

"I don't think they used those words, but it was bad, and they knew it. Today's shrinks call it 'bipolar affective disorder.' Must have come down from my father's side of the family. I see it in him, not my mother."

I have never been able to shut my mother's mental illness out of my mind for very long. It's a central theme in my book, *Memoirs of a Cold War Son* (2000), my first written word on a subject I had only discussed with John, Jeanie, and a few close friends. I wrongly assumed it was also my last written word. I had to know more. I was not merely acting as family custodian because I'm also a son who is prone to depression and a man who has never stopped wondering how he grew up or didn't. "Get over it" makes no sense to me. "Live with it" does. But what is it? So, in 2001, I requested and received files from the two Wisconsin institutions where she was hospitalized between the spring of 1945 and the fall of 1948, when she left Wisconsin for Texas and then Paris.

The second of them was Winnebago Hospital, now called the Winnebago Mental Health Institute. Early in the reunion, I tell John I might drive the Bug up to Winnebago and ask if he'd like to come. Though I don't say so, I think the Bug will help me see things. This will be our best opportunity to have the conversation I have looked for, just the two of us, ever since our mother's death in 1995. I'm not surprised when John declines. Last year, he asked me not to send him copies of Mom's records from the two hospitals.

"Can't handle it," he said.

Now, he admits he has repressed a lot more than I have. He thanks me again for having the courage to bring painful family memories to the surface in my memoir, but he has no desire to bring them up himself at Winnebago.

I borrow his detailed atlas of Wisconsin. In it, I locate the hospital on the west side of Lake Winnebago north of Oshkosh. Nearby, I spot North Asylum Bay, South Asylum Bay, and Asylum Point. It isn't "Mental Health Institute Bay." It's "Asylum Bay." It was named long before Mom went there and also before the advent of medications that might have prevented her collapse while they brought about euphemisms for "insane asylum." The words close in on me. I decide not to go.

Places kept my mother alive. My mind photographed them for the long term. They included old favorites like Vilas Park, where we swam together, and her brother's ranch, where she rode like a cowboy. And there were new places like Winnebago, where she was locked in. She was at Winnebago State Hospital from May 1947 to October 1948. Those documents only number seven pages after more than fifty years of winnowing, but that's enough to confirm my memory of her decline during the war and show she became so ill that she had to leave us for care. Dad and her Madison psychiatrist agreed on moving her to Winnebago because two years of periodic hospitalization and shock treatments had not improved her condition. Accompanied by attendants from Wisconsin General Hospital, she was admitted to Winnebago "as a voluntary paid patient from Dane County." After a month of tests and observation, the Winnebago staff confirmed the Madison diagnosis. She had paranoid schizophrenia. Seventeen months later, she was "released to husband, will live with mother; unimproved."

Dad drove to Winnebago every couple of weeks. Sometimes, he took us with him. We followed U.S. 151 to Fond du Lac, going through Sun Prairie, Columbus, Beaver Dam, and Waupun. Sometimes, we turned off before Fond du Lac on a shortcut to Oshkosh. Dad would always begin the trip with apparent cheerfulness, pointing out old barns, spotting trains, threatening to drop us off at the state prison in Waupun, laughing at Burma Shave signs, describing the Wisconsin Glacier, explaining how towns and lakes got their names, and challenging my map reading skills to trace the water routes across Wisconsin that French explorers learned from the Indians. We would usually eat lunch in Oshkosh, at the same café on the right side of the main street. Then we'd drive the short distance to the hospital on the shore of Lake Winnebago.

I can soon predict how the afternoon will go. If Dad grows silent as we reach Oshkosh, Mom isn't doing well and he won't appear with her on the broad front porch and signal us to come over. If the weather permits, John and I leave the car. Just in case, we keep the porch in view. We play catch, skip stones, or just fool around on the lawn or shore. If it rains, we stay in the car talking, reading comics, playing cards, drawing faces on the fogged windows, and listening to the tapping on the roof. When he returns to the car, Dad says Mom's tired but sends love and will see you next time. John and I don't ask when she'll come home. On the way back to Madison, I tell myself that's okay. We'll be okay. I'll be okay.

On the good afternoons, we join Mom and Dad on the porch and find chairs inside or benches under the tall elm trees on the grounds. Sometimes, her eyes say yes, I do love you and I'll come back as soon as I can. Sometimes they stare past me or down at nothing, as they did during the war when I began to suspect something was wrong. I don't tell Dad or John, but when I see her stare now, I know she won't come back and I wish we could drive away.

I wrote to the University of Wisconsin Hospital, formerly Wisconsin General, after hearing from Winnebago, whose records I had incorrectly assumed would be the more complete. The university hospital sent me a thick packet covering all of Mom's admissions from John's birth in August 1936 to her sinus trouble in the sixties before they moved from Madison to Princeton.

"Are you decent?" I would ask before entering my parents' bedroom when I was in high school and college. Now, without knocking, I began to read about my mother's body. I blush even as I remember this.

I was relieved to discover that her pregnancies for John and me were "uneventful." Her deliveries and postpartum condition were "normal." Mother and child were discharged (after two weeks in those days) in "excellent" health and "on breast feedings." I thought I would find wartime allusions to her state of mind because I had begun blaming Hitler for her vacant eyes before Dad said we had landed in Europe and would win the war. I found none until she was admitted on May 23, 1945. It was fifteen days after V-E Day, but what she and Dad told staff about hearing voices and feeling inadequate went back more than a year. Her doctor diagnosed "acute hallucinatory paranoid psychosis" on the discharge form dated July 3. She reentered the hospital two weeks later and came home on August 10, the day after Nagasaki.

We dined that night in the summer cafeteria of the University Club. On the way from the serving room to our table, I turned to see if Mom was okay behind me. I bumped into a doorjamb and dropped my full tray. To this day, I can hear the crash. I still thank the man who broke the embarrassing silence that followed by saying, "Well, son, if those atomic bombs don't make 'em surrender, that sure will!" After two more hospitalizations, one of them in Texas, the diagnosis was paranoid schizophrenia.

The files from the two hospitals corroborated the fears of the boy. What did this new evidence tell me? First, she had more shock treatments and came closer to a lobotomy than I had guessed. Dad and her mother and brother changed their minds about lobotomy. I'm appalled they had assented in the first place. Second, the references to suicide may or may not be alarming. Either the Winnebago staff saw the signs or they asked her, as a normal part of interviewing such patients, if she contemplated taking her own life. I do not remember fearing this, but the idea must have occurred to me and frightened me enough to repress it.

Third, her mention of family decreased over time. Was she trying to protect us from her interrogators and the slanderous voices she thought she heard? Or did it hurt her too much to talk about us? Or was she losing interest in us? It's hard to say. In June 1945, she said her husband "was entirely absorbed by his university work and left all the responsibilities to her, also the upbringing of the children." In July 1947, she wanted to go home to "take care of her husband and boys." Just before her release from Winnebago in October 1948, "she plans on divorcing her husband but would not say why." Finally, she had no choice but to leave us. I had hoped this was true when I was a boy, but children can never be sure why parents leave.

Of all these documents, the most heartbreaking for me was Dad's letter to Mom's doctor in April 1949. She had lived with her mother in Texas for several months after Winnebago. Then she left for France, alone, with several hundred dollars in traveler's checks.

Dad wrote, "Would you kindly write a brief letter stating your knowledge of my wife's long mental illness? I may need it to send to the Department of State to enlist their aid to find her if she managed to get to Europe. Her relatives in Texas let her plan it and leave."

No one knew where she was.

The most miraculous text was this, from her routine physical examination at Wisconsin General Hospital in April 1953, nearly a year after we returned from Paris a family again: "As well as I can determine, she is completely over her psychosis and seems, at least, to be entirely normal."

Abandonment often implies the intent of the one who leaves, so I don't like to use the word in Mom's case. But abandonment also implies the loss felt by who is left. This sense of the word certainly applies to John and me. Loss was something done to us, not by, for, or with. We resented having no say about her leaving. We learned not to trust any hope that she would come home. I don't remember blaming either parent then. I don't now, despite the fad for retroactive charges of parental abuse.

In dreams, I often search for something that will resolve a dilemma, but I can't grasp the problem or find the answer. It's that way with my mother. Understanding her illness is the key. The key to what? Knowing who I am? Or how to care for Jeanie and prepare for losing her? Or why we exist? What my life contributes to the sum of human purpose? Or is Mom the dilemma and the boy the key? The key to what? It's all so circular, elusive, and dreamlike.

What can I regard as true after driving to the reunion, being with John and Andy, and remembering? Dad at the wheel, smoking his pipe, showing John and me the countryside, and letting us wander on our own: that was real. So was the relief of getting away from the house that felt empty and letting the mind drift with the motion. So was the proof that we could still find beauty, tenderness, and solace. I lacked what my mother could have given me against loneliness, mistrust, anger, and self-doubt. I acquired a photographic memory for place, a need to ramble, a taste for solitude and quiet, and an eye for ways around and through. That's how, with Dad or alone, that's how I learned to read the country before I knew much about trails.

One morning before Andy awakes, John and I have our best talk in a long time about careers and retirement.

It begins when I ask, "Do you recall having fantasies or ideas as a teenager about where you would end up? Or was it all a blank?"

"It was largely a blank. I was thinking, okay, gotta get through high school and get into college. But I wasn't thinking much beyond that," he says.

"Did you think you'd end up being famous?"

"I hoped I would. But it depends on what you mean by famous. I wanted to do great things in whatever field I thought I was capable of. It took me a while to figure out that it was going to be philosophy. Around commencement time at Harvard, after majoring in history, I decided I'd try philosophy. I had some friends there who majored in philosophy. They ran circles around me, and I felt challenged. Then I began to realize that, to think about the things I wanted to think about, I needed tools. The only place to find them was in philosophy. So I signed up for courses in the summer session of '58 at Wisconsin. I lived at home and got enough credits to be admitted to graduate standing. I did a year there before active duty. I loved logic, and I was good at it, even though I was still kind of green. In the history of philosophy seminar, my mind wandered off. I said to myself, somewhat grandiosely, that I didn't want to study history. I wanted to make history."

"Somewhat grandiosely," I tease. We laugh together.

John didn't find it as easy to laugh at himself back then. Even now, there is an earnest reserve in the way he talks about himself unless he's relating a story about boyhood pranks.

"Had you initially thought of staying at Wisconsin for the PhD?" I ask.

"Well," he replies, "I was inclined to go elsewhere because of Dad being at UW. I finally wound up at Berkeley, which might not have been the right choice. But what the hell! I'd never seen the West Coast."

"Every Midwestern kid has to see California."

"Right, although when I came back from the army for a semester at Wisconsin before transferring to Berkeley, everything seemed so unreal. What are these people running around for? What does all this mean? What's the point? I guess the army does that to you. Good reason to serve. You must have had that experience, too."

"For me," I reply, "the unreality was compounded by going from the Berlin Crisis to cloistered Oxford. Oxford was changing because the British had just ended their national service requirement, so about half the undergraduates came straight from school. They had no calluses. My good British friends, Robert Gray and Anthony Goodenough, said to me after reading my memoir, 'How did you put up with us? We must have been insufferable twits.' I said, 'Well, yes, but not as bad as some or I wouldn't be seeing you now!' Back to the academy. We grew up assuming, because of Dad's example, that this was a worthy profession. I remember resenting it as a boy when people would slam professors, implying that Dad didn't have a real job. Then we got into the academy and found the public has some justification for calling it the 'ivory tower.'"

"Yeah," John says. "And academic politics can be vicious, petty, and very hurtful, wrecking careers and human beings. It seems to me that, in the humanities and maybe social sciences, a disproportionate number of faculty are insecure and don't have much courage, and so they can get manipulated by unscrupulous people."

"Yeah," I agree. "I still have the feeling from time to time that I'm not the same thing as a history professor. That was my job and how most of my colleagues saw me. It was one dimension, but that's not me. I can always do something else, as if I were still young. I guess this made it easier for me to retire."

John says, "For me, retirement was driven very much by how bad things had become in my department as well as the politics, committee, work and craziness. I'm very task-oriented, and I have wonderful powers of concentration. But I've paid a price because I don't know where a lot of people are coming from. I play the game by what I think the rules are. I play it straight. And then there are these other people who are sniffing around and picking up political smells that I miss. That's why the C students like Bush rule the world. Many of them have these political instincts about what others want, what will appeal to them and turn them off. I'm terrible at that, and I don't like it."

"One part of your problem, John, which is part of mine, and I think we inherited it, 'cause Dad sure as hell demonstrated it, is that we assume there's a kind of natural law of just desserts. That you will get what you merit and be recognized, and you don't have to kiss ass. Naïveté of that kind is part of the problem."

John replies, "It was partly naïveté and partly having been raised by Dad with an ethic that was becoming out-of-date. The academy started to change fundamentally in the fifties and sixties, maybe above all with the NDEA (National

Defense Education Act) of the late fifties as a result of *Sputnik* and so on. The academy became a path of upward mobility. Before, it had been a more genteel place where the department might have a star or two, but most were there to teach and interact with students and so on. When that changed, the sniffing increased, and the politics became more vicious. Anyway, a few years ago, I thought, life is too short and this crap isn't letting me do what I want to do. I still have a lot of ideas, and I want to get 'em out before it's too late. So I got out a sharp pencil and figured out I could afford to retire, largely because the stock market had gained so much in the nineties and Pat planned to continue working. It took me a long time to realize you could publish and perish in the academy."

"What do you miss?" I ask.

"I miss some of the collegiality and the teaching, not the paperwork and administrative stuff. I certainly don't miss committee work or the stresses and strains of watching idiots make a hash of things. I miss the interaction with young people with sharp minds. If it weren't for the strong thread of continuity with my research and writing and if I didn't feel I had ideas and things to say, I'd be in bad shape. I'd have to work a whole lot harder to figure out who am I and what am I doing, that sort of thing. It's a comfort and escape to get into my work. The world is going to hell at a faster rate than usual, crazy, so it's wonderful to be absorbed in something that you care about."

I say, "I think I've told you this before, but I find it really interesting that, all through our lives, especially when we were young, I was the more social and outgoing ..."

"You still are, Gaines."

"But now, apparently, I feel more need than you to be alone. Not having a lot of companionship doesn't bother me as much as you. I'm still in touch with a few former colleagues, but it's gotten to where I'm almost always the one who initiates the call. Friendship takes work, and now life is too short to do most of it myself."

"Well, I don't have a lot of companionship," says John. "I'm alone most of the time. Too much so. But Pat and I have an adequate social life, discussion group, book group, Sierra Club, and outdoors friends. We get together with people."

I reply, "You say you often write in a café so you can have live bodies around and a bit of white noise. But my gut is telling me to hunker down, shut off the noise, and get out of the way. I began to feel that years ago, probably when I was dean and probably because I was dean. The job of academic dean had changed a lot since Mr. Ingraham's long tenure impressed scholars like Dad and planted the idea in my head. Something said stop! What are these eighty-hour weeks doing to your family? Save time for yourself. Even though I'm retired now, I get frustrated that I don't have enough time alone. Some of that's my own doing, but not all of it 'cause I'm constantly having to do nickel-and-dime stuff. 'Nibbled by ducks,' I've heard you say. I miss that nagging but reassuring feeling that I've got a major project underway. You know, screw everything else, and leave me alone for the next four hours. No calls! I'm working! Guess I need to write another book. Maybe some more short stories. But who'll read them?"

"Well," John says, "it's wonderfully stimulating talking with you and Andy about politics, memories, and so on. I don't get nearly enough of that."

"I don't think many people are willing to invest the necessary time for ... how shall I put it ... conversational friendship," I say.

"In many ways, that's understandable," he replies. "Hell, it's hard enough just finding compatibility and mutuality of interests. In the university, for example, younger faculty are under terrific pressure to teach, publish, join committees, get tenure, get promoted, and apply for grants while often raising a family. They don't have the time unless it's a conversation that feeds directly into those requirements or is necessary for the game they need to play to get promoted. Often, the senior faculty is similarly preoccupied for different reasons. If you still vote and are on committees and so on, they'll call you. It is the irony of higher education and much else that is connected to education that the word 'school' comes from the Greek word, *schole*, which means leisure. And we have damned little of that in our educational institutions."

Andy comes downstairs. We urge him to grab some coffee before we solve all of the world's problems.

"Maybe I should have been a lawyer," I resume. "I wonder how much of a load I carried through my career while thinking of Dad's example, feeling uneasy about being in the same discipline with a 'Junior' tacked onto my name. I'm not saying this was a huge cross to bear, not at all. In fact, I was proud of it. I sort of liked being a chip off the old medieval bloc. As Dad used to say, I was a 'very modern chip' because I specialized in twentieth-century Europe. But, occasionally, since retiring, I think, God, I'm glad to be out of that because I'm not 'Junior' anymore."

Andy joins us at the table, stirring his coffee. He has just started a CD, Mahler's *Songs of a Wayfarer*.

"Well, Senior Counselor?" John asks.

Andy stops stirring and replies, "My therapist says the older we get, the more we become ourselves. The need to do all these things evaporates. It's all in the past."

"You don't have to be successful or famous?" I inquire.

"Right," John says. "And you don't have to feel as defensive."

"As alert, wary," Andy adds.

"I hope that's true," I say. "There are times I don't know who the hell I am."

"Join the club," says Andy.

"Still trying to figure out Mahler, Andy?" I ask.

"Yeah. And Pound."

On Friday, we make a pilgrimage to the Baraboo Hills and Devil's Lake. Skirting Madison's east side, we follow State 113 northwest toward the Wisconsin River. In Lodi, John recognizes the pea cannery where he worked for two summers in high school. I remember my attack of appendicitis at a café on Main Street. Andy notes the sign at Spring Creek Park that reads, "Home of Suzie the Duck."

"Remember her?" he asks. "I wonder how many generations of Suzies there have been."

We stop in the village of Okee to look at the old general store where John and I and Ed Ingraham bought ice cream cones. We cross 113 and drive up what John and I will always call Ingraham hill, even though Ed sold the property after his parents died.

"Somewhere along here, John," I point out, "we mined sandstone."

"Yeah," says John. "White sand underneath this brow. Used Ed's toy trucks and cement mixer."

"There's the new driveway to the hilltop," I say. "We'd come on Sundays with Dad after lunch at Devil's Lake, throw the football, or shag flies in that hip-high grass. You could see a contoured cornfield down toward the lake and the yellow cars of the North Western's 400 streamliner going by just this side of the lake."

"Right," says John. "And we built our doggerel hut in the woods out of poplar saplings. Called ourselves 'Doggerels One, Two, Three.' Had a little chant, 'We're Doggerels One, Two, Three. We're Doggerels One, Two, Three. We work a while and rest a while, we're Doggerels One, Two, Three.'"

"Doggerels?" Andy asks, puzzled.

"Yeah," John replies. "Don't remember how we got the name."

"I walked up there with Ed twelve years ago," I recall, "before our class reunion. Their old cabin was gone. The new owners had built a large, brightly painted house with decks, not right for the curves and browns and greens of that hill. Ed seemed more reconciled to the change than I. He reminded me that we flew a doggerel flag over our hut with three Ds on one diagonal intersected by the numbers one, two, and three on the other diagonal. The Ingrahams were so good to us when Mom was away, sharing their hill, showing us flowers and birds, and taking us on walks to places like Parfrey's Glen over near Devil's Lake. Dad talked geology. We picked up a lot from that generation."

"Not just the names of things," John adds, "but the whole attitude toward nature. Small things and quiet."

"Wisconsin, I mean, country like this right here, has a lot to do with that attitude," I continue. "And it's catching. Think of Muir and Leopold, just to name the state's most famous naturalists. Leopold taught at UW in the thirties and forties. Dad knew him, and the Ingrahams knew him well. My God, you guys, I just this second had a strange sensation about mortality. When we were kids, I thought Mr. and Mrs. Ingraham would live forever, not just the way kids think about old people but because their hill, birds, and flowers would always be here. I can't believe they are gone when I'm up here or that Mom and Dad are gone. Lupines and juncos don't disappear forever."

Soon we cross the Wisconsin River on the Merrimac Ferry, at the same location since the mid-nineteenth century for travel between Madison and Baraboo. The Colsac II, named for Columbia County on the left bank and Sauk County on the right, came into service in the sixties, succeeding the smaller boat that John and I had scrambled over as boys. The old Chicago & North Western trestle survives upstream from the ferry. Across the river, we turn right on State 78 for a few miles and then angle steeply uphill on a gravel road.

"Just up here beyond the sign for the sharp turn," Andy says near the top.

We park off the road and walk down a faint driveway. After the war, Andy's father bought the land at the crest of a thickly timbered hill overlooking Lake Wisconsin, as the dammed river is called above Merrimac. He then began clearing a spot for a cabin. It would be the father's escape from 2310, but he hoped it would be the son's as well.

Andy came up here with a few friends in the summer of 1949 after his freshman year at UW.

"My father was in seventh heaven," he recalls. "Here's his son and his friends, guys in the wilderness and all that stuff. We rolled rocks from over that way to build the foundation. The neighbor farmer trundled a cement mixer over here and laid concrete over the rocks. My father built the big fireplace at that end and the kitchen at this end. The place has changed. It's much less rustic. It isn't really a log cabin now, more like a weekend house."

"Did Stan ever come up?" I ask.

"No. Never while our father was alive. I've got a picture of Stan in front of the stone fireplace with the *Life* magazine issue about Kennedy's assassination. It's late 1963, the year after our father died. He hadn't taken good care of the cabin since the divorce. It was his only significant property when he died, and they were going to sell it to pay the estate lawyer's fees, so I bought it with help from Uncle Lue."

"I remember you spent a lot of time up here in the summers after that," I say. "When was it that we came down this way from the Porkies in two Bugs and your friend and I drove on to Madison while you and John stayed here?"

"John and I were trying to figure that out."

"What color was my Bug?" I ask.

"Beige," Andy replies. "We have a photo from in front of the Paul Bunyan restaurant."

"Right, two Bugs," I continue. "Yours with your canoe on top. I sold mine in Palo Alto in August of '65 before going to Germany. I figured I'd buy a new one over there. Sold the old one to Richard Alpert, Timothy Leary's buddy in spreading the LSD gospel after Harvard fired 'em both. This guy in sandals just walks up the driveway while I'm washing the Bug and introduces himself, says he saw my ad on campus. He looks the car over and says, 'I'll take it!' He gives me a check, and I thought, I'll be damned, I've just sold my Bug to Richard Alpert! I hope he took good care of her. He's become quite a guru. Calls himself Ram Dass. Where was I? Oh, Bugs and Porkies. Couldn't have been summer of '64 because I was home only for August and my girlfriend Anne came up to meet Mom and Dad."

"Right," John agrees, "I was helping them prepare for their move to Princeton."

"So we're talking about the summer of '63," I conclude. "The Lord Astor trip. I was home from Oxford. I had picked up the Bug at a dock in New York and driven home with John. I don't remember why he was in New York. When did you sell the place, Andy?"

"Five or six years ago."

"You kept it that long?" I ask.

"Yeah, kept it and kept it. Felt I had to," Andy says. "A hold on Wisconsin."

Andy pauses and looks down, as if he sees something in the grass. We stand in the clearing between the house and the road. A song sparrow calls from the woods. Andy raises his head.

"Well, that's it," he sighs. "That's the *locus vivendi*."

We drive back roads south of Baraboo. Named for a French trader (Baribault), the town was made famous by the Ringling Bros. Circus, which had its winter headquarters there from 1886 to 1918. Stan lived nearby in North Freedom while co-founding and stocking the Mid-Continent Railway Museum, one of the best of its kind in America. I introduced Jeanie to him there in the summer of 1972, on our way from Montana to Boston.

"What the hell," I reminisce. "I figured there was no better way to introduce her to Wisconsin and us. We stopped at the museum headquarters and I asked if Stan Mailer was around. They told me, yeah, he was about a mile out that way, working on an engine at a grade crossing. So we drove out there in my blue Bug. I could see Stan clambering around. I told Jeanie to stay put. I walked toward him and said, 'Hey, Stan!' He looks up, back, and up again with that inimitable double-take with his whole body."

"Yeah, yeah," Andy and John laugh.

"You know how uneasy he was around women," I go on. "Well, he liked Jeanie instantly, and she the same. We took him to dinner in Baraboo and then drove to Sauk City for milkshakes at that fabulous place near the bridge over the Wisconsin River, where we used to come all the way from Madison in the fifties and sixties just for those shakes. Remember 'em? Slept on his floor that night, in the upstairs apartment he rented in an old house in North Freedom."

We enter Devil's Lake State Park from the east side. The lake occupies a spring-fed gap in the Baraboo Hills, one of the oldest mountain ranges in North America. The Wisconsin Glacier's terminal moraine plugged the gap at both ends, rerouting an ancient river that drained Glacial Lake Wisconsin and probably became the Wisconsin River. Dad began teaching John and me that geology on our Sunday morning trips here when Mom was gone. We have always associated this place with him, his glaciers, and his grilling cubed steaks in one of the massive stone fireplaces built by the Civilian Conservation Corps during the Great Depression.

I would look for the moraine from the highway and picture the blue lake out of sight between the hills. Dad would read the Sunday paper while John and I scrambled up the trail and over the boulders of the steep ridge north of the campground. Once he brought us along to a picnic with university colleagues. One was a woman with a gnarled hand who showed us how to make Chippewa biscuits over the coals of a wood fire and pour honey into the hole left by the stick. Dad, moraines, stone fireplaces, cubed steaks, Chippewa biscuits, playing with John, and feeling good. Memory gathers all of these things together at Devil's Lake.

After Andy parks the car, John decides to climb the old trail. Andy and I walk along the former C&NW right-of-way, now owned and still used by the Wisconsin & Southern Railroad. Completed in the early 1870s, the line carried holiday passengers from Chicago to Devil's Lake and Baraboo. Many stayed in the Cliff House at the northern end of the lake, a fashionable hotel that Colonel William Vilas bought in 1879. Andy and I search for the spot where the three of us swam in September 1961. I had just returned from military service in Germany. Three weeks earlier, I had been weighing the chances that my nuclear missile battalion would soon be fighting World War III over the Berlin Crisis. Two weeks later, I would leave for Oxford University. At Devil's Lake, I hadn't a care for loading warheads or making the grade at Oxford. Cleaving the deep water between those different worlds, I was happy just being there with John and Andy.

Andy and I find the same spot, or so we want it to be, especially Andy.

"Pristine," he says as we walk along the tracks. "That day with you and John was pristine."

Only now, over forty years later, do I perceive Andy's world on that day when his slow recovery needed our all-too-infrequent company. Today, overweight but always an athlete, he hits the water with a lean splash.

I haven't brought my swimsuit and can't skinny-dip because of tourists on the tracks, so I soon leave to find John. I backtrack to the trail and start up, passing rocks and cavities where we played hide-and-seek or last of the Mohicans, ambushing each other and working up an appetite. I recognize the dark red, flat-top boulder above the trail where I lay in wait to drop pinecones on John as he came seeking. Yesterday, in Kettle Moraine State Forest, Stan described the cooking and layering of rock in the formation of the Baraboo Hills.

What are we to these rocks, I wonder. What is time to them? Are we in some way geological? Has life hardened me like this quartzite? Or am I made up of shifting layers that memory, like wind and water, reworks as it uncovers them? Some of both, I guess. My time is short.

I meet John about halfway to the top. We descend slowly, pausing to look at the lake and the cliffs. John's trained eye picks out rock climbing routes that the boy did not see. Near the parking lot, we stop at the Bird Mound that we somersaulted down as kids. Constructed about a thousand years ago by so-called Effigy Mound Builders, the bird's body is 155 feet long with a wingspan of 240 feet, according to the older of two plaques, the one I read over fifty years ago. Layers hit me again: mound-building, somersaulting, and returning are all in my history through that sign.

Andy is at the car, and we putter around for a while before leaving. West of the park, Ski-Hi Farms is closed for a summer holiday, but we walk down to the restored cabin built in the 1850s by the original owner on land he received for military service in the war against Mexico. Dad brought us here every autumn during apple season. We would buy a bushel of McIntosh and a five-pound bucket of clover and apple-blossom honey. The fragrance of the apples filled the car all the way home to Madison, mixed with Dad's pipe smoke. In time, the honey would begin to sugar. I would take the bucket from the cupboard and dig down into it for the hard honey and eat it off the spoon. The taste hasn't changed, as I discovered two years ago when I drove up the day before my high school reunion.

John Post at Devils Lake State Park, Wisconsin

Andy turns south on U.S. 12. John suddenly remembers a Burma Shave jingle, "'Around the curve, lickety-split. Beautiful car, wasn't it?'"

We drive past the Badger Army Ammunition Plant, called Badger Ordnance during World War II. Many of its temporary buildings from the war are still in use. We have lunch in Sauk City, at the milkshake place that was a dairy bar and milk plant in our youth. It's now a restaurant called Leystra's. I ask the waitress if they still make great milkshakes, "the kind we had here forty years ago when you put a pint of ice cream in the blender."

"Yah, that's what we do," she replies.

"Is the cheese in the grilled cheese sandwich the real thing?" I ask.

"Yah, real cheddar. We don't believe in serving false food around here. None of that rubber stuff."

The restaurant is full of elderly locals in full chatter. Three women sit at the booth behind me.

One says, "Yah, when the cows are ready to milk, they go up this ramp."

"Oh really?" one of her friends responds, as if this were a marvelous new procedure.

The waitress comes over as we finish eating.

"Was it as good as you hoped?" She looks worried.

"Absolutely," I declare. "Just hold onto that old recipe and keep doing it."

She smiles.

CHAPTER 6

▼

IN OUR TIME

On the way back to Oconomowoc, Andy and I recall driving his Bug to the Bois
Brule River in September 1961, following Devil's Lake and John's departure for
Berkeley. Mom packed us a lunch of cold fried chicken. We stayed our first night
with friends of Andy's mother in a small town where scenes were being filmed for
a movie based on Hemingway's Nick Adams stories. Next afternoon, we set up
camp beside the Brule. The river was too cold for swimming, but we waded until
our ankles went numb. We warmed up on Andy's strong coffee. He had dropped
a raw egg into the pot to harden over the grounds. We still call the technique
"Brule coffee." We pictured French *voyageurs* paddling by our tent on one of the
best trapping rivers in northern Wisconsin. We talked canoeing and Hemingway.

Almost every reunion conversation contains some mention of the North
Woods, Hemingway, or Camp Manitowish, references long embedded in our
oral tradition. We were boys during the Second World War and young men in
the fifties. We tried to prove ourselves in the North Country during the Cold
War. We read "Big Two-Hearted River," camped with Nick Adams, and

admired Hemingway's masculinity. We were unsure of ourselves around girls. Both innocence and injury lie back there.

Camp Manitowish was, and still is, a YMCA establishment on Boulder Lake near Boulder Junction, about fifteen miles north of Woodruff and ten miles south of the Michigan border. All three of us attended the camp as boys. Andy returned for several summers as a counselor. Manitowish offered the usual array of activities for a summer camp, but the emphasis was on canoeing: technique, loading, portaging, and tripping.

During a three-week session, you would take at least three canoe trips, starting easy with two or three days and finishing hard with a five-to six-day circuit in Wisconsin's best canoeing country with hundreds of lakes and thousands of acres of second growth forest. If you learned a smooth J-stroke at Manitowish, you would always cringe to see novices flail and swerve. If you heard loons on Trout Lake, you would never forget the lonely sound. If you imagined Indians gathering berries or putting up shelter for the night, you knew they were like you.

John remembers picking up his sons at Manitowish after their first summer there in the mid-eighties.

"Here was David Gaines walking back to his cabin, and then we went looking for Gavin. I walked into Nash Lodge, and there was my son walking toward me. Boy, did that hit me." John swallows and takes a deep breath. "I couldn't put all that together. What stunned me the most was that Manitowish hadn't changed much at all. The rest of the world was insane, but here was this island of stability and continuity."

"Is it the insanity that makes us try finding anchors to windward?" I ask.

"Yeah," Andy replies. "Like your conversation with the Osage woman. People in the hinterland who still resonate to basic friendliness, unlike big cities and road rage …"

"And uncontrolled sprawl," John interjects, "the metastasizing of things like Wal-Mart."

"That too," Andy agrees. "The virgin land our ancestors saw disappeared a long time ago. We have a few wilderness areas, but even they aren't safe around the edges."

"Well," I remark, "I've got to give conservatives some credit, though they blow it way out of proportion, for calling our attention to the need for Koestler's 'umbilical cord.' The need to stay in touch with the past and American values, whatever those are. We have deferred too much to the conservatives to make these points. We ought to be making them ourselves, in progressive or liberal or populist ways."

"Careful," John warns. "Some of these conservatives want it both ways. They want a return to religious fundamentalism and political autocracy as well as the sort of historical consciousness you want to keep alive. As for values, consider how much damage is done to the value of community when governmental entities are hollowed out and lack the resources they had a generation or so ago. You know what's happened to the United States in the last few years? It has become more and more like the South."

"Thanks in part to Newt Gingrich and company," I add.

"That's right," John says. "The politics have gone that way, but the far right is also using what's called 'deep lobbying' to shape people's political and economic philosophy through think tanks, publications, op-eds, talk radio, and so on."

"In place of real education," Andy says.

"Our ideal of education is anathema to both extremes," I argue. "You know, weigh all the evidence. Be skeptical about authority, and don't trust ideology. But as a moderate German conservative leader said about the Weimar Republic in the twenties, the greater danger to democracy in America today is from the right. I think of Weimar Germany whenever right-wingers accuse people like me of being un-American, like McCarthy calling Marshall a communist. McCarthy lives, and he always will in this country. Gotta have enemies at home."

"Too true," John says. "At the heart of the right's talk about values is a highly individualistic attitude toward law, taxes, infrastructure, welfare, public good, and so on. All the emphasis on the one and freedom and rights and little care for the many and safeguards and duties. Not much compassion in Bush's compassionate conservatism."

"So what keeps us at odds with the right?" I ask. "What makes us liberals? Why do we reject outlandish expressions of individual liberty and private property? Why don't we hate our neighbor? Where do we get the gut feeling that certain kinds of people and policy aren't fair? From our parents? From growing up during the New Deal and Second World War and coming of age with the New Deal's offspring, the New Frontier and Great Society? Or what?"

"Probably all of the above," John replies. "But I also think it's from having been raised and educated in Wisconsin with that northern European social democratic influence, as opposed to Anglo-Saxon Tennessee or Texas, where the liberty of Locke and the Founding Fathers has been taken to extremes."

"Samuel Johnson got it right," I declare. "The 'loudest yelps for liberty' came from the owners of slaves. That just needs updating, and it's not confined to the South."

"But there are regional differences," John insists.

"I know," I agree. "Hell, I just saw how the highway litter decreases as you drive north. 'Screw y'all, I'm Amurican!'"

"That's what I mean by the one against the many," says John.

"Back to what you said about the northern European influence on Wisconsin, especially German and Scandinavian. That helps explain why the progressive movement was stronger here than anywhere else a hundred years ago, Robert La Follette and company. Those democratic and egalitarian ideals were brewing on both sides of the Atlantic. Just look at words like progressive, reform, modernist, social democracy, Christian democracy, Christian socialism, liberal Catholicism, and enlightened Protestantism. Not the revolutionary extremes of Marxism, but a mix of reform and religion and pluralism. While you're at it, toss in some Tom Paine populism, old-fashioned New England communitarianism, and the beginnings of the conservation and preservation movements. All that stuff came into Wisconsin with nineteenth-century emigrants after the first wave, which was mostly Southern and border state. In fact, emigration from the Northeast and Europe hardly touched the South, where ethnicity remained essentially Anglo-Saxon white over African black until our lifetime. Up here in this mix, you couldn't easily maintain paternalism, sanctity of property, rejection of government intervention, and so on. You had people ready to fight autocracy, political corruption, corporate greed, intolerance, and social injustice. What this country needs is a new version of Wisconsin progressivism. And a Wisconsin president to go with it!"

"Steady, Gaines. Steady," Andy says. "More coffee?"

"Brule coffee?" I ask.

"Nope, no egg."

"Damn," I say.

"Let's see," Andy reflects, "back to Manitowish. That was the place. There you are, you've got it all, the natural beauty, the clear water, and all the things we revere. And Elmer Ott in the center of things at Nash Lodge. Good ol' Elmer, the benign head of camp. It's solid, and it's good."

"That's Hemingway," I point out. "Solid and good."

"Yeah, but I felt that about Manitowish before reading Hemingway," says Andy. "I took a canoe trip into the Quetico after the war. I was rinsing a metal plate in the stream, and it slipped from my hands. The sun reflected off it, flashing and dimming as the plate zigzagged down and away in the current. As I got older, that plate made me question what we were told about perception, that perception clarifies things the longer you look at them. Deep recall is that incident in reverse. Your memory searches for the plate and finally, zigzagging and flashing, it comes to the surface."

"Wonderful image. So Ott was a father figure?" I ask.

"Oh yeah," Andy replies. "And my counselors were older brothers."

"That's what you were to me," I say. "My father was not all that full of praise and support. John, well, I guess you were not an old enough older brother. It's no joke that John and I still call you Senior Counselor. I took the train to Woodruff my first time at Manitowish, during the summer of '50. When the bus off-loaded us at Manitowish, there were these wonderful tall trees and the big lodge made of logs and the lake beyond the trees. I could smell the pine needles. I thought, wow is this pretty! But I was scared landing in the middle of a bunch of kids I didn't know. And there you were, Andy, coming toward me smiling. I thought, it's gonna work, it's gonna be okay. Andy's here."

"Remember Art Thomsen?" John asks. "Ran the waterfront at camp and was sometimes a lifeguard at one of the university dorm piers. Boy, did I look up to him."

"Yeah," Andy confirms. "I got to know him at UW after the air force. His daughter married Jack Heiden. Their son is Eric Heiden, the Olympic skating champ."

"One summer in the late fifties I was talking with Art on his pier," I recall. "Somehow, his age came up. I thought, jeez, this guy is old, he's nearly fifty! He had the youngest-looking fifty-year-old body I'd ever seen. He was one of those classic watermen. He knew everything about boats, swimming, and so on. Terrific guy. I wonder if this whole thing about surrogate fathers is peculiar to our generation. Maybe because of the war? Or does every older generation identify heroes with its youth?"

"In every generation," John observes, "the young from both sexes learn, and are supposed to learn, from adults who aren't in the family. That's one of the things meant by 'It takes a village to rear a child.' It's one of the consequences of being a social creature."

"But notice how often during this reunion we've talked about heroes, and they're not just from the war and Wisconsin," I reply. "They're in movies, music, books, and so on. Andy plays his CD of Mahler's First Symphony a lot. Olivier's *Henry V* was better than Branagh's. The Lone Ranger looked better on radio than TV. We love books like *A River Runs Through It*. We keep coming back to Hemingway and so on. The 9/11 disaster has turned 'hero' into such a buzzword that it's hard to think historically about it. But I still think our generation is unusually hooked on heroes, and our pantheon is better than most."

"Well, maybe," John concedes. "A few years ago, I was really pissed off by a book debunking hero myths. Damned deconstructionist!"

"Exactly," I concur. "Debunk Roy Rogers and Gene Autry if you want, but leave Randolph Scott, Gary Cooper, and Alan Ladd alone! What about John Wayne?"

"He never quite made my hero list," John replies, "but he was awfully good in *Stagecoach* and *Red River*."

Porcupine Mountains State Park on Lake Superior, west of Ontonagon in Michigan's Upper Peninsula, is as close to wilderness as you will find in Michigan or Wisconsin. John and I and several friends began going to the "Porkies" in the mid-fifties. We used Section 17 cabin on the Little Carp River as our base camp, explored trails around Lake of the Clouds and down to Lake Superior, and avoided the black bear that periodically clawed the cabin's exterior for the smells inside.

We introduced Andy to the Porkies in the summer of 1963, shortly after I returned from Oxford. Andy and a friend of his joined us after a day of canoeing on the Big Two-Hearted River about two hundred miles east of the Porkies, near Grand Marais. They arrived at our cabin at the mouth of the Big Carp after midnight, soaked through by rain. Andy's headlamp shone through the door, waking us up.

"Is this Lord Astor's swimming pool?" he asked, cracking us up.

The Profumo Affair had just rocked Britain. Lord Profumo, Minister for War in Harold Macmillan's Conservative government, resigned after admitting that he had been sleeping with Christine Keeler, a call girl who also served a Russian naval attaché in London. Profumo first met Keeler at Cliveden, the country estate of Lord Astor, where poolside bacchanalia relieved the Cold War stress of some of Britain's elite.

A few days later, on our tandem way home in our Bugs, we ate a mammoth breakfast at Paul Bunyan's Logger Camp in Minocqua, making the restaurant regret its all-you-can-eat policy.

For FOWLs, that's the "Paul Bunyan" or "Lord Astor" trip, epigraph for the North Woods, pig-outs, Bugs, and fellowship. Mention of the trip guarantees laughter. Memories of it edge uneasily toward what the sixties became. A week after returning to Madison, John and I sat in the living room with our parents to watch the telecast of Martin Luther King's "I Have a Dream" speech from the steps of the Lincoln Memorial. Two weeks later, we left for grad school in California by way of Texas. In November, we would lose President Kennedy, who, unlike Eisenhower's generation of war heroes, was young enough to be our older brother.

Andy took his wife, Bobbi, to Manitowish country several years ago.

"We were standing on Cathedral Point at the narrows of Trout Lake," he says. "The name of the point came from tall pines, but the pines were gone—blown down by a great wind. I remembered my first canoe trip there during the summer of '43 or '44, one of my first years at Manitowish, during the war. We had pushed our canoes up the Little Trout River, and fish coming downstream bumped against our legs. When we reached Trout Lake, we hoisted ponchos between canoe paddles to sail downwind to the far side of the lake." He pauses. "When Bobbi and I got back to the condo in Minocqua, I said, 'I can't take this anymore.'"

"I can see the narrows," I say, nodding, "and the rocks at the point and the ponchos. We sailed our canoes through on a south wind. But what do you mean you couldn't take it?"

"It was the overwhelming memory of associations with the place and the awful disjunction between the present and that childhood at Cathedral Point," Andy says. "I waded out into the water at the point and felt the same little creatures nibbling at my legs. Nature hadn't changed. Had you guys been there, you would have understood. But Bobbi didn't."

"That would be hard for any spouse to understand," I say. "I don't think Jeanie would have."

"Nor Pat," John adds.

We talk more about our mothers than our wives and more about searching for love and losing it than finding it and staying married. Artists attracted us FOWLs. Among our old flames, one of John's became a Broadway dancer; one of mine, a painter; and Lilias, an expert on yoga. A few years ago, Andy tells us, his Dallas therapist suggested he try to locate Lilias and give her a call. She had gained a national following in the seventies and eighties through her PBS television show, *Lilias! Yoga and You*, but Andy had not seen her offscreen for over forty years.

"So I looked on the Internet," Andy recounts, "found her address in Ohio, and found that she has three children and still teaches yoga. I called and got her husband. I left a message. Sure enough, in about a week, I picked up the phone, and here's this low, sexy, loving voice saying, 'How are you?'"

Andy leans forward as he imitates her.

"Lilias," I say. "She was terrific and beautiful. I saw you two having water fights on your front lawn, heading off to play tennis or swim, laughing. You didn't have much time to throw the football with me that summer."

"Summer of '56," Andy says.

We compare the changing dimensions of our marriages after many years of living with the same woman: misunderstandings between Andy and Bobbi, Pat's preoccupation with her job, Jeanie's illness, and my worries about taking care of her.

"I regret that our generation's emphasis on lifelong partnership and monogamy locks us in and makes it difficult to enjoy the company of other women," I say. "I don't mean sex. Just close friendship and long conversation, and yeah, I suppose youth and beauty if possible. Walking around the Place des Vosges in Paris about five years ago, I noticed this attractive, dark-haired young woman sitting alone at an outside table at Ma Bourgogne, a picturesque café under the arcade at the northwest corner. I recognized her. She's an American actress I had seen in several films, including one of those potboilers with Harrison Ford, I think. She spoke French to the waiter. I thought, this is too good to be true. As she got up to leave, something in me said stop and introduce yourself. Maybe it was my long-standing regret that I lacked the courage to take the plunge in the early sixties when a beautiful French girl smiled at me as we happened to leave a Paris art museum at the same time. But, before I could decide whether to act upon impulse on the Place des Vosges, this nice-looking guy comes out of the restaurant and off they go, arm in arm. God, the might have beens."

"Many women like older men," John remarks, "because we've got something to say. On the other hand, damn! So many women! And it's forty years too late!"

When the laughter subsides, Andy says, "I feel more relaxed with you guys than with any woman or, for that matter, any other men. I don't have to explain anything to you guys. You've been there. We've been there together."

"Hemingway again," I note.

Our attraction to Hemingway's fiction goes way back. At the reunion, however, attraction turns into metaphor. I learn how much Nick Adams has meant to us, especially Andy.

"There was a lot of Hemingway in your father," I say one evening. "Guns in the house, hunting, doctor whose father was a doctor, war, caring more for men than women and children. That sort of thing."

"Yeah, that's right," Andy agrees. "An armory in the house, hunter, two wars, misfit after both, fears about losing vitality and virility, divorce, and his father a country doctor like Hemingway's."

"Like father and son in 'Indian Camp'?" I ask.

"Yeah, one of the best Nick Adams stories. My father always saw his own father as the ideal country doctor, driving his one-horse buggy through the country around Green Bay and De Pere. So he was drawn to this ideal as well as going off to war. It was an odd combination. But he was no Nick Adams."

Andy's father was born the same year as Hemingway (1899), died a year later (1962), and looked like him: square jaw, barrel chest, and glinting eyes. I assumed Dr. Mailer introduced young Andy to Hemingway.

"No," Andy corrects me. "I never saw him read anything but professional stuff. It was the movie, *For Whom the Bell Tolls*, with Gary Cooper and Ingrid Bergman, during the war while my father was away. Later, I started reading the novels and eventually got to the Nick Adams stories. I was hooked. Of all the prose I knew, and I read all kinds of stuff, Hemingway was the one."

"He wrote for a lot of us," I add. "The simplicity, descriptive detail, and, as you say, the rhythm."

"Unlike Henry James, for one," Andy laughs. "What did H. G. Wells say about reading a James novel? Like watching a hippo over in the corner of his cage trying to pick up a pea?"

"Wonderful!" John shouts with a single clap of his hands.

"I assigned *A Farewell to Arms* in my course on the First World War," I continue. "Fantastic account of the pell-mell retreat in the battle of Caporetto, which Hemingway sets up earlier by calling Caporetto a 'clean little town' and 'nice little place.' The boys dug the book, but most of the girls didn't. They didn't even like the bittersweet romance with Catherine. Jeanie loves his short stories and *The Old Man and the Sea*. She says the writing in them is honest and lean, whereas in the novels, he writes like someone who doesn't and can't love anyone but himself, and all the women are either bitches or insipid, except the gal in *For Whom the Bell Tolls*. But I think there's more to all this than prose. That picture you sent us last year, Andy, with you and two other guys and the antlers you had found in the woods. You look about eighteen. Two of you are smoking pipes."

"Yeah," Andy says. "Hero photo. I was twenty, and I would soon be in the air force."

"You look right out of Hemingway!" I continue. "That has nothing to do with literary rhythm. You, John, and I were looking for experience that mirrored what we liked reading and vice versa. At that time in our lives, that time in American history, we would have invented Hemingway if necessary. Remember all the bull-fight posters on dorm walls. *Corrida!* Well, I don't think it was the bullfight itself that captured us, at least not me. In fact, I refused to join that fad. But now that I can see our generation from a distance, I'll bet Hemingway gave us hope that we could attain manhood even though we hadn't been old enough to fight in the war that defined heroism for us. His style made those images, those aspirations, accessible. His descriptions of place drew us in."

By now, we are all three drawn to "Big Two-Hearted River" as if to our biographies. It's not just the river, but also what it means to Nick to go there, to the quiet of the North Woods. Unlike Nick, we saw no combat. Our war was the cold one. Andy was in the air force, John and I were in the army, and Stan was aboard destroyers in the Mediterranean and North Atlantic. No one shot at us, although Andy almost went to Korea. None of us suffered from the post-traumatic stress of war. But we and many of our generation carried wounds. They had begun or deepened during the Second World War, and they lowered our resistance to the normal flak from society. Like Nick, we still try to heal by returning to good places—Stan to railroads and their terrain, the rest of us to woods, water, and mountains.

"Nick has suppressed a lot of bad stuff," Andy says. "We sense that, but we don't know exactly what. Hemingway told George Plimpton, who interviewed him for the *Paris Review*, that he wrote his short stories on the principle of the iceberg. Most of it was underwater. In one of those interchapters between stories in *In Our Time*, Nick and Rinaldi have been badly wounded, and Nick says, 'You and me, we've made a separate peace.'"

"That's what Frederic says in *A Farewell to Arms* after Caporetto," I interrupt. "He has made his separate peace and will escape the war. Easier for him than for governments. The possibility of one of its members making a separate peace with the enemy scared the hell out of both alliances in that war."

"But we don't see the war in 'Big Two-Hearted River,'" Andy continues. "Nick goes back to the river, rides the train up, and walks along the tracks to reconnect with before the war, with the North Country he knew then, with the peacefulness of it all. With the routine that is comforting, how you put the grasshopper on your hook, how you set up camp, chop wood, and make coffee. Everything's gotta be just perfect because you're reconstructing your psyche. He looks downriver at this swamp full of low trees and thinks, swamp fishing would be tragic. Strange adjective until you see that everything's got to work just right. That's important to Nick, and it won't work in the swamp."

"Because he needs something to hold on to? It isn't just the place that's the handle. It's also the routine, accuracy, and neatness?" I ask.

"That's right," Andy says.

"Sounds like John loading his backpack," I say.

"Damn right!" John replies.

"Could be that's what we're doing now," I say. "Holding on to, well, each other."

"And on to West Lawn and Wisconsin and the Porkies," John adds.

"Right, good places," I say. "We can hold on to all of that, and we don't have to explain or justify anything to each other."

"That's how I feel," Andy says. "Sort of a separate peace."

Andy thought he had discovered a whole new vista on Hemingway's writing while preparing to write the seminar paper at Berkeley in December 1958.

"Did that discovery have anything to do with your crash?" I ask.

"Well, I was under a lot of pressure," he replies.

I go no further. I don't bring up Andy's having shot a deer while hunting with Dick Lamm in northern California two months before the Hemingway paper was due. It wasn't a clean kill, Andy told us yesterday, the regret still in his voice. I don't mention Hemingway's suicide in 1961 or Andy's long attachment to the cabin he had helped his father build. I hesitate to draw any more parallels between his father and Hemingway, or between Andy and Nick, or Andy and Hemingway. I get little help from John. His iceberg hides more than Andy's or mine.

I started the reunion thinking the long friendship and the week together might give us full portraits of each other, but I have begun to see the risks of reunion. It's possible to damage the closeness by going too far, by pressing Andy on Hemingway or John on Winnebago. That would be tragic, like swamp fishing was for Nick. Yet I wish they would press me more.

Several years ago, a cousin warned me not to probe too much into Mom's mental illness.

"I understand your urge to know," she wrote, "but you may find things you wish you hadn't."

I went ahead, obtaining the hospital files. But something changes during the reunion. Andy takes John and me where Mom would not, into breakdown and recovery.

"Let's compare scars," Mom said to Andy.

Andy's story is not the same as hers, but they are close enough. By telling us his, really for the first time, he speaks for her, soul mate and fellow survivor. Both of them made a separate peace. When I decide not to drive to Winnebago, maybe I'm saying, enough, I have enough now for telling or submerging what I will. Perhaps.

We spend two days with Stan, but he's with us all the time. Andy updates us on his brother's poor health. Parkinson's disease was diagnosed last winter after Andy finally persuaded him to see a doctor about unusual aches and pains. It was "like pulling teeth," Andy recalls. Since then, Stan has often skipped his medication, but he probably started it too late to help him much. His place is a mess, Andy warns, and he's feeble.

"His mind is still sharp," Andy says. "But he's depressed and doesn't even understand it."

Andy speaks affectionately, with overtones of guilt for not having reached out to Stan while we were young. On December 7, 1941, the family had driven to Davenport, Iowa, to go ice-skating.

"On our way back to Galesburg," Andy says, "the announcement about Pearl Harbor came on the radio. Stan reached from the backseat and turned the radio off."

"How could a seven-year-old kid know what that announcement meant?" I ask. "Did he know your dad would be gone for a long time?"

"Well, remember how attentive we were to radio back then?" Andy replies. "Adventure shows and so on? As for missing my father, no, Stan had already turned off in that department. He just couldn't stand hearing something so ominous and completely beyond his control."

"None of us could control that war," I say. "Thus our generation's silence?"

"Could be. By the time we moved to Madison, Stan had gone his own bullish, lonesome way. He had already found railroads in Galesburg, where an engineer saw him standing alone by the tracks near the house and gave him a ride in the cab. That was Stan's world. He just decided he didn't understand our world, school and all. His character, strength, and intellect became coupled to steam railroads and model railroads. Here was a world that his parents and older brother could not invade. He was king of that world, the champ. No one knew more about that world than Stan."

"At the same time," I add, "he used his world to shut out other people."

"Well, what did other people do for him?" Andy asks. "Our father always putting him down. Everyone telling him what to do and faulting him for not toeing their line."

After high school, Stan worked as a fireman for the Chicago & North Western. Then he joined the Navy and rose to the rank of petty officer third class in the engine room. When his destroyer docked in Boston, he wore his pea jacket to Harvard to see John. He dropped in and out of the University of Wisconsin, ran the art department of the University Co-op on State Street, and owned one of the first Bugs in Madison.

"When his passion for something was aroused," Andy recalls, "he'd go for it. Not just railroads but history. One day he said to me, 'Geez, if I had it to do all over again, I'd major in history.'"

"He writes damned good history," I affirm. "That book of his on the Green Bay & Western is just wonderful. He has the knack."

For a six-footer weighing about two hundred twenty, Stan had extraordinarily nimble fingers that sketched quickly and assembled HO-gauge engines and cars without a bobble. Clutter surrounded his basement layout and bedroom desk, including half-assembled models, unopened kits, books, photos, wires, tools, small bottles of dope (which meant only paint to Madison kids then), assorted fragments in boxes of various sizes, candy bars, and remains of lunch. If he couldn't find something, he'd blame gremlins or fairies.

"That screw was right here! Right here! Some goddamn fairy got it when I wasn't looking! Those goddamn fairies!"

Everything smelled of glue, solder, dope, and electric motors.

Stan could imitate the sounds and motions of anything mechanical, from locomotives to airplanes to Buicks rounding corners. He could mimic any character, from bossy school principal to smooth-talking Jaycee to starched German officer. He reminded me of Jonathan Winters, who has never gotten over being ridiculed by his parents, and of Steve McQueen in *Sand Pebbles*, a loner who knew his gunboat's engine cold. I think of Stan whenever Dan Ackroyd plays a furrowed-brow specialist explaining esoterica.

We take Stan to lunch on Monday. He rents a room in a bungalow in a quiet neighborhood on Milwaukee's north side, near Whitefish Bay. He's sitting on a chair in the driveway under the eaves of the house, looking out to the street like an old man waiting for his grandkids. We help him into the car. But his mind is indeed sharp. His memory is exhaustive. He still narrates stories like nobody else. His humor is as quick and caricatured as ever, such as this one about finding Andy's fencing gear in the attic.

"Here's this foil. I'm trying to figure out how you could kill somebody with that funny little button on the end of it," says Stan.

"File it down, Stan," I recommend.

"Yeah. 'What are you doing, Johnny?'" he says in a woman's voice. "'Never mind,'" in a little boy's voice.

John and I praise Stan's history of the Green Bay & Western Railroad, published in 1989. It's crammed with historical and geographic detail and illustrated with maps and photographs, among which are many of Stan's. It's movingly written. John hauls out his copy and asks Stan to sign it.

"Oh my God," says Stan. "Well, that's nice, John." His hand quivers. "Sorry, I'm a little on the shaky side these days."

Stan laments the passing of American railroads.

"There was this sharp guy," he says, "an economist out on the West Coast, although he came from Chicago. He said back in the sixties that railroads were doomed because of the decline of the coal and steel industries. He was right. Plus trucks and interstate highways, of course. There was this precipitous curve. We finally got to the point where there were too many unused railroads, and they just said to hell with it. Same thing had happened to electric urban railroads back in the twenties. By 1930, there were just a few interurban lines that made a profit. Soon, they were gone, too. The steam railroad, electric railroad, and automobile had been about neck and neck in the early twenties."

Stan has always been a nostalgic pessimist. Because of human nature—autocracy, dishonesty, stupidity, and greed—things are bound to change for the worse.

"The whole country's going bankrupt," he grumbles after John says Tennessee is. "All of a sudden, the bills are coming in on all the things we've been doing. And you start realizing they were robbing the bank."

Add to this outlook Stan's own thin skin and nonconformity and you end up with his resignation from the Mid-Continent Railway Museum more than fifteen years ago. Now, understandably, I also hear forebodings of mortality. One of his closest friends at Mid-Continent stayed on after Stan left.

"A little while back," Stan says, "he did a beautiful job of restoring a fifty-foot coach. Gorgeous. Silk-screened the inlaid plywood of the clerestory, everything meticulous and polished. But he got to the point where he was too discouraged to go on. Everybody good was dying. So he quit."

But Stan doesn't complain about his illness, and we all want to dwell on the good stuff: our faithful dogs, Inkie and Barbos; our first Bugs; blasting tin cans and cow pies with cherry bombs; sacking out on the sandy shore of Lake Michigan after a day at Sheboygan's International Bratwurst Festival; war games during World War II; and FUBARs from our service in the Cold War. Stan's Bug keeps coming up, a 1956 with sunroof and oval rear window. It was the last model with that oval. In July 1956, he and I drove north in it. He had just bellowed from his front porch, "Hey, Gaines, wanna go to Duluth?"

He soon loaned it to Andy to drive Lilias back to New York after summer school.

The FOWLs: (left to right) Gaines Post, Stan Mailer, Andy Mailer, John Post

"She charmed everyone," Andy says, "even Stan."

We parked it near the beach outside Sheboygan in the summer of 1959, where we listened to classical music on my newfangled transistor radio as we searched the night sky for *Sputnik 3* and *Vanguard 2*.

"'*Music 'til Dawn*,'" Stan recalls the name of the program. "'WBBM Chicago, 780 on your AM dial.'" He sounds just like the announcer of old.

As we pull into his driveway late that afternoon, Stan is praising the Bug's impudence in the fifties when it took on Detroit.

"Those American fins," he says, snorting. "And those Dagmars."

"Dagmars?" I ask.

"Yeah, those two big boobs on the front bumper," he replies.

We confirm plans to see Stan on Thursday. We head back to Oconomowoc, trying to make the best of what we have seen. Sure, Stan walks slowly and trembles some. He has difficulty keeping his balance, and he speaks softly with a bit of a slur. But he's still great company. He's still able to split our sides. We stay upbeat until Andy puts on a CD of Frank Sinatra's songs and selects "It Was a Very Good Year." The person in the song remembers being seventeen, twenty-one, and thirty-five, but has now entered the autumn of his life. Stan is well past autumn.

We return to Milwaukee on Thursday morning determined to show Stan a good time. We have decided to tour the northern unit of Kettle Moraine State

Forest, northwest of Milwaukee. Stan can no longer explore on his own, but he loves the Wisconsin countryside. He learned its geology through self-teaching and a couple of university courses, as had Dad a long time before. Dad showed John and me features around Fort Atkinson that are now part of Kettle Moraine State Forest's southern unit. The glaciation of Wisconsin has been popularized since then, thanks to the expansion of this forest and its visitor centers; the establishment of the state's Ice Age Park and Trail Foundation in the late fifties; the creation of the Ice Age National Scientific Reserve in 1971, which the State of Wisconsin and the National Park Service administer jointly; and the designation of the Ice Age Trail as a National Scenic Trail in 1980. We have an incomparable guide in Stan, and I'm ready to pick his brains, partly as a way to reconnect with Dad.

The day is clear and dry. Stan is glad to see us. John gets us started by playing a tape of zany songs by Spike Jones and His City Slickers.

"For you, Stan," he says. "We saw these guys with you at the Orpheum after the war."

Stan beams. We turn off U.S. 45 onto a county road near the boundary of the state forest.

"This is nice. Real nice," Stan says. "Those hills point in the general flow of the Wisconsin Glacier."

He's just warming up. We stop at the forest headquarters, surrounded by hardwoods and conifers, to pick up a map and read a few explanatory signs.

"You're talking heat," Stan enthuses about types of rock. "God, think of it. Imagine how hot it must have been to change sedimentary rock into metamorphic rock. Really cooking."

"Is that what was going on around Devil's Lake?" I ask.

"Yeah. Take a look at Van Hise Rock on State 136 just north of Rock Springs. That thing is nearly two billion years old, almost half as old as the earth. I've seen it, two layers of quartzite. Came up at an angle like this or got tipped up. Don't know which. Tells you the origins of the Baraboo Hills."

Van Hise Rock is named after University of Wisconsin geologist Charles Van Hise, who used this monolith to teach principles of geology in the late nineteenth century. The National Park Service designated the rock a National Historic Landmark in 1999.

Later, at the Ice Age Visitor Center, I corner Stan on the balcony while John and Andy continue looking through the displays inside. I need Stan's gift for reading geology like a story.

"That's a terrific example of a kame over there, isn't it?" I ask, pointing to a mound about eighty feet high.

"Yeah," he says. "And there's another one out of sight around the corner."

"I understand kames, but what exactly is a kettle?"

"They were formed when great hunks of ice melted, and that process lowered the mass of sand and debris that had covered the ice. In the end, when everything has melted and settled, you've got a depression. Sort of like pouring sand over an ice cube in a drink and then letting the water out the bottom."

"And a kettle moraine?" I ask.

"Oh, that's a hodgepodge of stuff the ice pushes around and leaves behind where two ice lobes have come together, as they did along here, called the Lake Michigan and Green Bay Lobes. It's sort of a ridge, but it's not as clear as the end moraine where the glacier stopped, like you have over at Devil's Lake. Lots of interesting features over there near Baraboo. Moraines, cuestas, you name it."

"What's a cuesta?" I ask.

"You know how we used to drive up Highway 12 to Sauk City for milkshakes? How you go to the top of the ridge at Springfield Corners and start down the other side? That's a cuesta," Stan explains. "You've got a heavy layer of rock like this from one era going over the top of another layer like this." He gestures with his hands. "You can tell one from the other by the fossil record. There are other scientific ways to do that now, but the traditional way, back when I took the course forty years ago, was to check the fossils. All kinds of stuff died and sank down into layers of silt and mud, from big stuff to little animals and foraminifera and shells and so on. It's a whole world of detecting and trying to find out whether there's a missing link between two layers of material. That's how they date the stuff, using fossil records. Not just for mastodons but also for the little guys."

"Stan, you make those rocks and formations and fossils sound like an extended family," I say. "And you probably know Wisconsin better than most geologists, having traipsed all over looking for grade crossings, fills, bridges, and so on. Your book is full of landscape. In fact, that's where I got most of my information on the Fox River."

"Yeah. In my book," he says with an effete accent. "Well, in it, there is a lot about the Fox. Building the canal in swampy country to connect the Fox and the Wisconsin, which was too shallow and always needed dredging. Trying to make a permanent steamboat route from Green Bay to St. Paul, starting before railroad days and then losing to rail. Now there's a good example of trying to make something out of what wound up being nothing. I don't feel sorry for the big guys who got their money back after the whole thing collapsed. That's typical. But you gotta hand it to 'em for having the concept. And you can't say it was absurd to try because nobody knew they couldn't pull it off."

"Look at that." I point to a large bird in flight in the direction of the kame.

"Hawk. Four-engine hawk. Looking for lunch," Stan says.

"Stan, you would have been a terrific teacher."

"Really?" he asks. He's serious.

"Really."

We take a time-out from geology for hamburgers and beer at the Crocodile Bar and Grill in Dundee. We tell more stories of the old days on West Lawn, about fireworks, street games, bullies and fights, farmers selling fresh corn and tomatoes from their pickups, trucks from Redbird Fuel delivering coal down our driveway into the bin that fed the furnace before Dad switched to oil, and walking and biking around our domain, from Vilas Park to the University Arboretum across Lake Wingra and the shops along Monroe Street. Stan recalls a friend's model train line, the Sand Hill Interurban Traction. The friend chose the name just so he could paint the initials on the cars. John says that inspired him to recommend "Students Here Incensed Totally" when someone he knew at Berkeley in the early sixties was contemplating acronyms.

And, of course, there are more tales of Inkie and Barbos. No doubt about it, Inkie was the best cocker spaniel, and Barbos was the best black lab–golden retriever mix that ever lived.

"Barbos was a great watchdog," I reminisce. "If John or I came through the basement door and yelled, 'meter man!' Barbos would bark like hell from the top of the stairs, even after smelling us and wagging his tail. Remember that couch in Dad's study? Barbos used to sit there with his head over the back of it. He could hear Dad's car a block away. That bushy, black tail would start thumping the couch."

"Before Inkie, we had Nicky," Andy says. "Stan and I always needed soft kinds of stuff. Our neighbors in Galesburg had a baby and unloaded Nicky on us. He was named after the last tsar. The man was a White Russian, and his mother had taken him across Siberia after the revolution to get them both out of Russia."

"Trans-Siberian Railroad," says Stan. "Hook heem up to locomoteef and hee puull!"

At the northern end of the state forest, we stop in Greenbush for a look at the white frame exterior of the restored Wade House. The marker reads, "One of the earliest stagecoach inns in Wisconsin." This house "became the most important stagecoach stop on the plank road between Sheboygan and Fond du Lac. Meetings for the discussion of Civil War issues and early railroad constructions were held in the inn."

Stan knows the place from his scouting of railroads.

"That plank road," he says. "That was quite a trip in those days." He begins coughing. "Boy, I get coughing fits."

We have supper at Smith Bros. Restaurant on the waterfront in Port Washington. John and I chose the place because Dad took us there in the late forties and ordered lake trout that was firm and sweet. But commercial fishing is now banned on Lake Michigan because of pollution, so our fish come from one of the other Great Lakes, probably Huron. We dine on whitefish, served on a plank to give it a smoked flavor.

Driving back to Milwaukee, Andy says, "There's no three people I'd rather be with than you three."

It has been that kind of reunion, remarkable. The four of us, Mailer and Post brothers, are together for the first time in over forty years. Stan is unsure on his feet. I had to help him today, just like I would normally help someone in his eighties. Stan knows he's dying. He's lonely; he needs his two tomcats, both of which found him as strays, and he worries that one has gone AWOL.

When we drop off Stan at his house, he says, "Please come back," and, "When can we do this again?"

By the way he looks at John and me, I know he doubts he will see us again. Stan shakes hands with Andy. Then he stands in the driveway with his head down and right hand stopped at the handkerchief he has reached for in his back pocket. At first, I think he's having difficulty removing the handkerchief. I saw him fumble for it during the outing. His lip starts to tremble. He stays like that for eternal seconds. The rest of us freeze, inept. I'm searching for something to say when Andy embraces Stan. It's the first time I have ever seen either brother take the other in his arms.

Stan sobs and murmurs, "I hope I can handle this."

Andy hugs him again, holding him for several minutes. Then all of us try to cheer each other up.

"Thanks for the geology lesson, Stan," I say.

He grins. "That Kettle Moraine was nice," he says. "Real nice. And that was a good dinner we had. Not every fish gets to end up on a piece of wood like that."

John leaves early Saturday morning, set on making it back to Nashville in one day. I expect the cumulative emotion of the reunion to show as we embrace, but there are no tears. There are just smiles and slaps on the back, as if to say congratulations to us all, we did it, let's do this every year from now until the end. Soon,

Andy and I pull away from the condo. He's in the lead. Three boys about eight or nine years old sit on a board fence in front of the adjacent building. They point at my Bug, jump down, and race over toward me, smiling and waving. I stop.

"Spin the tires!" they shout.

"Sorry, boys, I won't do that," I say. "You wouldn't say that to your grandmother, would you?"

They laugh, say no, and ask how old my Bug is. I tell them I bought it in 1965 and have been driving it for thirty-seven years. "That's a little longer than you've been alive."

They look puzzled, but then they do the math.

"Oh, yeah," they say.

Grandmother, I think as I drive on. I used the same analogy a few days ago when I had the Bug's oil changed at a service station in Oconomowoc, the only time that I drove it during the reunion. I handed the keys to a lively young blonde with several pieces of silver imbedded about her face.

"What are you doing here?" she asked when she saw my plates.

"This is my home state," I said.

"Boy, you oughtta go back to California where the weather is decent."

"But I love this overcast and drizzle," I said. "California gets boring after a while."

She didn't believe me. I showed her how to find reverse and first gears. She eased the Bug into the garage where a young man took over. I told him the valves were knocking a bit louder than usual, but he agreed that I could probably wait until returning to California to have them adjusted. While he changed the oil, I struck up a conversation in the waiting room with a guy in his thirties, maybe early forties. He sported a crew cut and a red sweatshirt and spoke with a Wisconsin accent. He had seen the woman drive the Bug into the garage.

"You let her do that?" he asked.

"Yes," I replied.

"Well, I don't let anyone touch my pickup," he said. "That's a really clean Bug you got. Really nice shape." He drove a 1961 Chevy pickup and did the engine work himself. "Good therapy," he said.

"What do you mean?" I asked.

"Well, at the end of the day, after supper, I go out and work on it and feel a lot better about things."

We wished each other luck.

"Safe trip," he said.

The mechanic came inside to write up the bill and said to a colleague behind the counter, "He's driven this thing all the way from California, without a radio."

"Yeah," I said, "and no air-conditioning or cell phone."

They looked astonished. As I paid, I thanked the young man and woman for the care they showed my Bug.

"I appreciate your kindness," I said. "That car's like my grandmother."

When did my Bug become a grandmother? I wonder as Andy and I turn west on I-94. I called her "old girl" back in the late eighties when the six-volt battery could no longer run her central nervous system. Grandmother must have occurred to me soon after that. It was certainly on my mind when I gave her fresh paint, new chrome bumpers, and a new engine last year.

She looks great, but that new engine is, after all, a transplant, and how much longer can the original transmission last? My God, I thought, I'm old enough to be a grandfather. Remember that young woman in the grocery store parking lot a few weeks ago? "My grandmother had one just like it," she said.

After registering at a hotel in Middleton, Andy and I drive into Madison in his car for a last look at West Lawn, West High, university, Capitol Square, and the big house in Maple Bluff. On the east side of town, the Chicago & North Western's station has vanished, its space now taken by a small garden and enormous power plant. On the west side, the Milwaukee Road's station houses a restaurant and shops. We stand on the platform where Andy and his mother met his father returning from the war with his chest full of ribbons. It's where I waved good-bye to my parents in August 1955 when they left for a year in Italy. I would soon go east for my freshman year at Cornell. Mom later told me they felt sorry for me as their train pulled away.

She said, "We were leaving our little boy all alone to go to college."

Off Capitol Square and overlooking Lake Monona, the city built the Monona Terrace Community and Convention Center after all the Mailers and Posts, except Mrs. Mailer, had left Madison. The center retains some of Frank Lloyd Wright's original design. When we were boys, officials who disliked the man had rejected the design along with the idea of placing any building so as to block their view of the lake from the city's most exclusive club.

"The Badlands will clear my brain," I say at one point. "I'm just so cluttered and overloaded with memories. Can't sort it all out."

"I know," Andy agrees. "I don't recognize half of this stuff. Then we'll hit a street corner, and something clicks, like I rode my bicycle here."

"Or I scuffed my knee on that curb," I add.

Over lunch at the Brathaus, Andy says he, like his father, was afraid of father-
hood.

"I was petrified at the thought," he recalls. "That's one of the main reasons I
didn't pursue my relationship with Lilias after that magic summer of '56. I probably picked that up as a boy. Well, that and other fears."

"But you, I mean, we also picked up a lot of good stuff, didn't we?" I ask.
"One of the things that has struck me this week is how often you refer to old high
school friends as terrific guys. That makes me think not only that you like and
attract terrific guys but that Madison probably had more of them per capita than
most towns in America in that period. No way of proving that, of course."

"No, but it may be true. We're blessed to have grown up where and when we
did."

We return to Middleton by way of University Avenue, passing the former
Wisconsin General Hospital.

"I was born there," I say. "There I was in those records I told you about, from
pregnancy to delivery to nursing. Eerie. Back to the beginning."

"Yeah, chapter one," Andy reflects. "'I grow old ... I grow old ... I shall wear
the bottoms of my trousers rolled.'"

"One of your favorites?" I ask.

"Yeah, T. S. Eliot."

I have arranged to see Mary Mohs late in the afternoon. As Mary McKenzie,
she was my girlfriend at Dudgeon School. An only child with an overbearing
stepmother, Mary had pigtails and was talented at the piano. She was impressed
by how far I could kick a football and enchanted by my stories about Texas cowboys because she was madly in love with Roy Rogers. We drifted apart as soon as
we hit seventh grade at West Junior High, where worldly eighth-grade boys lay in
wait. She eventually married another classmate, Fred Mohs, son of the famous
Dr. Frederic Mohs, whose technique for removing skin cancers became known as
"Mohs Micrographic Surgery."

Mary and Fred attended the University of Wisconsin and later became pillars
of Madison society, supporting the university, arts, and other civic causes.
Stephen Ambrose appointed Mary to his founding board for the National D-Day
Museum in New Orleans. She was a power in the state Republican Party when its
platform coincided with her moderate views, but it has since moved far to her
right. Fred, a prominent attorney and popular member of the university's board
of regents, has strongly promoted historic preservation and traveled widely. They
live near the state capitol.

With a little time to kill, I park my Bug at the curb on the southeast side of
the capitol. Completed in 1917, its perfectly proportioned, white granite dome

was recently cleaned and is now whiter than I have ever seen it. Except for a monstrous, glass-paneled building on the northeast side of the square, Madison has not allowed new construction to block citywide views of the capitol. It's unlike Austin, Texas, where imperious high-rises conceal and truncate the lovely red granite edifice of the 1880s.

I walk over to the bronze statue of Hans Christian Heg. The inscription reads, "Colonel, 15th Wisconsin Volunteers; born in Norway December 1829, fell at Chickamauga, September 1863; Norwegian Americans gave this memorial to the State of Wisconsin."

Returning to the Bug, I pass the wooden bench where three old men sat when I parked here in 1990 before returning my rental car to the airport. Their conversation drifted through my open window.

"It's thirty-four seconds after … Wait, it's three forty-seven … riiiight now!" said one.

"Aaaah shit," grunted one of his companions.

"Pretty good watch?" the third man asked.

"Yeah, correct time all the time."

"Aaaah fuck."

"Had it for twenty years. It's a special. Special Timex."

"That's what I've got. Had it for years. Correct time all the time."

"Aaaah shit."

I figured I'd be sitting on a bench like that in another twenty-five years. I wondered if I'd be one of the Timex guys. Or would I, like their friend, ignore the conversational seconds and mark a different kind of time with expletives? Today, I'm twelve years closer to that bench.

Leaving the square, I stop to take a photo of the Bug with the capitol in the background. It's my way of introducing two old friends. Outside Mary's, I pause on the sidewalk, not ready to ring the doorbell, like a boy expecting his girlfriend's parents to come to the door.

Mary looks great. She's dressed casually for her but elegantly to my eyes. She has a warm smile and reddish brown hair. She's as slim and pretty as the girl I knew at Dudgeon School. We had been out of touch after high school until our class reunion in 1990 when she and Fred invited me to dinner. Polly, the older of their two daughters, had just graduated from college with a major in history. Before dinner, she and I adjourned to the study to discuss graduate school and the profession.

Mary told me later that Polly came into the kitchen afterward and asked, "How did you let him get away?"

Fred and Mary and a friend of theirs, another Republican, questioned my liberal views without any of the snide invective that their party had used against Michael Dukakis in the presidential campaign of 1988.

When Mary sounded exasperated, I said, "Good thing we broke up."

Wisconsin State Capitol, Madison

As we walked out to my car, Fred said, "You've really had an interesting life. Done a lot of interesting things. I admire that."

I returned the compliment.

Now, Mary and I talk in the small library at the rear of their graceful old house and begin picking up where we left off two years ago when I came to Madison to give the keynote speech at our 45th class reunion. We cover families, worries, classmates, and Stephen Ambrose, of whom I'm not really a fan. We talk about Madison then and now and the politics of Bush's War on Terror. On this subject, I tread softly in her home. She wonders why I still wear glasses instead of contact lenses and why I didn't go out for high school football since I could kick farther than anyone else in the class. I tell her I'm happy to stick with glasses. I explain I was too light for football, but I sometimes wish I had tried out for the squad anyway.

After confiding something personal, she says, "I've never told that to anybody except my two closest friends, both of whom are now dead."

"Don't worry," I assure her. "I won't say anything to anyone."

"I know you won't," she says.

She asks about John, and I bring her up to date on his retirement, adding how great it has been to spend a week with him and Andy.

"Well," she says to my surprise, "I always thought your brother didn't look after you enough."

"What do you mean?" I ask.

"I mean when your mom was away and you were so vulnerable."

"Well, so was he. And who looked after him?"

Mary is facing the window. Suddenly, her eyes widen as she looks beyond me. I turn around to see a young man crossing the backyard. He walks up to the porch and opens the kitchen door as if he owns the place, oblivious to my having moved into the kitchen to intercept him.

"What are you doing here?" I ask.

An African American in his twenties, he stops and flinches as if waking from a dream.

"Oh, I'm sorry," he mutters. "Guess I have the wrong place. I was looking for a friend's house."

"Well, this isn't it, so just go back the way you came in."

He says, "Okay. Sorry. Didn't mean it."

I follow him across the backyard and out to the front sidewalk, where he changes his tune.

"I shouldn't have done this. I won't do this again. I'm really sorry," he says. He looks bewildered.

Back inside, Mary calls a policeman friend and a college boy around the corner who often looks after the house. The policeman guesses the intruder was high on drugs and looking for money. Fred is away for the weekend on a fishing trip. I offer to stay the night if Mary wants me to. Then I call Andy at the hotel to warn him I'll be late meeting him for dinner and that after dinner I might spend the night at Mary's.

Mary and I talk a few minutes about the scare. Then I change the subject.

She interrupts me, "Gaines, you were very brave then."

"What?"

"You were very brave. I'm really proud of you. You're my hero."

"How very strange," I reply. "This must be exactly how anyone feels who says, 'I was doing my job.' You know how often we hear that. Not the least bit heroic, whatever that means. I was just responding to a problem."

"Well, you didn't hesitate," she says. "You jumped right up and did it. Probably your military training. Don't be so damned Midwestern modest."

Mary says she'll be okay, but I promise to call her after dinner. I meet Andy at Tony Frank's Tavern on the west side of town, a popular hangout beyond the city limits when built after the war. We agreed to dine there tonight for old time's sake, not for the old-fashioned cholesterol. It's hard to get Mary off my mind, and Andy sympathizes.

"I'm sure she'll be fine," I tell him, thinking that may be truer about her security than her spirits. "I feel good about what I did, but I wouldn't call it heroism. The country has gone so gaga over heroes since 9/11 that everybody seems to want to be one. Hell, me too. But let's not get carried away."

I keep mum about Mary's memory of John, hesitant to question older brothers on my last night with Andy. Some of John's remarks during the reunion got under my skin, as in "Well, if we forgot anything [at the store], we'll send Gaines back for it." That's old and unnecessary big brother stuff, but it's also harmless.

Mary took me back to moments of a different kind when I learned a double lesson. Sure, you have to be able to swim on your own, but, at the end of the day, you're all alone. Even with family and among FOWLs.

Back at the hotel, I call Mary and offer again to stay with her. She insists she'll be safe by herself. She has called Fred. He said he'll come home tomorrow morning. All the doors and windows are locked. The police will send a patrol car by the house every hour or so.

"Fred thinks you should have called 9-1-1," she adds.

"Well, I didn't," I reply. "Didn't even think about it. All I wanted to do was get that guy out of your house."

"When you got up, you waved your arm at me to stay put. You said, 'Mary, I'll handle this.'"

"Did I say that?" I ask.

"You certainly did. I'll never forget it, and I'll never let you forget it."

"I'll call you in the morning," I say.

"I love you, Gaines," she says.

"I love you, Mary."

The word, love, comes naturally now. It's a lifetime after my crush on Mary that I had no words for. It's two years after she learned from my memoir about my mother's absence and told me how lonely she, too, had been. We have few secrets left. It's just as well that I don't stay the night.

CHAPTER 7

▼

WEST AGAIN

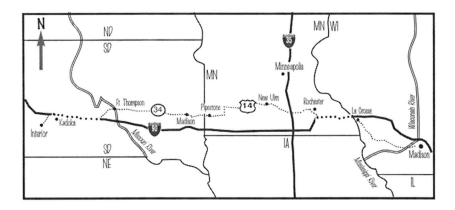

Sunday, June 9

I call Mary from the hotel while Andy and I drink a last cup of coffee in our room. A friend is with her. Fred will arrive soon. She asks me to stay in touch. Andy and I say good-bye in the parking lot. Again, there are no tears, but the bear hug bespeaks undying affection. I did not know until this reunion how vulnerable Andy was at the time of his life when he was All-American in my boyhood book. My criteria for All-American have grown up since then, thanks in part to my mother's struggle and recovery. Andy still qualifies.

I head west on U.S. 14, talked out and happy to be back on the road. Even the best of conversation with the oldest of friends demands response. Solitude comes only in fragments at such times. Driving long distances again in the Bug will free me to locate the reunion on my own map of things. Before leaving Claremont, I thought the reunion on Wisconsin soil was the point of the journey, just as returning home inspired ancient Greek songs about survivors of the Trojan War, no matter how many verses along the way. Now, I know my time with John and Andy was episode, not destination.

The cloudless morning is opaque with the summer haze that overspreads southern Wisconsin between occasional dry fronts from Canada. There's little traffic, much birdsong, and an aftertaste of last night's bratwurst with sauerkraut and Swiss cheese. Between Middleton and Cross Plains, a sign welcomes motorists to the Black Earth Creek Watershed. I have felt welcome there since the outing that Mom arranged for my birthday during the war in 1943 or 1944. She, John, I, and some neighborhood boys rode out in a Milwaukee Road caboose, climbed a hill, and had a picnic in autumn sunshine. It's one of the few days I remember from the war when Mom smiled enough for me to think she'd be okay and we'd win. That wasn't long ago.

The Green Bay Lobe of the Wisconsin Glacier ended at Cross Plains, where the terrain abruptly changes to the steep hills, narrow valleys, and sandstone out-croppings of the older Driftless Area. Recent rains have greened the valley of Black Earth Creek. Some of the prosperous farms have three or more silos. The cows are freer than those I see crowded together in California, where the cheese industry fertilizes its droll television ads with bullshit about happy bovines. In fact, I haven't come across a large dairy feedlot in Wisconsin or more than fifty cows in the same enclosure, a large pen next to a milking barn.

On the old Milwaukee Road line, a tourist train out of Middleton slows as it approaches Mazomanie, which began in the 1850s as a village for crews servicing the Milwaukee & Mississippi Railroad Company. The M&M engineer who named Mazomanie thought, incorrectly, that the word was Sac for "iron horse." His company completed its line from Milwaukee to Prairie du Chien in 1857, the first to cross Wisconsin from Lake Michigan to the Mississippi River. The timing was unfortunate for the M&M. The recent Crimean War had deprived Europe of Russian grain. The resultant surge in American farm exports had helped accelerate railroad building in the Old Northwest. Peace in Europe and over-expansion in America led to the international financial panic of 1857, probably the clearest sign to date that the economies of the New and Old Worlds were bound together. The resultant depression ended in 1859. The Civil War disrupted Mississippi River traffic south of the Ohio, and west-east trade across Wisconsin rebounded. In 1863, the Milwaukee & Mississippi became the Milwaukee & St. Paul, which became the Chicago, Milwaukee & St. Paul in 1874. "Pacific" was added when the railroad reached Seattle in 1909.

The old part of Mazomanie has been blocked off for a weekend fair. I don't keep my Pie Town promise to Candace to look up her theater friend here. At a small café just off the highway, I order their basic breakfast of eggs and hash browns. The waitress brings it right from the grill, the fresh over-easy eggs untouched by infernal warming lights.

I'm not far from the street that we must have walked from the caboose to the bottom of our picnic hill south of town sixty years ago. After the birthday cake, we rested in the sloping pasture below the hilltop woods. I sat next to my mother. The sun warmed our backs. The town, fields, and hills looked like cutouts from colored paper. Everything fit together. There was no war in the valley. I wasn't afraid.

It was the kind of Wisconsin autumn day that John Steinbeck describes in his *Travels with Charley*:

> There was a penetration of light into solid substance so that I seemed to see into things, deep in, and I've seen that kind of light elsewhere only in Greece. I remembered now that I had been told Wisconsin is a lovely state, but the telling had not prepared me. It was a magic day. The land dripped with richness, the fat cows and pigs gleaming against green, and, in the smaller holdings, corn standing in little tents as corn should, and pumpkins all about (Steinbeck 1961).

West of Mazomanie, a marker remembers the village of Dover:

> Beginning in 1844, nearly 700 settlers were brought into this area by the British Temperance and Emigration Society, organized the previous year in Liverpool, England.

Dover soon decayed, the marker continues, for the Milwaukee & Mississippi built its local depot in Mazomanie and did not stop here. Dover's most famous boy who made good, John Appleby, invented the "knotter" for the grain binder, the idea having come to him "as he watched the monotonously regular movement of his mother's hands in knitting."

The hills recede as I enter the valley of the Wisconsin River. When John and I wore knickers, Mom seemed fine, and Dad drove the old black Chevy that he would put up on blocks after Pearl Harbor, we came out to see two famous hills south of the river near Spring Green. On one of them, a tower, gravity, and cold water had turned molten Wisconsin lead into shot from the 1830s to the eve of the Civil War. Into the other hill, Frank Lloyd Wright had built Taliesin out of native oak and sandstone. I remember the dark hole at Shot Tower Hill, the natural aura of Taliesin, and the inaudible promise from an invisible source that I would understand these things some day.

Highway 14 crosses the Wisconsin River in Spring Green, about twenty miles below the site of the Battle of Wisconsin Heights. In July 1832, Black Hawk led his band of Sac and Fox, together with a few Winnebago and Kickapoo, west from the Rock River, through the isthmus of the Four Lakes, to the "Ouisconsin." They reached the river at a point several miles downstream from where the tribe had once had a village, near our milkshake joint in Sauk City. This was not a ruthless war party but a hopeless migration, looking for some way to recover tribal lands east of the Mississippi. While women, children, and the elderly crossed the river, Black Hawk and his warriors fought a delaying action against pursuing militia volunteers commanded by Colonel Henry Dodge and General James Henry. Some of the Indians fled southwest down the Wisconsin and were decimated by troops from Fort Crawford before reaching the Mississippi. The remainder made their way west overland, hoping to gain sanctuary across the Mississippi. Many of these died in the Battle of the Bad Axe, on the east bank of the Mississippi or trying to swim across it. Sioux killed many of the survivors because they were out to settle scores despite a recent peace treaty with the Sac and Fox.

Black Hawk surrendered to Colonel Zachary Taylor at Fort Crawford. Lieutenant Jefferson Davis escorted Black Hawk to detention in St. Louis. General Winfield Scott, who had taken charge of the campaign in June, subsequently apologized to the Indians for the killing of women and children at Bad Axe. Black Hawk, in his autobiography, praised Scott as a great leader whom the Sac would not have abandoned for the British had he been America's "Great Father" in 1812 (Black Hawk 1964).

Twelve months after the Battle of Wisconsin Heights and no longer a prisoner, Black Hawk came down the Wisconsin River in an open boat. He took the same route from Lake Michigan that Indians had used for centuries. Marquette and Joliet had canoed it in 1673, as had Jonathan Carver in Britain's first exploration west of the Great Lakes from 1766 to 1768 after defeating the French in the French and Indian War, or Seven Years' War. Green Bay, Fox River, Fox-Wisconsin portage, and the Wisconsin River all lie in the diagonal trench of the Green Bay Lobe.

Black Hawk was born in 1767, the year after Carver entered Wisconsin. Few whites lived in Wisconsin then. Many of them were rough French *coureurs du bois*, or freelance traders and woodsmen, who had adopted the wilderness ways of the

Indians and taken native wives. In 1833, his sixty-seventh year, Black Hawk was returning to his home in the Iowa Territory after several months in the East, where he finally saw the truth. America's young men, as President Jackson tersely warned him, were indeed as numerous as leaves in the woods. In three years, Wisconsin would become a territory, Dodge would govern it, and the isthmus of the Four Lakes would be chosen as the site for its capital. Black Hawk died in 1838, the last Sac leader to defy the United States.

The Wisconsin River is high, bending bushes that have ventured down its banks. About ten miles west of Spring Green, U.S. 14 turns northwest, following the Pine River into rolling country. In Richland Center, a pretty town settled in 1849 and surrounded by hills, American flags mark a "Purple Heart Memorial." Northwest of Richland Center, the highway winds up and down folds of the Driftless Area plateau that extends to the Mississippi. Among the castellated pinnacles and buttes of dark sandstone, layering and shearing has revealed bright yellows.

Two markers near the village of Boaz recognize firsts. In 1897, two farm boys found large bones protruding from a streamside after heavy rains, the first recorded discovery in Wisconsin of the remains of the American mastodons that came here after the last glacial retreat. A spearpoint found not far away supports the thesis that Paleo-Indians arrived in Wisconsin about the same time, probably along the lower Wisconsin River Valley. The farmhouse here, constructed and wired for electricity in 1917, became "the first in Wisconsin to obtain central station electric power from a rural electric cooperative," in 1937.

My Bug takes the hills in stride. In third gear, it rolls along at forty-five to fifty miles per hour, ideal for obsolescence in the Driftless Area. I love this car, how reliable and self-contained it is, and how its circumference reminds me that few possessions are essential. I need nothing else. No one depends on me. Nothing rattles, flaps, or flutters. I still have my old cross-country way of packing the Bug. I have the same routine and everything is in its place, like Andy on Nick Adams.

A blackbird flashes brilliant scarlet shoulder patches in flight. Farms tucked into hollows are smaller than those around Black Earth, but they still offer hope that the family farm will survive in Wisconsin. Off to the right, one of them has diversified. At least fifty cars are parked on the lawn and adjacent field. A modest, handmade sign reads, "Dairy Breakfast." The farms grow larger and richer on the flattened uplands, and the temperature cools. I drop into another watershed. On the dark green lawn of a white farmhouse, a grandfather or great-uncle guides a boy's hands on the steering wheel of a large mower. In Readstown, I cross the Kickapoo River and add it to the names of Wisconsin's rivers that have come back to me since I entered the state: Pecatonica, Sugar, Rock, Bark, Fox, Wolf, and Yahara. Cars and pickups line the highway's shoulders near a country store called "Mrs. D's Gifts."

Viroqua lies atop the Driftless plateau, elevation nearly thirteen hundred feet, about six hundred feet higher than Spring Green. At the south edge of town, a trailer park sprawls next to a pasture that has been denuded for the sale of trailers and towing rigs. In the middle of this ugly, man-made moraine, a sign proclaims, "Jesus Saves." The town itself is one of the cleanest I have seen in Wisconsin. It has an attractive main street, several old buildings, and a prosperous look. Dad, who gave every syllable a chance, pronounced it "Vee-ro-qua," not the Wisconsinese "Vro-kwaah." The origins of the name are uncertain, but the favorites seem to be a paddle wheeler on Ohio's Muskingum River and a legendary daughter of Black Hawk who killed herself to avoid capture by white men. Jeremiah McLain Rusk moved here from Ohio in 1853, fought in the 25th Wisconsin Infantry in the Civil War, and served three terms as Wisconsin's governor and one as America's secretary of agriculture from 1889 to 1893. In May 1886, Uncle Jerry, as he was fondly known, came under pressure from employers who feared revolution was at hand. He ordered the local militia to use force if necessary against Milwaukee workers, many of them Polish and German, who marched and struck for an eight-hour workday. Several workers were killed. Afterwards, the governor said he had done his duty.

Westby, as high and tidy as Viroqua, was named after Ole Westby and remains largely Norwegian American. *Velkommen* and Viking ships decorate blue and white banners on Main Street. I pass Lutheran churches, the statue of a Viking, and storefronts bearing Norwegian names. The highway bears west and drops steeply into a lovely valley below round hills covered with forest. A New Beetle passes me without a wave from the driver, another case of historical amnesia. In the village of Coon Valley, where the trim, redbrick Norwegian Evangelical Church and its simple spire watch over a quiet cemetery, I walk among the graves of families that cultivated this watershed.

The valley of Coon Creek lies in what is called the "coulee country" around La Crosse. The little coulee that bounded Hamlin Garland's childhood universe is scarcely ten miles north of here, near the La Crosse River and the village of West Salem. Several years after returning from the Civil War, Hamlin's father decided to move west "in search of the perfect farm." Hamlin's grandfather warned, "Ye'd better stick to the old coulee. Ye'll find none better."

He was right. Thirty years later, discouraged by failure at farming wheat on the open lands of the Golden West, Hamlin's parents moved back to Wisconsin, where, during their absence, dairy had replaced grain as the foundation of the state's agricultural economy. The Garlands lived in the frame cottage their son bought for them in West Salem with a view of the hills he had known as a boy. It was a homecoming for Hamlin as well as his parents. While they prepared to return from the West, he moved from Boston to Chicago.

"I belonged here," he had learned. "My writing was of the Middle Border" (Garland 1927).

I drove this highway to the Mississippi in August 1964 in my first Bug. I was on the way to California for my second year at Stanford. I would cross Minnesota, South Dakota, Wyoming, Idaho, and Oregon, camping and hiking along the way. I marveled at the beauty of this wedge of land between Madison and La Crosse, but I was eager to get out there beyond the Mississippi to bigger country that was new to me, the northern Great Plains, Badlands, Big Horns, Wind River, Grand Tetons, Snake River, and Cascades. I know that country now, but I have found none prettier there than this. Maybe I should stay a few hours in this valley.

What tugs on me? What holds me back? It's the roaming and reminiscing with John and Andy, the ancient friendship with Mary, and the memory of the hillside at Mazomanie. It's the feeling, stronger now than at any time since boyhood, that I belong in Wisconsin, where I began to understand that I had to leave home. That world was too small, especially after the year in Paris. I had to live beyond it. But the Wisconsin boy came with me. He took his bearings from the land and remembered them. He loved open fields and hilly woodland. He made friends easily and spent hours in the large storage box in the attic, where he could hear the rain on the roof, alone but safe.

After the reunion and because of it, I see why I have always been intrigued by openings that lead away into the hills. This is more than curiosity and wander. When things don't fit together, these clefts offer refuge. I ask protagonists in novels, where will you hole up? In the landscapes of Courbet, shadowy ravines draw me in. No matter where I travel or how pleasing the panorama, my eye for the land looks for quiet places where I can sort things out. This instinct is contoured by Wisconsin.

I decide to move on, saving time for Ansel Wooden Knife and Two Creek Ranch. The West will always hold something new for me. The memory of taking this road in 1964 wants to repeat itself, out into the excitement of the unknown, Bug willing, kit handy, and open space still available. Wisconsin boys need trails to be Westerners.

About a mile beyond Coon Valley, a marker salutes America's "first watershed project." In 1933, the U.S. Soil Erosion Service (now the Soil Conservation Service), the University of Wisconsin, and local farm leaders agreed to launch a large-scale soil and water conservation effort in the Coon Creek watershed. Their methods, including improvement of woodlands and wildlife habitat as well as crop rotation, terracing, and erosion control, spread throughout the Midwest.

The road climbs steeply out of the valley through woods and rocks and traverses another broad divide with large farms. Then it goes down and up again and again. The country is every bit as captivating as my dreamiest memories of rural Wisconsin. I vow to bring Jeanie here for autumn color in Steinbeck's light. A black-and-white sign on the side of a red barn advertises "Bossy Mootel." I drop toward the Mississippi, see high bluffs on both sides of the river, and enter the arc of commuter homes spreading out from La Crosse.

On the southern outskirts of the city, the Bug jounces over the double tracks of the Burlington line that was completed between Minneapolis and Chicago in 1886. The Milwaukee & Mississippi had been the first railroad to reach La Crosse in 1858 when the town, not to be outdone by St. Louis, boasted itself as "Gateway City." Around 1948 or 1949, Dad took us and our next-door neighbor, Tom Stevens, on a two-day train trip. Tom's father, like mine, was nuts about trains, and I think this was Dad's way of thanking the Stevens family for their many kindnesses to us after Mom left. We took the Milwaukee Road from Madison to La Crosse, where we spent the night in a hotel near the station. Next morning, we climbed aboard the Burlington Zephyr, America's first lightweight, stainless steel streamliner. Introduced in the thirties, it was named for the Greek god of the west wind. We sat in the Vista Dome all the way to Chicago, and we hated to leave it for the pedestrian Milwaukee Road back to Madison. "I rode on the Zephyr" was worth a lot of points in neighborhood score-keeping.

At a traffic light, a balding man about my age stops in the lane to my right.

"Nice car!" he yells over, giving me the "O" sign with thumb and forefinger.

It's much warmer here, at an elevation of about six hundred feet, than atop the Driftless Area. Highway 14 crosses the Mississippi on an old, two-lane steel girder bridge a few miles below Interstate 90. Pleasure boats ply the "June high" on the river that had been well known to French and British traders before Lieutenant Zebulon Pike (1805) and Major Stephen Long (1817) followed it north from St. Louis.

At the mouths of two of Wisconsin's rivers, the French had already named Indian villages Prairie du Chien (after the Fox chief called "Dog") and La Crosse (after the game played there by the Winnebago). Pike learned that most of the Indians and white traders up this way preferred Britons to Americans. The British occupied Prairie du Chien in 1814, having enlisted support from several tribes in the area, including the Sac and Fox, Kickapoo, Winnebago, and Sioux. Long encountered the same bias, although the British had lost the War of 1812 and Astor's American Fur Company had replaced the British-owned North West Company as the major trader in the Upper Mississippi.

Pike and Long showed the flag in a region that most Americans have never viewed as fancifully as the Great Plains and Rockies. I regret this disproportion because I learned to portage a canoe and recognize wild rice in the *voyageur* country of northern Wisconsin. Likewise, I have developed a certain reserve toward Frederick Jackson Turner, the famous historian who grew up in Wisconsin, taught at its state university, and loved its North Woods. He argued from the 1890s until his death in 1932 that the American character was shaped by the energy, freedom, individualism, and optimism of advancing always westward. My trouble with Turner isn't that his "frontier thesis" has been disproved, as has his fear that democracy in industrialized America would flounder because, according to the U.S. census of 1890, the frontier had disappeared. Rejection awaits every sweeping historical proposition, and I admire Turner for making his so compelling.

My problem with Turner is that, unlike John Muir and Teddy Roosevelt, he failed to grasp how the North Woods, if sufficiently preserved, could forever sustain certain frontier values. Among these, no matter how much myth and contradiction surrounds them, is the need to live with wildness rather than tame it.

At breakfast yesterday, we talked about Norman Maclean's books, *A River Runs Through It* and *Men of Fire*. We agreed that no one had written so beautifully about clear waters since Hemingway and Maclean gratified our hankering for the Rockies. I wish it had occurred to me to point out that Maclean's generation is the same as Hemingway's and our fathers'. They were born at the dynamic turn of the century when the back-to-nature movement flourished. We were born in the dismal Great Depression when escapist cinema thrived. They connect us with a more romantic time. I doubt that we give our fathers enough credit, certainly not as much as we do Maclean, for taking us back there.

Interstate 90 runs briefly beneath bluffs that Major Long found:

> of an exceedingly wild and romantic character.... Here might the poet or bard indulge his fancy in the wildest extravagance, while the philosopher would find a rich repast ... in tracing the wonderful operations of nature that have taken place since the formation of the world (Long 1978).

A gigantic RV pulling a four-door car stifles my musings about exploring up the Mississippi or crossing it to discover the West. The Bug feels terribly small, and there's no refuge between exits. I find consolation in remembering how Jeanie spelled me when we drove this Bug on this highway—some sections of it still two-lane U.S. 16—from South Dakota to Wisconsin in the summer of 1972. After I had sent the manuscript for my first book to the publisher, we left Austin, camped and backpacked our way up the Rockies from New Mexico to Montana, and then proceeded to Wisconsin and Boston. Jeanie was strong. She had a dark tan and black braids. Outside the visitor center at Little Big Horn Battlefield National Monument, several tourists from a bus presumed she was Indian. They looked sympathetic, embarrassed, and uneasy.

I can't take more than an hour of I-90. Adding insult to injury, another New Beetle, a blue one at that, passes without salute. Oh, to hell with it.

The land flattens out, quite a change since western Wisconsin and the Mississippi Valley. I have skirted the small piece of Driftless Area in Minnesota's southeastern corner and entered glaciated country again. Altitudes aren't much higher than those around Madison. A steady wind from the south pushes the Bug to the right.

At a rest area southeast of Rochester, a plaque commemorates the Mayo brothers. I'm reminded of the poignant baseball film, *Bang the Drum Slowly*, based on the novel by Mark Harris. Robert De Niro plays a sweet, naïve catcher whose terminal illness is diagnosed at the Mayo Clinic. The favorite song of his guitar-playing teammate is "Streets of Laredo." I picture Stan in his driveway. Then Jeanie. From plaque to movie to loved ones, you can't control this kind of road pinball.

I gladly leave I-90, bypass Rochester, and rejoin U.S. 14. This stretch of 14 is called the "Laura Ingalls Wilder Historic Highway." Minnesota is one of several states that have preserved her homesteads. The signs for them aren't as numerous as those that say "George Washington slept here" back east, but it's the same idea. Like Hamlin Garland, Laura's first home was in Wisconsin, but her family became the more celebrated.

The terrain has begun to look like the Plains, not the smaller grasslands east of the Mississippi that the French called "prairies" before their word moved west. I gas up in Owatonna, just off I-35, which I crossed in Oklahoma going east two weeks ago. Again, I think of my first job with PhD in hand and our first home, down the 35 in Texas. But what is I-35 doing this far east? Time to look at the map. I see, I-35 angles northeast in Wichita for Kansas City, Minneapolis, and Duluth. Laredo to Lake Superior? Sounds strange.

The white-haired woman at the next pump looks over. A black T-shirt stretches around her portly midriff.

"Very nice Bug," she says.

"Thank you," I reply.

"I had a '70, and I loved it."

"Mine's a '66. Bought it new in Germany. Just had it fixed up," I say.

She looks at the Bug maternally. "I *love* that car," she coos.

The nostalgia I read on her face brings to mind E. B. White's account of searching the countryside north of New York City for a horse-drawn sleigh to ride on a winter's day about fifty years ago. When farmers' wives at their front doors apologized they no longer had one, at least not one in working order, he could see them remember the sleighs of their youth. You never forget your first Bug.

The wind grows stronger and warmer between Owatonna and Mankato, reaching thirty to forty miles per hour with gusts well over fifty. I have to steer left constantly, easing off only in the lee of farm buildings or copses. When eastbound trucks pass, I react quickly after absorbing the first shock wave. Then I turn hard left against the second, which combines wake and wind. I use guesswork, experience, and profanity to stay between the right shoulder and the cars that have stacked up behind the trucks. Highway 14 on this flatland is a thoroughfare, not the meandering byway of Wisconsin's Driftless Area. With nerves on edge, I'm all the more nettled by the sight of a wooded campground near Waseca crammed with RVs and other rigs with no tents in sight, and by drivers pulling into my lane from side roads immediately ahead as if the Bug were … well … a bug.

Corn is the major crop in the widening fields. Grain elevators have begun to appear along the railroad line built by the Chicago & North Western in the 1870s and 1880s as it expanded west from Winona on the Mississippi. Together with the Milwaukee Road, Burlington, and Rock Island, the C&NW was one of the four so-called Granger railroads that dominated the grain trade after the Civil War from Wisconsin and Illinois to Kansas, Nebraska, and the Dakota Territory. Having benefited from federal land grants, the four companies boosted profits by manipulating rates for shipping and storage. The National Grange of the Patrons of Husbandry, founded in 1867 with modest social objectives, grew large and political, forcing states and, eventually, Washington in the landmark Interstate Commerce Act of 1887 to regulate the railroads. Of the four Granger railroads, the C&NW, my employer in the summer of 1956, had the best reputation among farmers as wheat prices fell sharply in the 1880s and among workers as unrest against robber barons spread during the last quarter of the nineteenth century. The North Western suffered the least disruption from the great railroad strike of 1877 and the Pullman Strike of 1894, the latter led by the American Railway Union recently founded by Eugene Debs.

Satisfied to reach land between Old Northwest and new, the North Western refrained from expanding beyond eastern Wyoming. The northern transcontinental latitudes, which Secretary of War Jefferson Davis ordered the army's Topographical Engineers to survey in 1853 along with other possible corridors to the Pacific, were left to the Northern Pacific, Great Northern, and Milwaukee Road. Instead, the C&NW collaborated with the Union Pacific and the Central Pacific. In 1867, the North Western reached Council Bluffs, Iowa, the first line to connect Chicago with the Union Pacific. Daily passenger service began from Chicago to San Francisco several days after the completion of the transcontinental railway in 1869. In December 1887, the Overland Limited became the first regular deluxe train service between the two cities.

I cross the Minnesota River at Mankato, where the river's bend was called the "Crescent" when the ubiquitous Major Long led his 1823 expedition up the Minnesota to the Red River. The high water this afternoon doesn't surprise me after having seen the Mississippi twice in a week. I have entered country that the Santee Sioux fought to keep in the 1860s, but I find no roadside advisories on the subject. In fact, except for the plaque at the rest area on I-90, I've seen no historical markers since entering Minnesota, in sharp contrast to Wisconsin. At least I'm able to decipher the "WELS" on small signs pointing to churches off the highway. It stands for "Wisconsin Evangelical Lutheran Synod."

I follow the shallow valley of the Minnesota to New Ulm and find a simple motel managed by a Pakistani couple. Their color jars me for a second in this very Caucasian part of the country. I chose this destination last night, liking its sound and presuming I would take U.S. 14 most of the way across Minnesota. Old Ulm had charmed me while stationed in Germany, especially its Gothic cathedral (Muenster), Lutheran since the Reformation, with choir stalls exquisitely carved in the fifteenth century; the old Fishermen's Quarter down near the Donau (Danube); and the German family who served me tea in their apartment overlooking the cathedral. They waved good-bye by curling fingers toward themselves. "So you will come back," the mother said.

German emigrants founded New Ulm in 1854. Thirty years later, they erected a large statue of Hermann, patterned after the colossal monument at the site of the battle of the Teutoburg Forest, where German tribes united under Arminius (Hermann) annihilated a larger Roman army in AD 9. The opening scene in *Gladiator* takes place nearly two hundred years later, but it conveys the horrors of forest combat between these civilized and barbarian forces.

I was stationed in Giessen, about seventy miles south of the *Teutoburger Wald*. My friend, retired General Hermann Floerke, who fought in both World Wars and took the long view of military history, spoke of the ancient battle as if it were modern.

Hermann, New Ulm, Minnesota

The Santee (Dakota) Sioux under Little Crow did not have the success of the Germans under Hermann. The Sioux rising of 1862 roiled the Minnesota River Valley between the Upper Sioux Agency (near Granite Falls) and Mankato. The Santee had retreated to this area after selling or surrendering almost all of their land to the United States since the 1805 agreement with Lieutenant Pike that provided a small site for a military outpost at the junction of the Mississippi and Minnesota Rivers. Treaties of the 1850s surrendered Sioux title to more than twenty million acres, preserved only small reservations along the Minnesota, and opened the gates wide to immigration and statehood in 1858.

The Santee had long called themselves "people of the farther end." They guarded the eastern edges of the larger Sioux domain that had spread from the woodlands of Wisconsin and Minnesota to the northern Great Plains. This migration began around the middle of the seventeenth century when Algonquian-speaking tribes, notably the Ojibwa, or Chippewa, spread west of the Great Lakes and pushed the Sioux before them. Humiliation at having failed this duty, continued white encroachment, misunderstandings and broken promises, government annuities drained by dishonest traders and duplicitous agents, poor crops and bad hunting, agency warehouses guarded by soldiers, starvation, thefts from white farmers: all of this came to a head at the same time whites began killing each other in the Civil War.

Little Crow had signed treaties in the 1850s. In the summer of 1862, however, he finally agreed with younger men to make war to recover the Minnesota Valley. Unable to take Fort Ridgely, the Santee moved downstream and attacked New Ulm, burning most of the town before being thrown back. They surrendered a month later. A military court sentenced 303 Santee to death, a number reduced to thirty-nine by President Lincoln. Little Crow fled west to kinsmen on the Dakota plains, only to be killed the following summer by settlers when he came back to Minnesota to take horses from whites who had taken his land. Most of the surviving Santee were forcibly removed to a reservation on the Missouri River in what is now South Dakota. New Ulm's Germans had become Romans.

Hermann stands in a park on a hillside in this lovely town of wide streets and redbrick Victorian houses with white wood trim. A woman walking across the street toward one of these houses looks at the Bug. Then she looks at me and grins broadly. Germany is everywhere, from Martin Luther College to restaurants with names like *Kaiserhof*, banners saying *Willkommen*, Glockenspiel carillon clock, Schell Brewery, neat houses and yards, *Marktplatz* (downtown mall), and U.S. Post Office in German Renaissance style. The Chamber of Commerce touts Oktoberfest, Heritagefest, Bockfest, and Kinderfest, adding St. Patrick's Day Parade, Shakespeare in the Park, and Riverblast as afterthoughts.

I choose the Kaiserhof for supper. The *Schweinekotelett*, *Spaetzle*, and *Strudel* are very good, not the real German thing but as close as you'll find in Middle America. My waitress is tall, blonde, and inquisitive. She congratulates me on my profession. Her boyfriend loves history and combines it with an education degree so he can teach history in school. She also prepares for a teaching career in Spanish. Both attend Martin Luther College, which trains young people for the ministry or teaching in Lutheran schools. The college is affiliated with WELS, the most conservative of the three Lutheran synods, she says.

Pointing to the long list of beers served by the Kaiserhof, I ask, "What about drinking?"

"Oh no. That's not a problem," she replies.

The boss/bartender/cashier is just as cordial and asks about my trip. I congratulate her on the German cooking and thank her for cashing a traveler's check. Her "you betcha" is straight from Berlitz Minnesota/Wisconsin.

Exploring the old part of town in the dusk, I think of John and Andy. On the rainy third afternoon of the reunion, we walked around Oconomowoc. We saw the main intersection where Indian trails once met. We learned that the first white settler arrived in 1837 and the Milwaukee-Watertown plank road in 1850. The town was named in 1846. From the 1860s to the 1920s, it called itself the "Newport of the West" because its two lakes attracted many wealthy summer residents from Milwaukee, Chicago, and St. Louis. Some grand old houses still lined the isthmus between the lakes.

After the history and architecture lesson, we ducked into Winger's Tavern for a beer and our own stories.

"Ale's the thing!" John cried, and we raised our glasses in salute.

"Sounds familiar," I said.

"A. E. Housman," John said. "*A Shropshire Lad*. Mom gave me the book in high school. 'And malt does more than Milton can/To justify God's ways to man/Ale, man, ale's the stuff to drink/For fellows whom it hurts to think.'"

Hearing us mention Madison, the barmaid told us her daughter had just gotten her master's degree at the University of Wisconsin. The regulars at the far end of the bar near the big-screen TV and Green Bay Packers banner had already accepted us after a once-over.

"Port in the storm," John said halfway through our first round.

"Yeah," I concurred. "The neon signs are probably on all day. But, in the rain or at night, they give you the feeling you'll survive another day and you can stop here if you need to. Same way I feel about French cafés and British pubs."

"Like Hemingway's story, 'A Clean, Well-Lighted Place,'" Andy said. "Great story. There's an old man at a café. He's the last customer, and it's after midnight. There are two waiters there. The young one has a wife. He wants to close up and go home, so he tells the old man to leave. The older waiter says you shouldn't have done that. There are people like this old man who don't want to go home, who need these places at night."

I'm tempted to find a place like that after dinner in New Ulm, my first evening in a week without company. But I don't feel lonely, and I'd rather walk than sit. After returning to the motel, I call Jeanie.

About the burglary incident at Mary's house yesterday, I conclude, "I just didn't have time to be afraid. The guy must have sensed that and backed off."

"Well," she replies, "it's more than that. You're good responding under pressure. Not at the little things, but the important stuff. Something about you tells people to settle down, things will work out okay."

"So I'm better reacting than worrying?" I ask.

"Yes, I think that's right."

"Then why do I worry so much?"

She laughs. No difficulties at home, she reports. The apricots are turning orange, but I'll be back in time for picking. The peaches are still green, and the tree is fuller than ever. She misses me, but she enjoys time for herself. I miss her, too, but I'm not ready to come home yet. I'm looking forward to meeting Ansel and seeing the Dalys.

"Love you," I say.

"And you," she replies.

I call Dennis and Nancy Daly at Two Creek Ranch near Douglas, Wyoming. We have stayed in touch since their spring cattle drive of 1990.

"Come see us whenever you can make it," Dennis says, "but get here soon if you want to help me move some cattle. I want to move 'em tomorrow, but I'll wait 'til Tuesday if you can get here tomorrow night."

"Dennis, this is Minnesota. I'm still in the Midwest, and I was hoping to spend some time in South Dakota on the way to see you," I say.

"Well, how 'bout Wednesday?" he asks.

"Okay. Look for me on Tuesday night."

"Okay," he says. "Be careful."

That changes things. I had planned on a couple of days for Ansel Wooden Knife and the Lakota Sioux, arriving at Two Creek Ranch on Thursday or Friday. Now I'll have to hustle across South Dakota and cut my time south of the Badlands, which will give me too brief an introduction to the Lakota.

Monday, June 10

The Bug's engine knocks sharply in the early stillness. I open the engine compartment and listen. The noise abates as the engine warms up, but it's still there. Maybe I should have the valves adjusted soon, before home. Gotta be valves, I think. Maybe a rocker arm. Can't be a rod, not loud enough, not with only thirty-five hundred miles on the new motor. After forty-two years of listening, I know something isn't right.

West of New Ulm, I see a sign for Wall Drugs in Wall, South Dakota. A boyhood friend on West Lawn, whose family drove to the Black Hills on U.S. 14 for a summer vacation, came home with more souvenirs from Wall Drugs than

Mount Rushmore. The wind is already up this morning, and high winds are predicted for South Dakota. The first few eastbound trucks in the south wind mean a rough day ahead. It's a little over four hundred miles to Interior, where Ansel lives just outside Badlands National Park. I'd call it about eight hours from here.

In this level country, you can tell at great distance where the farms are, or were, by the groves of trees planted against the wind. They are the thickest on the northwest side of the house. In Sleepy Eye, named for a friendly Santee chief, the temperature is sixty-eight degrees at the town offices and seventy-five degrees at the bank. The Knights of Columbus have put up a sign advocating "Right to Life." I have seen several like it on this trip, but none supporting the woman's right to choose. I pass a large Del Monte canning plant west of Sleepy Eye and a pretty park in Springfield. Between the two towns, I detour around construction on U.S. 14. Local farmers driving pickups flash no greeting, unlike in rural New Mexico and Texas, and they seem surprised when I do. A sign points off to a farm that has preserved a sod house from the 1880s.

I stop for breakfast at a joint where Highway 14 intersects U.S. 71, which I took north from Carthage, Missouri, about ten days ago. A notice on the door warns the café will be closed on a certain day "for our daughter's wedding." I sit at the counter, and when the waitress pours my coffee I ask if it's her daughter who's getting married.

She looks startled for a second. Then she smiles and says, "No, no. Someone else's."

I suddenly realize that the waitress may be in her thirties, but she looks to be in her forties. She shows no umbrage as she cheerfully takes my order for scrambled eggs. I overhear her telling the guy two stools to my right that she'll have to close her car windows if it rains.

I ask her, "What's the forecast?"

"Just a chance of rain here, but heavy stuff and flooding up north," she says. "We need the rain. Had about four inches a week ago, but we need more. The wind really dries things out."

"Is this wind typical?"

"Doesn't always blow this hard in the summer. When it does it's usually from the south. But the north winds in the winter are really something else, I'll tell ya."

The other customer says, "We're between fronts. That brought the bugs out like crazy. They've been just awful the last few days."

"Yeah," the waitress says, "but they don't seem to be biting much."

"No, they aren't," he replies.

I file this information away for my bug-splat guide to American geography. The woman doing the cooking comes out to join the conversation.

When I see an opening, I ask, "Am I in wheat country yet? Or is it mainly corn?"

"Mainly corn and beans," the man says.

"What kind of beans?" I ask.

He looks at me as if I asked who's buried in Grant's Tomb.

"Soybeans, of course," he replies.

"Of course," I say sheepishly.

Back outside, I spread my map of the Dakotas on top of the Bug. I had never before noticed that four of the five east-west federal highways crossing South Dakota go through Madison, Wisconsin: 12, 14, 18, and I-90.

Two men arrive in a muddy pickup. The younger one in clean Levi's goes right into the café. The older one in oil-stained khakis stops.

"That's a pretty little car," he says.

I tell him something about its history.

"Well, what are you doin' in these parts?" He looks up from my front license plate. "California? You're a long way from home."

I explain.

"Oh," he says. "We was in Wisconsin last winter. Had a coupla beers."

"Then came right back?" I ask.

"No, no. Stayed a coupla weeks."

I should have winked as I asked.

In a few miles, I cross the Cottonwood River, flowing full to the Minnesota near New Ulm. I'm humming a tune. It nothing I've heard before, not an "Ogal-laly song" about the road. It's just a ditty on driving with my elbow out the window and a toothpick in my mouth after breakfast.

Grain elevators cluster near the railroad tracks in Lamberton. Again, it's the old C&NW line. The size of the fields, most of them larger than anything I saw in Wisconsin, suggests agribusiness. Some of the farmhouses betray the nonchalance of managers. Walnut Grove, at last, is "Childhood Home of Laura Ingalls Wilder," the one before her family moved on to the Dakotas. Another detour takes me due south, and I floor the gas pedal to maintain fifty miles per hour against the headwind. Seeing few cars and no trucks, I assume the regular users of U.S. 14 know something I don't. When the detour bends northwest, I'm too irritated with 14 to rejoin it, so I turn south on State 59, then west on State 30.

State 30 runs straight through good farmland that rolls gently and tilts upward. Pastures and beef cattle appear, having been scarce across southern Minnesota. At the crest of a rise, the flat metal likeness of a buffalo, about thirty feet high, is silhouetted against the sky. I cross a branch of the Rock River, which flows south to the Big Sioux that continues south to join the Missouri at Sioux City. Several miles back, I left the watershed of the Minnesota and Upper Mississippi. I have entered the northern range of tallgrass prairie, where explorers found native grasses as high as their heads.

The town of Pipestone lies at about seventeen hundred feet. I've climbed eleven hundred feet since La Crosse, seven hundred this morning since Sleepy Eye. If I read meridians correctly, Pipestone is about one hundred fifty miles east of the comparable altitude in western Oklahoma two weeks ago. Up here, still six hundred miles east of the Rockies, I'm close to a continental divide. Upland runs northwest from Pipestone into South Dakota. French traders named this terrain the Coteau des Prairies. Streams rising in these hills feed not only the Minnesota and Missouri Rivers, but also the Red River of the North, which empties into Lake Winnipeg. The lake is a remnant of the vast glacial Lake Agassiz that covered parts of North Dakota, Minnesota, Manitoba, and Ontario before it found channels across the Precambrian bedrock of the Laurentian Shield to drain into Hudson Bay. Beneath the prairie are several hundred feet of composite sediment, drift from pre-Wisconsinan glaciation.

At the southern end of the Coteau des Prairies are outcroppings of red quartzite. Among these, Indians quarried soft, red catlinite stone for ceremonial pipes. From the eastern woodlands came Santee (Dakota) Sioux, Sac and Fox, and Ojibwa. Teton (Lakota) and Yankton (Nakota) Sioux, Pawnee, and Oto came from the western Plains. The stone is named after George Catlin, who saw the place in 1839, brought back samples of rock, and portrayed the quarriers on canvas.

In 1838, the French-born scientist and geographer, Joseph Nicollet, led an expedition west from the Minnesota River to these pipestone quarries before going north to Lac qui Parle. The Army Corps of Topographical Engineers sponsored the expedition and assigned Lieutenant John C. Frémont as Nicollet's assistant. Both men delighted in this new landscape. Nicollet recorded in his journal:

> The prospect changes and becomes more cheerful, more varied due to the undulating surface of the ground that presents before us summits which are lost in the mists of the horizon, making us believe in high mountains far away that, however, sink back to the general level of the ground as we approach (Nicollet 1976).

Frémont wrote:

> Approaching [the Coteau], the blue line which it presents, marked by wooded ravines in contrast with the green prairie which sweeps to its feet, suggested to the *voyageurs* the name they gave it, of the Prairie Coast. At this elevation … the prairie was invigorating, the country studded with frequent lakes was beautiful, and the repose of a few days was refreshing to men and animals after the warmer and moister air of the lower valley (Frémont 1970).

As a kid, I was right to imagine the West beginning out there on the other side of the Golden Gophers. Like Nicollet and Frémont, I can feel the change in the land. This is where Santee and Teton met, Eastern and Western Sioux. Wisconsin lies back there. The West starts right around here. Can you belong in both?

I fill the tank in Pipestone. My mileage is down. I made twenty-five miles per gallon on that last tank, my lowest average so far. Must be the wind and the steady climb that morning. On the marquee of radio station GLOH is "God Bless America." I have seen this entreaty by the hundreds since leaving Claremont, always assuming it's an invocation, especially during a time of national crisis like the aftermath of 9/11. This morning, for unknown reasons, I hear something peremptory in "God Bless America," as if it's our commandment and God might not.

West of Pipestone, Minnesota 30 becomes South Dakota 34. The speed limit increases from fifty-five to sixty-five. I keep the Bug at fifty-five. Overcast that has thickened in the last hour drizzles off and on. In the shallow valley of the Big Sioux River, bison and llamas graze in separate pastures, but Black Angus and Canada geese share the green verge of a pond.

The sign at the entrance to an ethanol plant flashes, "Roses are red, violets are blue, cows eat corn, cars can too."

A marker commemorates the "Lone Tree," planted in 1881 by Mrs. George Cameron. She did so, according to the marker:

> little thinking that this tiny seedling would grow into a stately tree which would be a beacon signal in a blizzard to save the life of a teacher, Emma Clancy, and her little flock of twelve children …

Many years later, this concrete highway choked the tree's roots and killed it.

The overcast breaks around Madison, where a Baptist church signboard preaches, "Honor thy Father and thy Mother." I do. Madison owes its name to settlers from Wisconsin who were reminded of my hometown, but that's a stretch. These lakes do not really form part of the town, and grassland surrounds this Madison. This is my fourth crossing of the Dakotas. The wind has been bad every time. Once a headwind from the west held my speed to forty on the flat. That was in my first Bug with the engine whining and prairie ambling by. Living in this wind, whatever its direction, would drive me bonkers.

But I'm grateful to South Dakota for markers. One introduces Miner County:

> Named for Captain Nelson Miner, Company A, 1st Dakota Cavalry and territorial legislator ... The ancient Sioux trail from Pipestone Quarries to the ... Missouri passed through the county.

The first road across the Dakotas came through here, the Fort Ridgely and South Pass Wagon Road, in 1857. So did the Minnesota and Powder River Road, in 1865. The county's first white homesteader arrived in 1879, the first train two years later.

The marker's short history lesson opens up time. Driving east to Wisconsin, I met successive generations of Europeans and Americans making their way west by river, trail, road, and railroad. I moved historically from exploration to emigration to settlement, through waves of Indian removal westward. I have reversed this progression since leaving Madison. I have gotten ahead of Hamlin Garland, the Chicago & North Western, the Civil War, and the removal of Santee Sioux from Minnesota.

I place one of my imaginary transparencies over the Great Plains and date it 1853. Federal wagon roads do not cross the Dakotas. Prospectors have not discovered gold in the headwaters of the Missouri. No wagon trains cut through Sioux hunting grounds in the Powder River Basin to reach mining towns in Montana. I'm on the Sioux trail between the Minnesota and Missouri Rivers. White trappers and traders have used it, but this is Indian country.

In the fifty years since the Louisiana Purchase, Americans have established a handful of forts hundreds of miles beyond the frontier, along major waterways from the Mississippi to the Rockies. Forts Pierre (in present South Dakota), Union (North Dakota), and Benton (Montana) secure the Upper Missouri River. Forts Kearny (Nebraska) and Laramie (Wyoming) guard the Emigrant Trail along the Platte and North Platte. All but Kearney began as trading posts, and some of these four still provide more trade than firepower. Washington's policy of removal has shifted westward along with the frontier since the early plan to push Indians beyond the Mississippi. States and territories now occupy the entire west bank of the Mississippi. Between them and forts far upriver, the Great Plains have been judged undesirable for white settlement and allocated to Indians.

From bases on the edge of the frontier, such as Fort Leavenworth on the Missouri, one of the army's tasks is to settle disputes among the Indians. Another is to keep whites from encroaching on Indian lands. But removal has increased intertribal tensions by throwing woodland Indians out onto the Plains, where the Lakota Sioux have already made enemies by pushing the Kiowa, Crow, and other tribes out of the Black Hills. Settlers spreading west from Iowa and Missouri violate Washington's Indian treaties and lobby for territorial status. The territorial question draws the Great Plains into America's own intertribal dispute. Will the new territory of Nebraska, proposed in Congress this year, prohibit or permit slavery?

By the Fort Laramie Treaty signed two years ago in 1851, the Sioux, Cheyenne, and others allow limited emigration across their lands as well as the construction of forts and roads. These terms will no doubt help the army keep the peace. I can imagine the usefulness of a road from Fort Ridgely on the Minnesota River, where construction of the fort has just begun, to Fort Laramie and South Pass. The road needn't interfere with Sioux travel to their pipestone quarries. But the Plains are about to change fundamentally.

Now more than ever, Manifest Destiny expects white migration to civilize the West, with God on the side of white peoples. In less than a decade, America has become a continental nation, expanding to the Pacific and adding immense territory west of the Louisiana Purchase. It has acquired Texas, Oregon Country, and, after the defeat of Mexico, the Southwest from Colorado and New Mexico to California. The discovery of gold in California has increased emigrant traffic and gilded the world's images of the American West. This summer, transcontinental railroad survey parties start across the Plains. Indian lands are under increasing pressure from emigrants in transit, prospectors, traders, missionaries, buffalo hunters, squatters, entrepreneurs, railroad speculators, expansionists like Frémont and his father-in-law, U.S. Senator Thomas Hart Benton of Missouri, and a federal government willing to break treaties for the sake of freedom and progress.

New forts and wagon roads will connect older ones on both sides of the Great Plains. They will also, both inadvertently and intentionally, militarize the Plains, close in on the Indians, and encourage white Americans to expropriate tribal lands and rid them of buffalo.

I'm on my own again on the Plains, transported by trails that mean nothing to John and Andy as they return to Nashville and Dallas on interstate highways. But I can sense the reunion staying with me. Many things at their best stick with me, such as Jeanie's roast chicken; old red Burgundies; Joe Montana to Jerry Rice; stained glass at Chartres and Bourges; romping on the floor with Kate and Dan when they were little; students carrying discussions on their own; and water purling under a well-rowed eight.

This is different, like the first time I grasped geometry in tenth grade. For a couple of weeks, I did not see lines and angles fitting together in discernible patterns that could always be measured according to certain rules. Miss Krueger insisted, very patiently. One day, I got it. I saw the patterns, used the rules, and solved problems. QED, I thought, what a kick! I have forgotten much of Euclid since then. But I still tell myself that, if I can catch on to geometry, I can assemble all kinds of puzzles, including people.

The Post and Mailer brothers went back to origins and patterns last week. We relived West Lawn, reviewed our adult lives, and confronted aging. Each of us revealed interior shadows along with escape routes to bright country. Andy opened up the most. A visual kind of guy, he has fought off mental illness by finding places where nature, literature, and memory meet. Clear water, separate peace, and palimpsest, words like these come easily to him because he has needed them for most of his life. Stan clung to railroads and the Wisconsin landscape for hope that he could handle Parkinson's disease. John held in the most. I'm sure he took to mountain climbing because it enabled him to escape and perhaps conquer emotions he would not or could not express. His feelings run deep and true. On the first night of a backpack trip in Wyoming's Bridger Wilderness in the summer of 1986, he, Pat, and their boys had just sacked out in their two tents. I was alone in mine about twenty yards from them.

Suddenly, John shouted over my way, "I love you, little brother!"

I treasure that memory.

I can live with my mother's illness because I have to. I recognize signs of her absence wherever I go, but I also see her return. Both are features of my interior landscape. Looking ahead, I'm not certain how I will deal with my own depression and Jeanie's decline. I'm not suddenly a new man. My instinct for shelter is still intact. So is my need for privacy. But maybe I'm getting it. A lot of things came together at the reunion. It was solid. It was good.

Quiet and empty, South Dakota 34 is a perfect road for listening to names that a solitary historical marker evoked. It is also perfect for feeling the continent shift from Central Lowland to Great Plains and imagining thousands of buffalo on native grassland that the loessial loam deposited by millennia of winds enriched. Grazing is more evident than plowing. Serious wheat country lies to the north and west. Most of the cattle are Angus, but I occasionally spot what my Uncle John would have called "integrated" herds of Angus, Hereford, Charolais, and mixes.

The crystal song of a meadowlark pierces the thrumming of the Bug. The wind abates and shifts to southwest. It's cooler and drier now, thus easier to roll the Bug's windows against rubber and felt. I cross the James River. Its wide valley is several hundred feet lower than the Coteau des Prairies behind me. Two road-runners race across the highway outside Woonsocket, named by a Milwaukee Road superintendent for his hometown in Rhode Island. Roadrunners in Woonsocket would be great material for W. C. Fields. I can hear him elongate the "woon."

After Wessington Springs, I climb onto another rolling tableland, the Coteau du Missouri. This part of the Great Plains' Missouri Plateau, separated from the rest of it by the great river, forms the western limit of glaciation and the left shoulder of the Missouri River Valley in the Dakotas. Large, tilled fields occupy some of the flatter terrain. Farmers and ranchers still don't initiate greeting from their pickups, but most of them now reciprocate if I raise fingers from the wheel.

Like West Texas, this is the kind of country where the word "yonder" works best and people still use it, helping the eye take in every detail from hat brim to horizon. Whenever Granddad Post, Uncle John, or my grandmother, Miss Ada, said "over yonder," my eye flew there and my brain worked on it. In the middle of a pond off to the right, over yonder, a small heron stands motionless. I guess it's a black-crowned night-heron. And then something peculiar occurs to me. There's plenty of roadkill today, but there are no buzzards.

"Welcome to Crow Creek Sioux Indian Reservation," the sign says.

Santee Sioux have struggled here since their expulsion from Minnesota in 1863. The Missouri River cuts a steep cleft through the plateau. I drop toward the river and enter Fort Thompson. Once the site of an outpost where whites held councils with "friendly" Missouri River Sioux during Red Cloud's fight for the Powder River country after the Civil War, Fort Thompson is now an impoverished village on barren terrain. The United States Army still controls the Missouri. I head south on State 37 and cross the river atop one of the many dams on the Upper Missouri that the Corps of Engineers operates. There are bulky power stations all around, sagging webs of high-voltage transmission lines, and skinny lakes upstream and down. This is no river. What a lamentable crossing.

I cannot picture the Indians' pipestone trail, or the expedition of the La Verendrye brothers in the 1740s, French-Canadian fur traders who came to the Dakotas from Fort La Reine in today's Manitoba. I can't hear the prophetic, almost fatal, argument between the Corps of Discovery and a band of Teton Sioux not far upstream from here in September 1804, which provoked Lewis and Clark to call these Sioux, unlike the friendly Yankton downriver, "pirates" of the

Missouri and "the vilest miscreants of the savage race." This is no place to rendezvous with the explorers and trappers whom I met at Arrow Rock as they came up and down the Missouri. I have lost my way back to them, their West.

Cedar trees, the first I've seen all day, dot the hillsides as I climb out of the valley. Sleek horses and colts graze off to the right: paints, sorrels, whites, and browns. Indian ponies. The Lower Brulé, one of the Lakota's seven historic subtribes, have a reservation on this side of the Missouri. An ad for their casino takes some of the gleam off their animals.

I must take I-90 to the Badlands if I'm to find Ansel before evening. But I hold out briefly and parallel the interstate on old U.S. 16. I wave to a kid on an ATV, probably the first time I have acknowledged anyone driving anything called "V" and not made in Germany. I fill the tank in Kennebec. The mileage remains disappointing, only twenty-six miles per gallon since Pipestone. Again, I blame the wind. In the small convenience store, two women and two girls queue outside the women's restroom.

"You have to wait now," the older woman says to an antsy girl as I pass them on my way to the men's room.

"It's easier being a guy," I remark. Then I find door to the men's room locked. "Uh-oh," I mutter.

They all laugh. The older woman looks grateful that I helped make her point. "We always have to wait," she says.

"Yeah, that's one of my wife's biggest complaints," I reply.

Outside, the father of the family parked next to me is looking over the Bug.

"Nice, car," he says. "Really good shape. California? Jeez, you drive all this way?"

"Yeah, but I wouldn't have done it without a new motor," I reply.

He laughs. "Don't you have a radio in there?" he asks.

"No."

"No air conditioning?"

"Nope. No cell phone, either."

He shakes his head. His daughter, with curly brown hair and about ten years old, scoots up carrying a quart-sized soda and sees my license plate.

"California? Gee, how did you get here?" she asks.

"In this," I say.

Her brow wrinkles as she reverts to her straw.

I sneak onto I-90 and nudge the Bug up to sixty. This stretch of interstate is easier going than the others I have tried because semis don't own it. Still, my senses begin to dull. I know I'll miss details that go with driving fifty miles per hour on a two-lane road. You can't miss the billboards. Far enough from the interstate to be legal, these are commensurately larger than their cousins along other kinds of highway. They widen the interstate's gash across the Great Plains and deny travelers the golden chance to see prairie all the way to the horizon. The most numerous billboards promote Wall Drugs:

"As told by *International Herald Tribune*"
"As told by *Time*"
"As told by *Western Horseman*"
"See the Western art collection"
"Entering Wall Drug Country"

Also up ahead are "Death Row," a reptile garden; Mount Rushmore; Deadwood; "shootouts with the deputy sheriff"; Flintstones; "1880 Town, *Dances with Wolves* epic filmed in South Dakota"; and "see prairie dogs free."

My change of plans now rules out the Black Hills, where I had intended to mine parking lots for curiosity about the Bug. But I would have suffered there. The road will never open my mind to merchandizing beautiful country into unsightliness and transforming the West into a carnival. See the Old West on a movie set? No way. Boycott Wall Drugs! Free the prairie dogs!

A man and woman ease past on a muffled motorcycle. Dressed in matching black leather outfits, they are pulling a small, two-wheel trailer. They nod and smile, as if to say, "Nice rig yourself."

I spot another heron. This one is a great blue. The phony skeleton of a tyrannosaur stands on a hill just before "1880 Town." A human skeleton leads it by a rope.

Clear sky, dry air, light southwesterly wind, and temperature in the eighties, it's such a beautiful afternoon. The land changes as the Missouri Plateau rises steadily west of the hundredth meridian, which I crossed near Kennebec. Murdo lies at about twenty-three hundred feet, Kadoka at nearly twenty-five hundred. The soil, dark brown east of the Missouri, is light brown and red here. Grasses are shorter and thinner, lighter green and tan, and more resistant to drought. Eroded ridges and bluffs off to my left mark the valley of the White River. As they grow larger, their gray changes into bands of color.

I first saw the color when I was a boy, in the parlor of the Post house in Haskell, in a small glass jar of layered sand, a gift from a friend of my grandfather's who traveled farther from Texas than he ever did. I first saw the source in August 1964. I made camp in the dark on the prairie beside a dirt road off U.S. 16 near Kadoka. I had driven nearly seven hundred miles from Madison that day. I was young, and I had gained an hour by entering Mountain Time in Murdo. It was my first night ever on the Missouri Plateau. I put up my small A-frame tent, placed sleeping bag and pad outside, and lay on my back to look at the stars. There was no moon, not a cloud. I saw no dome in the incandescence overhead. The heavens seemed as flat as the land, as if I were looking down on them. When I awoke, the sun had struck the jagged brow of the Badlands off to the southwest. Since those two night and day revelations at one stop, I have understood why some Westerners prefer High Plains to Rockies.

West of Kadoka this afternoon, the Badlands spread north as I near the national park. An ancient combine rusts in a field, a real dinosaur. In the Buffalo Gap National Grassland, I pull into a roadside view area and stop as far as possible from other cars. This is more like it. There are no billboards. You can't shut out the highway noise, but you can turn your back on it and see nothing but shortgrass prairie to the skyline. Walking around behind the Bug to include it in a photo, I'm struck by the ecology of this car. It has the body of a grazing animal and the color of the sky. It makes a simple statement of utility. The Bug looks right on the Plains. As I leave, a middle-aged man wearing a Green Bay Packers shirt points to the Bug and gives me a thumbs-up. Good guy.

In a few minutes I exit I-90 and turn south. A marker explains that the Civilian Conservation Corps (CCC) offered work to thirty-one thousand unemployed men in South Dakota in the thirties. They lived in camps where the U.S. Army provided food, clothing, medical care, recreational and educational programs, and pay. The National Park Service supervised construction projects in what was then Badlands National Monument, such as a pump house on the White River, ditches and pipelines, and a reservoir. I shall never accept the GOP's attempts to make the Reagan of trickle down as great a president as the Roosevelt of public works.

A mile or so beyond the site of a backbreaking homestead on sandy soil, I flash my Golden Age Passport at the northeast entrance to Badlands National Park. I cross the narrow end of the park and head for Interior, two miles beyond the park's boundary. At the southern edge of the village, near the road down to the Pine Ridge Reservation, I find Wooden Knife Café.

CHAPTER 8

▼

RED CLOUD'S GRAVE

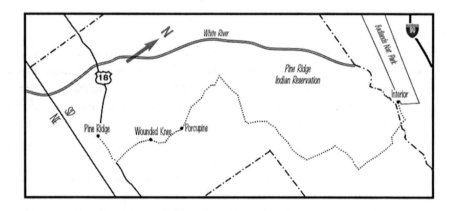

"Wooden Knife Café. Indian Tacos & Much More. ARTS-CRAFTS."

The blue, black, and red words on the white sign surround most of a circle. The circumference of the circle is divided into quarters painted red, yellow, black, and white. Four radii meet at the center, painted the same four colors as the circumference. I turn off the highway and park on gravel in front of a low, white building with an A-shaped peak in the middle. The small café faces east. In June this far north, the afternoon sun slants shadow across the rectangular front deck. I walk inside and ask the auburn-haired woman behind the counter where I can find Ansel Wooden Knife.

"Right there," she says. "My husband."

A stocky, serious-looking man with dark hair has just come out of the kitchen. Ansel Wooden Knife, a Teton (Lakota) Sioux in his forties, is a friend of my daughter's neighbors in Los Angeles. I haven't warned him I'm coming. We've never met, but I presume, like a typical retiree, that he can drop everything for a long conversation. He cannot.

"This is a family operation," he says with a hint of rebuke. "I have to start work at four o'clock."

And he won't be free to have breakfast with me next morning. But he looks at his watch and says, "Now's best."

He packs a lot into the half hour he can spare. When I remark that the '66 Bug out front has carried me from California to a reunion in Wisconsin and I'm on my way back, he begins nodding.

"You are on an odyssey, a quest," he says, as if identifying a familiar plant.

"Yes, I guess I am," I reply.

"Then tomorrow you must drive down to Wounded Knee and the Pine Ridge Reservation. And be yourself," he says. His dark eyes size me up.

"What do you mean?"

"You would probably call it 'aura,' but we call it *wakan*," he replies. "It means what is true about yourself. Everyone has *wakan*. Tomorrow, you must be open. Open yourself up. Let things come in. Look at everything. Accept what you see as what is. People will want to see you as you really are. Let them. Let them see you. When you are open, anyone who sees you will know your *wakan*. If they do not know, they haven't seen you. Even if you talk to them, they won't see you. Don't worry about them."

He pauses. "There is power here," he continues. "To us, the Badlands are not bad. They are holy. I had my first vision quest there. Many young Lakota do. I go to a place there, a tree, just to be alone and think about things. There's power there. And where you are going tomorrow."

Soon I thank Ansel for his time.

"I'll be back for supper," I add. "Are you doing the cooking tonight?"

"No, my wife is, but it's just as good when she cooks," he says.

I register at a modest motel up the road and drive into the national park. French trappers called this area *les mauvaises terres*. However, because of Ansel's words and the restoration of prairie grasses, the Badlands appear less hostile than my first impression of them nearly forty years ago. Ridges of eroding shale break the prairie's surface like the spines of Cretaceous sea dragons. Their reds, grays, and buffs deepen in the late afternoon. Mixed grasses, short and tall, cover flatland and sod tables, probe gullies, and cling to ledges. Blue grama, buffalo grass, bluestem, cordgrass, and needle in thread, all hold on, holding together what is left after rain, snow, and wind.

I return to Ansel's café for supper. His amiable wife says he has left and is unlikely to return before they close. I order the house specialty, Indian tacos made with fry bread. Locals say they are the best in the region, and the Smithsonian sells Ansel's fry bread mix. Delicious. I sit at a small plastic table on the front deck, grateful for the open country beyond the road as well as the sweet evening smells of grass and sage.

Four young Lakota men share another table. Their two dogs roam the deck for scraps. The Indians and I exchange respectful looks, but I hesitate to open a conversation, lest I appear to be some strange white guy trying to connect with the Lakota, which, of course, I am. I'll leave it to them to start, and they don't. When the dogs come my way, the men call to them, but I raise one hand to say it's okay and lower the other to scratch the animals' ears. The men nod, and we resume eating. Soon, they hop in their car and head south toward the Pine Ridge Reservation. The car is a heap.

"What's the point of a new car?" Sacred Eagle Woman said two weeks ago in Oklahoma. "Just get something for a couple hundred dollars that will run for few years. Don't worry about maintenance and depreciation. Easier and cheaper that way."

The young couple at a nearby table ask me to join them for dessert. Lisa Nipp and Mel Antonen have just arrived from Nashville, where she does photography for the *Nashville Tennessean* and he covers baseball for *USA Today*. Mel majored in political science at Vanderbilt, but he did not encounter my brother on campus. He knows Roger Angell and admires him enormously, says Angell always does his homework, knows his history, never stints, and writes beautifully.

"And he understands the Red Sox," I add. I tell them of my boyhood adulation for Ted Williams and my lifelong suffering as a Red Sox fan.

"I'm ripe for omens about the Sox after talking with Ansel this afternoon. So I think meeting Mel means the Sox will go all the way this year," I say.

Mel laughs. "Don't bet on that!" he warns.

He and Lisa like my plan to use retirement for writing without footnotes. They appreciate good writing, find it rare among journalists, and bemoan how little the youngest generation in their profession knows about history and literature. They have begun a two-week vacation of hiking in the Badlands and Black Hills. I wish them good hiking, and they hope I'll have a good day tomorrow. Nice people.

Before returning to the motel, I drive about a mile back toward the park, stop, and walk onto prairie between the highway and the serrated ridge to the north. A light wind, still from the southwest, feels cool on my exposed arms. The sun, just before setting, touches the tops of the grasses, coloring them soft greens and browns up to the solid shadow that creeps toward me from the ridge. Meadowlarks sing. I want the sun to stop where it is.

Back at the motel, I exchange greetings with the family staying two doors away. They live in Virginia, but they always stop here on the way to see parents in Buffalo, Wyoming. They sit outside their room in lawn chairs.

"We love this place," the man says. "No television or telephone. Great view. Quiet."

"I know what you mean," I agree.

Before sleeping, I read most of the book I purchased at the park's visitor center, *The Sacred Pipe: Black Elk's Account of the Seven Rites of the Oglala Sioux.* Black Elk was the last of three wise men to whom the former "keeper of the sacred pipe" had handed down these traditions orally. Black Elk was determined to "bring to life the flowering tree of his people" before he died because, if the Sioux forgot the pipe, they would lose their "center" and perish.

In the first few pages, I run into a problem. According to the Lakota, the "red road" runs north and south. It is straight and good. But the "blue" or "black road," running east and west, is full of error and distraction. Deciding my road since Claremont has been oval, I read on. Black Elk tells us that the Great Spirit, *Wakan-Tanka*, dwells at the center of the circular universe, where all single things come together in a whole. This center is, or ought to be, replicated in the "sacred hoop" of all peoples as well as the Lakota nation and in the community, lodge, and individual. *Wakan* is a holiness or power that comes from the Great Spirit, and it resides "within all things." Rituals remind you of this and take you closer to the Great Spirit, helping to "make you *wakan*." By "walking in a *wakan* manner," you have "the power to make others *wakan*."

In a footnote, the editor explains:

> The 'power' (really the sacredness) of a being or a thing … is in proportion to the ability of the object or act to reflect most directly the principle or principles which are in *Wakan-Tanka*, the Great Spirit, who is One (J. Brown 1953).

Having taught Western civilization and modern European history during my academic career, I naturally turn to Western philosophy for handles on *wakan*. Brown's footnote reminds me of the ancient Greek notion of virtue, that is, the virtue of anything is its skill or ability to do well that which it is intended to do. A person lives well who is wise, courageous, and just. A knife cuts well when it is sharp and so on. I also summon the French writer, Albert Camus, as I always do when I want to translate religious teachings into ethical norms accessible to everyone. Common decency, Dr. Rieux says in *The Plague*, is the only means of fighting injustice. We have that capacity for decency inside us (Camus 1972). Neither Greeks nor Camus prepare me for Red Cloud's grave.

Tuesday, June 11

A stiff wind, now from the north, moans through the window screen on one side of my room when I open the door at the other. As I breakfast in the motel's café on all-you-can-eat sourdough pancakes for three dollars and fifty cents, the grandfather of this family operation brings his coffee over to an adjacent table and says hello. Slight and soft-spoken, he wears glasses, cowboy boots, a straw hat curled up at the sides, jeans, and a long-sleeved shirt with glass buttons. He removes his hat with one hand and brushes strands of gray hair back with the other.

"How do you like those hotcakes?" he asks.

"Very good. Very good," I reply. "Real sourdough, just like the menu says."

"That sourdough is a hundred and two years old. I got it from an Idaho woman when I was out there one time. Brought it back here," he says.

"I didn't know that stuff traveled east."

A few teeth are missing at both sides of his wide smile.

He says, "No, usually goes west, doesn't it? Back in the old days, they didn't have refrigerators, no ice or nothin'. That sourdough just sat there stubborn until you were ready to use it."

"When my wife and I were running a starter soon after we got married," I say, "we noticed that certain kinds of milk wouldn't work. Just too homogenized or something. What kind do you use?"

"Two percent," he replies.

"That works okay? I thought you needed whole milk."

"No, two percent works fine."

"I guess you never leave the starter alone for long."

"We do in the wintertime. But not now in the summer, 'cause it gets a goin' all the time," he says.

"Do you have to add milk in the winter to keep it alive?"

"Actually, what my wife does in the winter, why, she just adds flour and water and stuff like that to keep it goin'."

"I see."

"Sometimes, you wanna add potato water," he continues.

"That spices up the starter?" I ask.

"It does somethin' to it. Helps it. You take your starter, put it out on the table, add potato water, and cover it up with cheesecloth. That starter gets yeast outta the air. Can't do that with the air-conditioner on."

"There's a lot of yeast blowing around this morning," I say. "That wind is pretty bad."

"Yeah, it's bad, but it's not unusual. The wind's a real problem 'round here, but it's also a blessing, 'cause without it, the summers would get hot as blazes. Then you'd have to turn on the air-conditioner all the time, and there goes the sourdough. It won't rain today. Rain here usually comes from the northwest. When it clouds up out that way, you know you're likely to get some. If the rain comes from the east, it really comes down hard."

"Is that from Gulf air coming up from down south?" I ask.

"Yeah, that's right. Either way, we sure need the rain. My wife and I got a little ranch on the other side of the Badlands."

"Most of the cattle I saw coming across the state yesterday were Angus, both black and red. Also saw some Charolais but not many Herefords. Why's that?" I ask.

"Used to be folks 'round here said, if it wasn't red 'n white, it wasn't a cow," he replies. "But then they wanted to branch out. Besides that, your dressin' percentages are better on Angus than Hereford or any other breed for this climate. I really like Red Angus."

I say, "Well, my uncle raised Herefords in West Texas. He had a small ranch and ranched all his life. I used to help him out. We lived in Wisconsin, but we went down there in the summer. His Herefords dressed better than anyone else's, and the buyers knew it. He was very careful in his breeding and grazing, and you could tell. His cattle had what I call a long wheelbase, the distance between the front and rear legs. It was just longer than other Herefords. He taught me what to look for in a healthy animal."

"I know what you mean," he says. "There's some kinds of cow that are naturally long, like some of those from France and Germany over there. Others have just lengthened out, like your uncle's Herefords. There's the Charolais and the Limousin." He pronounces the latter like the long car. "Simmental, that's my favorite. Big, gentle animal. And they're just easy to handle, and o'course, the older you get, the more you look for somethin' like that. My wife and I handle about a hundred fifty head by ourselves."

"Do you hire help to gather 'em or anything like that?" I ask.

"No, don't really need to. Got our pastures and pens set up so we can move 'em and load 'em ourselves. We just finished cakin' 'em 'bout two weeks ago."

"Cottonseed cake?"

"Yep."

"You don't cake in the summer?" I ask. "My uncle used to do a little in the summer just to keep his cattle trained so he could keep a close eye on 'em. He'd go out in the pickup and honk the horn or rattle the bucket full of cake, and they'd come up for a handout. That routine gave him a good start on gathering the herd at branding time. He rode and gathered right up to his stroke. After that, he sure missed riding at branding time."

"Well, I used to gather cattle and ride horses all the time, that sort of thing. But a couple years ago, I had a horse buck me and messed up my back. Then I had a heart attack and open heart surgery."

"Good Lord," I say. "That's a lot to pile on one guy."

"Well, I'm still here," he chuckles.

When we exchange good-byes, he brushes his hair back and puts on his hat.

I drive south from Interior, the Badlands creased with their own morning shadows. The air is cool and clear, and the tailwind promises good mileage for the Bug. As I approach the bridge over the White River, an extended family of wild turkeys scurries across the highway. I slow and stop, allowing time for the stragglers that never seem to catch up to the main party in such peregrinations. I drive on. In a matter of seconds, another covey crosses the road. Again, I stop. It isn't turkeys this time. I think it's sharp-tailed grouse. While hens and chicks run for the brush, several males cover their rear, strutting and chattering toward me with neck and breast feathers puffed out. I slowly pull away, giving the valiant guardians reason to add '66 Bugs to their genetic memory of successful deterrence.

In nearly fifty years of hiking, camping, and driving back roads, I have never seen turkeys and grouse in quick succession. I never so readily subordinated myself to birds. I feel a thrill, yet also say to myself, well, why not? Why not see them? And why not today?

The White River has the color of its Sioux name, "earth-smoke." South of the bridge, I enter the Pine Ridge Reservation, established in 1878 for the Oglala subtribe of the Lakota as Washington began to dismantle the Great Sioux Reservation of 1868 after Little Big Horn. I climb out of the White River Basin into a geological area called the Pine Ridge Escarpment, magnificent country of mixed grass prairie, ridges clothed in ponderosa pine and crested with sandstone outcrops, and inviting valleys formed by creeks named Bear-in-the-Lodge, Potato, and Medicine Root. You can't begin to capture this country with a camera. You barely begin from anything moving faster than a horse. Meadowlarks greet me from fences and telephone lines. Their limpid song follows me as if they flew alongside or I stood still, defying Doppler.

Ansel's words come to mind. I wonder when my trip became an odyssey. Probably before I met Dick Ferguson in Carthage, Missouri, who called me "a man from Wisconsin who's on an odyssey." He viewed Wisconsin as my Ithaca, even though my Bug had California plates. Perhaps Ansel meant something more than going home. When is an odyssey also a quest? I suppose it's when you search for something beyond the adventures you hope to have along the way, like any good Arthurian, even if you don't believe in grails at the end. At the reunion, I sought my childhood in a very different time. On the road, I sought my way through. As for being open, hell, in the past hour, I have let in sourdough yeast and wild fowl.

Well then, what is my *wakan*? What's the self in there that is truest and least changing? What could be possibly be holy about it? There must be some connection between Ansel's own *wakan* and his name, Wooden Knife. Suppose the Lakota named me after something I had done or seen. When and for what? They threw away the childhood names of young warriors and gave them man names. Slow was renamed Sitting Bull after his first war party. So why not a new name after I began teaching and another one after I retired? From, say, "Tracks Young Minds" to "Old Bug Man"?

I play with these musings intermittently. They are not heavy with portent. A sign at an intersection enjoins, "Vote Yellowbird Steele for President." I pass Porcupine School, "Home of the Quills." I smile at life. Until I stop at the historical marker just south of the village of Porcupine that reads, "Chief Big Foot surrenders."

Near this spot, on December 28, 1890, Big Foot and his band of about three hundred fifty Minneconjou and Hunkpapa (Lakota subtribes), two-thirds of them women and children, surrendered to Major Samuel Whitside of the 7th U.S. Cavalry. Dismayed by the recent fatal shooting of Sitting Bull at Standing Rock Agency, the Indians were on their way to seek refuge at Pine Ridge with the Oglala under Red Cloud, who had lost sway among younger Lakota for not joining Sitting Bull and Crazy Horse on the warpath in 1876. Whiteside marched Big Foot's Indians to a camp along Wounded Knee Creek. Next day, as the soldiers began to disarm them, an errant shot quickly escalated into massed fire from the cavalry's carbines and Hotchkiss guns, killing Big Foot and more than half his people. About thirty soldiers died. Wounded Knee has been called the "last bat-tle" between Indians and the United States. Little Big Horn was a battle. This was a massacre.

At Wounded Knee, the small, circular visitor center uphill from the creek and below the cemetery is run by the American Indian Movement (AIM), not the tribe or Bureau of Indian Affairs. The gist of the displays inside would be clear even if it were not written on the whitewashed wall: "The Indian Wars are not over." That belief prompted AIM members to occupy the Wounded Knee site for two months in 1973, where they were harassed by a coalition of federal agents and the GOON (Guardians of the Oglala Nation) Squad of Dick Wilson, tribal chair of the Oglala. The conflict between AIM and GOON Squad continued for several years after the occupation ended, but AIM's actions helped solidify Lakota rejection of Washington's offer of financial compensation for their loss of the Black Hills if they would surrender their legal claim to that land.

A woman and her son sit at a table, tending the center and making artifacts for sale. She looks about thirty and wears a light blue dress. As I approach, she places her unfinished dream catcher on the table.

"Some of the proceeds go to AIM," she explains graciously, implying that, otherwise, she would not think of charging what seems a reasonable price to me.

I buy a dream catcher and a small bundle of sage. The Lakota use the sage, smoldering, to purify the dwelling or ceremonial place.

My dream catcher measures about ten inches in diameter. Inside the hoop, made by warping a green willow branch, spiral webbing catches bad dreams while good ones escape through a small hole at the center of the web. A small, red feather hangs from the edge of the hole. She apologizes that it's not an eagle feather, but strict rules limit tribal use of these. Sage wraps the top half of the frame. Five short lengths of buckskin hang from the bottom portion. Each is secured to the frame with four beads that are colored red, black, yellow, and white. The four colors, sacred to the Lakota, represent the directions of the compass where the four winds live. Black Elk refers to the "four quarters of the universe" and the "four powers" residing there.

"This is lovely," I say. "I would like to know your name so I can tell my wife who made it."

"First-Born Woman," she replies shyly. Then she says the Lakota words, repeating them several times until I get it right. "My father taught me how to make the web, and I am teaching my son." She says this affectionately, proudly.

The boy, whose eyes have been darting back and forth from me to his work, looks up at his mother and grins. I tell her my grandmothers and parents were teachers and driving alone across the country gave me a lot of time to remember them. She nods. I compliment her son's dream catcher in progress, thank her, and go outside.

A car has just pulled up near mine. The driver comes over as his wife and kids enter the visitor center.

"Nice Bug," he says.

A middle-school teacher from Ohio, he loved the two Bugs that got him through college. He has been attracted to this country since reading Dee Brown's *Bury My Heart at Wounded Knee* years ago.

"Ever since then," he confides, "I have felt scarred. I have felt deeply scarred. So I come back here whenever I can. You gotta watch out though. In northern Nebraska yesterday, we told an Anglo woman we were sympathetic toward the Indians and regretted the abject poverty we had seen on the reservation. She snapped back, 'It's their own damned fault. They just take welfare all the time and don't work.' But I just can't think that way. I'm not a liberal, but I think there has been injustice done. It's not in their culture to behave the way we want them to."

I climb up the cemetery hill that overlooks the massacre site. A short pillar over a mass grave pays this tribute to the dead and their leader:

> Big Foot was a great Chief of the Sioux Indians. He often said, 'I will stand in peace 'til my last day comes.' He did many good and brave deeds for the white man and the red man. Many innocent women and children who knew no wrong died here.

Among the names inscribed on the pillar are Spotted Thunder, Shoots the Bear, Tooth its Hole, No Ears, Charge at Them, Big Skirt, Brown Turtle, Blue American, and Kills Seneca.

Single graves date from the 1890s to the present. Some contain the remains of men who fought in America's twentieth-century wars. Strips of cloth flutter from wooden poles at the four corners of many of the graves, but nothing can break the haunting silence of this hilltop. I sit amid the graves in the shade of a lone tree, alone. I don't want to stay in this valley, where the victims found no shelter. When I return to the visitor center, I ask First-Born Woman about the grave markings. She tells me the ribbons and poles mark the four directions.

"Sometimes, we wrap a bit of Indian tobacco inside one of the ribbons, a gift to the departed person," she says.

Meeting First-Born Woman eases the sadness and anger I feel as I leave Wounded Knee. She helped me concentrate on the Lakota. I need a dream catcher. My bad ones have not retired. I prefer the smell of sage to that of incense. I like the Lakota emphasis on place, on knowing corners, directions, and centers. Remembering Ansel, I wonder what First-Born Woman and her boy saw in me. Like Ansel and Sacred Eagle Woman, she nodded at the man in his mid-sixties traveling alone and far from home. Whites usually nod at the Bug.

Cemetery at Wounded Knee, South Dakota

I turn west on U.S. 18 and drive through Pine Ridge, one of the poorest towns in America. I continue north on 18 for a few miles to the Heritage Center and Red Cloud Indian School. The several buildings include the school constructed in 1888 with the help of Jesuits and Franciscan Sisters, whom Red Cloud had invited to assist in the education of Lakota children. The trim redbrick church, its white spire suggesting a lodge pole, was built in the nineties to replace the hundred-year-old original after a fire. The museum contains a reconstructed schoolroom with old desks, maps, and a timeline of educational policy. By tracing the policy, one can infer the increasing paternalism and racism of white Americans in the nineteenth century.

The Bureau of Indian Affairs, the timeline informs us, was established in the War Department in 1824. History tells us that the federal government was then forcibly removing Indians to areas west of the Mississippi. In 1851, the Indian Commissioner:

> reconfirmed that the 'civilization' of Indians was the object of the government, while describing the Indian as 'intellectual, proud, brave, generous … devoted to his family, his country, and the graves of his fathers.'

In the Fort Laramie Treaty that year, the government recognized Indian rights and claims to their land. Both parties swore "to maintain good faith and friendship … and to make an effective and everlasting peace."

By 1886, the tone had changed. No reference was made to Indian virtues. The commissioner:

> ordered Indian schools to use English for all instruction, as the use of Indian languages was considered detrimental to the cause of 'civilizing' Indians.

This order came ten years after the humiliating defeat of the 7th Cavalry at Little Big Horn, the climax of Indian defiance of the white encroachment that violated the Laramie treaties of 1851 and 1868.

In 1889, the commissioner emphasized the "inculcation of patriotism" in Indian schools through praising American heroes, singing patriotic songs, and observing national holidays.

That same year, Congress reduced what was left of the Great Sioux Reservation to six smaller reservations. The Ghost Dance spread across the Plains, heralding an Indian messiah and igniting white fears of a red uprising. It was the year before Wounded Knee.

Not long after the Fort Laramie Treaty of 1851 pledged "everlasting peace," the Plains Wars began. The peace was doomed by white emigration, military expansion, cultural resentments, conflicting ideas of treaties and political authority, intertribal rivalries, infighting between the War Department and Department of the Interior over Indian policy, and gold. In 1854, a Sioux warrior killed and butchered a cow that wandered away from a Mormon wagon train near Fort Laramie. This incident escalated into bloody retaliations by both the Lakota and the army. In the largest of these, September 1855, General William S. Harney led over twelve hundred troops against a Lakota camp, killing eighty-six Indians. None were warriors. Harney imprisoned seventy women and children in Fort Laramie.

After Harney's attack, the number and determination of hostiles increased. They resented the army's further attempts to build roads, such as the Fort Ridgley and South Pass Wagon Road from Minnesota to Fort Laramie that opened in

1857. They ridiculed their "hang-around-the-fort" brothers for continuing to trust the word of whites. Tension subsided on the northern Great Plains during the Civil War, but the Colorado gold rush that began in 1858 led to the massacre of Southern Cheyenne and Arapaho by Colorado Volunteers at Sand Creek in November 1864. That shocking event, a year after the discovery of gold in Montana and the expulsion of Santee Sioux from Minnesota, hardened the resolve of Plains Indians from below the Arkansas River to the Dakota Territory who would resist white invaders and confinement to reservations.

The museum's main gallery displays exquisite examples of beadwork, including moccasins, purses, dresses, vests, dolls, and a doctor's bag. I also find two handsome leaders' shirts, made from buckskin in the 1870s and decorated with long strings of black horsehair. Next to one of the shirts is a rifle said to have belonged to Red Cloud. I leave the museum in search of his grave.

On the way to the adjacent cemetery, I pause to read a large sign titled, "Red Cloud, 1822–1909." Born near the forks of the Platte River, he got his name from the "ball of fire meteorite" that crossed the sky from west to east the night of September 20. "His family had no tradition of chieftainship, but he became a great war chief counting 80 coups. He represented the fighting Sioux from 1865 to 1870."

In what became known as Red Cloud's War, he led the successful military campaign against white incursions along the Bozeman Trail to Montana through the Powder River country between the Big Horn Mountains and the Black Hills. That was the last remaining hunting ground for his people, and he was determined not to lose it as the westward migration of white Americans surged after the Civil War.

"The white man," he said, "was raised over the great waters, and his land is over there. Since they crossed the sea, I have given them room. There are now white people all about me. I have but a small spot of land left. The Great Spirit told me to keep it" (quoted in D. Brown 1972).

The Fort Laramie Treaty of November 1868 acknowledged Red Cloud's remarkable victory, confirming the withdrawal of American troops from the Powder River country, closing it to whites forever, and recognizing a Great Sioux Reservation that included today's South Dakota west of the Missouri River. Or so the Lakota thought.

The cemetery is larger than Wounded Knee's and has more traditional headstones. The only visitor, I stand for a few moments where the path enters the cemetery until I'm drawn toward a grave over on the west side. It is Red Cloud's. I read the inscription and reach for my camera. With no warning and no apparent cause, I begin to weep. I look away, bewildered. I fumble my camera back into its case and turn back to the grave.

Red Cloud speaks. I hear no voice. I only hear the message. He says I must be brave, wise, and kind. That's all, simple and personal. I stay at the grave a few minutes longer. Still expectant, I hope he has more to say. He doesn't. I turn to leave, walk a few steps, stop, turn again, look toward the grave, and, involuntarily, put my hand on my heart.

Until this encounter with Red Cloud, my sentiments about Indians have been typical of many Americans. I have had a guilty conscience for white injustices, romantic visions of buffalo hunts, fascination for ceremonies and artifacts, distress over poverty and alcoholism, and sympathy for the Sioux in movies like *Little Big Man* and *Dances with Wolves*. Jeanie and I contemplated adopting an Indian child when we knew we could not have our own. We were more sympathetic than hurt when we encountered tribal resistance.

Now, none of that counts. All that matters, utterly new to me, is a moment of human contact with one dead Lakota. Until today, I doubted that the supernatural, if it existed, would show itself to me except for the epiphanies that have hit me while backpacking in wilderness, listening to Beethoven's Late Quartets, meditating in ancient churches, or suddenly feeling the presence of a deceased parent. Now, I have set foot in spirit.

"God is awesome," the old Marine veteran of the Korean War said two weeks ago in the restaurant parking lot in Lamar, Missouri.

I do not subscribe to the Marine's theology, but awe, intangible and indescribable, strikes me at Red Cloud's grave. Ansel was right. There is power here. It is a holy place. Spirit is real, my gut tells me as I drive south into Nebraska.

My mind begins to take over the soliloquy, puzzled by revelation and bound for plausibility, but now, really for the first time in my life, defying reason. Why did this happen at Red Cloud's grave? Why does he care about me?

Because we are related. The Lakota revere grandfathers and grandmothers. *Wakan-Tanka* is the grandfather (and father) of all humanity. Earth is our grandmother (and mother). Even if we doubt the existence of God or cannot grasp the "sacred hoop" of the Lakota, we can believe in a spirit that joins us to them. In western Oklahoma, where the highway crosses the Western Trail, I saw my grandfather, Henry Post, heading cattle north through Indian Territory. He was born during Red Cloud's War. Red Cloud, too, is my grandfather. Our three paths meet here. The spirit joining us lives in the land, if it is not the land itself. That's where we begin, walk, and rest. Place is our bedrock. So it makes no sense to call the spirit supernatural for it is of the soil beneath us. I have opened up, in Ansel's meaning, enough to see these things, enough for Red Cloud to see me.

The trip itself has done the opening, just as Lakota rituals require preparation for releasing a soul, having a vision, or returning to the center. Had I taken this northern route to Wisconsin, I would have heard nothing at Red Cloud's grave. Talking with strangers would not yet have lowered my guard very far. I would not have read enough trails, markers, and family tracks to see the West as a whole and feel I'm not just in the story but beneath the footprints. Sacred Eagle Woman would not have gotten under my skin by challenging me to "get inside the Indian mind."

The reunion would not yet have assembled four singular lives on common ground. Andy would not have taken me inside mental illness and used "Big Two-Hearted River" as a metaphor for healing. I would not have gone back to West Lawn Avenue, where my roads began before I was old enough to know their numbers or destinations. A stone's throw from my house, Monroe Street was also U.S. 18, making its way from Milwaukee to Wyoming. My brother and I rode our bikes out Monroe Street to explore the fields and woods southwest of Madison. We knew high adventure waited beyond our frontier but not that we could have followed the same road to Red Cloud's grave. The reunion returned me to that beginning and pointed me out here.

I met Ansel Wooden Knife after driving more than three thousand miles alone in the Bug. It's fitting that he lives in Interior. He understands that odysseys are journeys inward. He may have guessed something powerful would make me weep.

"It is good to cry at this moment," Black Elk says about a stage in the ceremony for the releasing of the soul, "for it shows that we are thinking of the soul and of death, which must come to all created beings and things" (J. Brown 1953).

For some time, I have been wrestling with what my soul is made of, what it owes to my ancestors and says to my wife and children, and how it will get me through what remains of Jeanie's life and my own.

You have a center, Red Cloud tells me. I have seen you there. Let others see you there. Things won't always fit together there. That is part of you. Think about these things alone, where it is quiet. That is part of you, too. You will know when things are too far from the center. You have many memories and have seen many trails. It is good that they carry you back and away. But you have your own path. You are not at the end of it. Walk it in a *wakan* manner as you sing out names. I shall think of a Lakota name for you, perhaps something to do with birds.

CHAPTER 9

▼

"I COULD SEE THEIR SIDE OF THINGS"

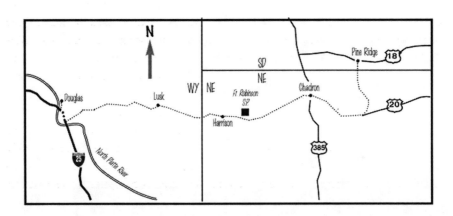

Red Cloud accompanies me the rest of the day. Suppose the universe and humans do have centers where things meet and spirit resides. Does that not mean concord among different characteristics? Restraint instead of excess? Is there a parallel between Lakota belief and the Greco-Roman ideal of moderation? Can the wholeness of the Lakota universe be reconciled with the Judeo-Christian dualism of man and nature? I carry this inquiry into the heart of the Plains Wars.

On U.S. 20, a few miles short of Chadron, Nebraska, I stop at the Museum of the Fur Trade, built next to the remains of a creekside trading post that the American Fur Company owned from 1837 to 1849. James Bordeaux operated the post independently from 1849 to 1872. Born near St. Louis in the French settlement of St. Charles, Bordeaux left home while still a boy and followed the fur trade up the Missouri and North Platte. He joined Pierre Chouteau's American Fur Company, which acquired Fort William on the North Platte from Jim Bridger and others in 1836. They had bought it a year earlier from the men who built it in 1834, William Sublette and Robert Campbell. They renamed it Fort Laramie.

Young Francis Parkman, who met Bordeaux at Fort Laramie in the summer of 1846, found him "a stout, bluff little fellow, much inflated by a sense of his new authority" as the temporary *bourgeois* (boss) there (Parkman 1949). By the 1850s, Bordeaux had married twice, sisters of Swift Bear, head of a band of Brulé Sioux. Whites and Indians from Fort Laramie to Fort Pierre regarded Bordeaux well enough to have him serve as occasional translator and mediator, but he could not prevent the bloodshed that followed the cow incident near Fort Laramie in 1854.

William Bent had no better luck ten years later, three hundred miles to the south. He had been a good friend of the Southern Cheyenne and fostered peaceful relations on the Plains since he, his brother Charles, and Ceran St. Vrain built Bent's Fort on the Santa Fe Trail in 1833. Like Bordeaux, William had married Indian sisters (Cheyenne in this case), one after the other died, and like Bordeaux, he tried to mediate as tempers frayed on the western Great Plains. But compromise was out of the question for Colonel John Chivington, who commanded the Colorado Volunteers. In 1864, he resolved to attack the Cheyenne-Arapaho camp at Sand Creek, even though it had been guaranteed military protection. He damned any man who did not want to kill Indians. Intermarriage and mixed-race families, common among trappers and traders since the early days, could not reconcile whites and Indians in this new West. As soon as America spanned the continent in the middle of the nineteenth century, the land was no longer wide enough for both cultures.

The Bordeaux trading post has been intelligently reconstructed. Commerce focused on buffalo robes, which had saved the fur trade from Bent's Fort north to Fort Union after the 1830s as beaver grew scarce and silk replaced it in the fashionable hats of America and Europe. Bordeaux received his wares from Fort Laramie. In 1842, a buffalo robe had an estimated value of three dollars. For one robe, Bordeaux offered a knife, five yards of cotton print, two pounds of small beads, twenty-five dentalia shells, or fifty bullets and a pound of powder. Three robes bought a blanket or a pound of vermilion. Five robes bought a flintlock gun.

The small, excellent museum brims with artifacts of the fur trade. Among the patent medicines in the Upper Missouri were Seidlitz powders for headaches; Jayn's vermifuge for worms; Mexican mustang liniment for sore muscles; Perry Davis vegetable painkiller; Opodeldoc, for cuts and sprains; Thompson's eyewater; and Rogerts' liverwort and tar for lung infections and jaundice. From clothing to weapons, you can see the belongings of trappers and mountain men, traders, *voyageurs*, Indians, and buffalo hunters. Judging from displays and maps, the French were far ahead of the British and Americans in reaching the Upper Missouri and getting along with the Indians. One kind of scalping knife evolved from French cooking knives. John Russell Cutlery Company of Greenville, Massachusetts, warranted every blade of its famous Green River knives, which were named after its Green River Works back east, not, as I had long supposed, the Green in Wyoming.

One room contains the largest collection of frontier guns and rifles I have ever seen. Too many, I decide after a few minutes in this room. It's disproportionate and mind-numbing compared to the simple and evocative display of Red Cloud's rifle next to the Lakota leader's shirt at the Heritage Center an hour or so behind me.

Soon, I'm yanked back into America's present by the Wal-Mart at the western edge of Chadron. I couldn't find tapes for my recorder at several shops in the old business district. There is nothing moderate about this store, which would dwarf some of the town squares the company has disabled. Staff members are cheerful. The atmosphere is fastidious and patriotic, as if to say, "We are the most all-American of all. Don't you just love us?" It's like the Dallas Cowboys on artificial turf claiming to be "America's Team." What can possibly be *wakan* about such posturing?

West of Chadron, which lies at an elevation of thirty-four hundred feet, I reenter the valley of the White River and follow it uphill toward its source near Harrison, a steady climb of about fifteen hundred feet through pretty country with rocky ridges, grassland, large pastures, and a few wheat fields. Just beyond Crawford are the restored buildings of Fort Robinson, called Camp Robinson when it was established in 1874, a fateful outpost during the Plains Wars. The fort quartered troops who fought at Little Big Horn, closed down the Bordeaux trading post for supplying arms to Indians, and killed Big Foot's people at Wounded Knee.

Crazy Horse died here in September 1877 of stab wounds that may have been accidental. He had surrendered to General George Crook, a rare army commander who dealt in good faith with the Indians. They called him "Three Stars."

With assistance from Red Cloud, he promised Crazy Horse and his Oglala followers a reservation in the Powder River country, a pledge given honestly but never fulfilled. Thirteen months later, Dull Knife and his band of about one hundred fifty Northern Cheyenne surrendered near here. They were trying to reach Red Cloud, having recently separated from a smaller tribal group under Little Wolf, who insisted on returning to the Tongue River Valley north of the Big Horns. Together, Dull Knife and Little Wolf had fled northwest from the reservation in Indian Territory, where Washington sent their people in 1877 as it dispersed and punished the Cheyenne and Sioux after Little Big Horn. In January 1879, many of Dull Knife's band were killed attempting to escape Fort Robinson when the War Department ordered them back to Indian Territory. There, and in Kansas and Nebraska, where railroads promoted the carnage, the buffalo herds had been wiped out before Little Big Horn.

At Fort Robinson and Wounded Knee, like Little Big Horn, I lose my panoramic view of the West. Tribes and regiments on the move in this country look grand on the large screen, but they acted out tragedy in small places. When I gaze at bloody ground, I do not see big sky.

I crank up the Bug's engine outside the headquarters building. A man in his seventies comes over and asks, "Is that a diesel?"

"No, why?" I say. "Because of the racket?"

"Yeah. Ya oughtta have it looked at."

"I will. Thanks."

The noise has indeed increased since leaving New Ulm. Again, I blame maladjusted valves. I can have that fixed in Wyoming, if necessary. I stop for gas in Harrison, about ten miles short of the state line. I add a quart of oil, but that doesn't reduce the clatter. A friendly guy, about forty years old, wanders over.

"What model Bug is that?" he asks.

His accent sounds surprisingly thick Southwestern for northwestern Nebraska. I summarize both the model and the trip.

"Boy, it's sure in good shape," he says.

"Thanks. I've taken good care of it, but I also had it fixed up last year. New paint and motor," I reply.

"Well, I tell ya, I painted a pickup, an old Ford pickup. Wasn't doin' much last fall so I painted that sucker. Won't never do that again."

"Why?"

"'Cause it's hard work. I stripped it down and hand-painted it. Looks pretty nice, but I won't do it again."

I tell him I'm worried about the engine.

"Let's hear it," he says.

I start it.

"Well, I don't know enough about that kind of engine to say," he says. "There's an ol' boy in town with a dune buggy, but he's away today. He might have been able to tell ya. I know a character who owns horses 'round here and all the way up to Canada. One day, he pulled up at the café. It was winter, and he left his old Chevy motor running to keep the car warm. Kapokata-pokata-pokata. I heard that and went inside. I asked him how he was doin' and where'd he drive in from. He said 'Canada.' Boy, I couldn't do that. A car would quit on me if I drove all the way from Canada. But that fella, he's got a way with cars."

A marker west of Harrison identifies the location of Coffee Siding, named after Charles F. Coffee, who trailed cattle from Texas to Cheyenne in 1871. He stayed and became one of the first to establish large ranches in this area. The Fremont, Elkhorn & Missouri Valley Railroad, which the Chicago & North Western controlled and later took over, built the siding in 1886 as a loading point for shipping Wyoming and Nebraska cattle east. Ranchers pastured their cattle along the Niobrara River before shipment.

Somewhere this side of Harrison, I have come over the narrow divide between the headwaters of the White and Niobrara Rivers. Indians and trappers prized both. Although only a few miles apart here, the rivers soon diverge when the White bends northeast toward the Badlands. They drain their northern shares of the Great Plains along separate courses eastward to the Missouri, just as I saw the Cimarron and Canadian do their southern portions to the Arkansas. A few miles into Wyoming, I cross the Niobrara and a double-track line of the Union Pacific, which, in 1995, acquired the Chicago & North Western and its trackage from the Wyoming coalfields to Chicago.

Several miles east of Lusk, I stop where U.S. 20 crosses the Texas Trail. "Texas to Montana 1876–1897," the marker says.

The trail brought longhorns to Wyoming, Montana, and the Dakotas to "replace the fast vanishing buffalo and build civilization on the northwestern Plains," according to the plaque dedicated by Wyoming's Historic Landmark Commission in 1940.

Prairie stretches from the marker to the southern and northern horizons, but I see no obvious depression of the kind that cattle made where I crossed the Western Trail over five hundred miles to the south as the crow flies.

The cattle brands in the concrete below the plaque include "N-N," "JA," and "XIT." I ran into the N-Bar-N Ranch northeast of Amarillo on my way to Wisconsin. Charles Goodnight operated the JA Ranch, located south of Amarillo in

Palo Duro Canyon. Goodnight is the model for Woodrow Call in Larry McMurtry's *Lonesome Dove*. Goodnight's sidekick, Oliver Loving, is Augustus McCrae.

Texas Trail marker, near Lusk, Wyoming

In the late 1860s, Goodnight and Loving were among the first to trail cattle northwest from Texas through New Mexico and Colorado into Wyoming. The Goodnight-Loving trail was one of several routes called "Texas Trail" by the time they converged in southeastern Wyoming and continued north to Montana and Canada. About ten years later, Call and McCrae took another route. From the lay of the text, they stitched together portions of the Chisholm, Western, and Texas Trails from south Texas to Fort Worth, Dodge City, Ogallala (Nebraska), the Powder River, and Miles City (Montana). They must have crossed this Wyoming latitude west of here, between Lusk and Douglas (McMurtry 1985).

The XIT Ranch belonged to the Chicago combine that Texas gave three million acres of Panhandle in 1882 for building the state capitol in Austin. The XIT trailed large herds to Wyoming and Montana until the mid-1890s, but they also helped doom long drives by building barbed wire fences on their vast holdings, as much as fifteen hundred miles of fence by 1900. Cowboys said "bob wire." Plains Indians called it "the devil's rope."

Edward C. "Teddy Blue" Abbott rode through here a number of times. He recalled 1883 and 1884 as "the biggest years there ever was" on this trail when "all the cattle in the world seemed to be coming up out of Texas" (Abbott & Smith 1991). From a hilltop near the North Platte in the summer of 1883, on his first drive to Montana, he could see the dust of more than twenty herds. Good grass and water from the Powder River Basin on into Montana enabled cowmen to fatten their herds before shipping them east on the Northern Pacific, which reached Miles City in 1881.

After the mid-1880s, however, the northern drives declined for a number of reasons, including the persistence of "Texas fever" that longhorns carried, the superior quality of northern shorthorn stock, the increasing reach of railroads and fences as settlers occupied the Great Plains, the habit of overgrazing acquired during a few deceptively good years for grass, and the severe winter of 1886 to 1887 when arctic temperatures and heavy snows killed 60 percent of Montana's cattle in what was called the "Big Die-Up."

"Everything on the range dates from that winter," said Teddy Blue.

Teddy had little respect for the army and none for buffalo hunters. Going by the book of military regulations did "no earthly good on the Plains." The army usually moved slowly and allowed small troubles to get out of hand. Buffalo hunters were "smelly, lousy and proud of it," and they would "sleep with women that cowpunchers wouldn't even look at." Slaughtering the buffalo "was a low-down, dirty way of doing business."

Like a good number of cowboys, Teddy Blue sympathized with the Indians and respected their courage and sense of honor. Even more, he liked them as people. "I could see their side of things," he said. He admired the Northern Cheyenne above all, calling them "the bravest Indians on the Plains." He was in Nebraska in 1878 when they came through "like a prairie fire" after breaking out of their reservation in Indian Territory. "They killed eighteen cowboys down there when they was making that break for home. They come pretty near getting me, too, but if I'd been in their place, I'd have done the same."

In Montana in 1884, Teddy witnessed mix-ups between ranchers and the Northern Cheyenne under Little Wolf, who had been given a reservation on the Tongue River in 1879. Teddy joined a posse and had an "awful narrow squeak." From then on, he sided with the Indians "because I saw that when trouble started, more often than not, it was the white man's fault" (Abbott & Smith 1991).

Teddy Blue's friend, Charles M. Russell, was of like mind. They met in Montana in 1886, before Russell turned from punching to painting for a living. Russell often painted at the N-Bar-N's ranch in Montana, and the Niedringhaus family owned many of his works. During one of their frequent conversations on horseback, which Teddy called "augurs," Teddy repeated what a Sioux recently told him about living on the Plains before the white men came.

"God," he said to Charlie, "I wish I'd been a Sioux Indian a hundred years ago."

"Ted, there's a pair of us. They've been living in heaven for a thousand years, and we took it away from 'em for forty dollars a month."

After settling down in Montana, Teddy Blue married the half-Shoshone daughter of his boss, Granville Stuart, owner of the DHS ranch in the Musselshell country east of the Judith Mountains. To Teddy, Mary was a "daisy dipped in dew." They had eight children (Abbott & Smith 1991).

My great-uncle, John James Ballard, reached this section of the Texas Trail six months after Wounded Knee. In May 1891, at the age of nineteen, he joined an outfit that trailed three thousand steers from central Texas to a railhead at Quanah, not far south of the Red River or west of the old Western Trail that his older brother, Tom, had ridden. Uncle John did not know he was about to discover "other cow countries besides Texas." To his surprise, the herd's owner, a Mr. Converse, rehired the men to accompany the cattle by train from Quanah to Wyoming and then trail them to North Dakota to the AHA Ranch near the confluence of the Missouri and Little Missouri Rivers.

"Until now," he recalled, "[cattle] had been driven all the long weary miles, even as far as Canada. But now they began shipping as far as practical and driving from there to the various ranges."

They unloaded the steers from three cattle trains at Orin Junction, on the North Platte downstream from Douglas, "happy to [be] on the north side, leaving the turbulent stream behind without having to swim it." Each of the seven cowboys had eight horses in the remuda. On their second night, Uncle John had crawled into his bedroll as if he were still in Texas, wearing his union suit. Something spooked the cattle. Determined to be the first to reach them, he ran for his horse without his clothes, boots, or hat. While he helped settle the herd, "there came a thin, cold wind right off the snows of Laramie Peak. I almost froze and this was in June—I was learning things."

They moved northeast to the Texas Trail and followed it north, fording the Cheyenne River at flood stage. They veered away from the main trail toward the Dakotas, passed west of the Black Hills, and saw Devil's Tower off to their left, a holy place for Indians, who named it "Rock Tree." They crossed the Belle Fourche and kept the herd together during a violent electrical storm. They passed the deserted blockhouses of Camp Crook on the Little Missouri River in northwest South Dakota; continued down the Little Missouri; crossed the Northern

Pacific tracks west of Dickinson, North Dakota; and turned the cattle loose on summer pasture about sixty miles north of Dickinson, not far from Teddy Roosevelt's Elkhorn Ranch on the Little Missouri. They were short only thirteen head, "a very light loss." The drive had taken them forty-five days, covering over six hundred fifty trail miles if Uncle John's estimate of about fifteen miles per day is accurate, a fast pace, even for steers (Draper 1979).

Among the ancestors on both sides of my family who migrated to Texas in the nineteenth century, Uncle John Ballard was the only one who moved on. A few months after returning from North Dakota, he left Texas for good because Haskell County was "too crowded." He drifted north and west to ranch on the Cimarron River in the Oklahoma Panhandle. Then he went to Colorado, Wyoming, Montana, Idaho, and Oregon before settling near Winnemucca, Nevada, where he raised cattle into his eighties. In Haskell, my brother and I heard stories about Uncle John from his sister, Rachel, our Grandmother Post. Granddad Post, who thought the world of the cowboy Ballards, added color. Since we normally slept on pallets on the floor, we were particularly impressed when they told us that Uncle John was so used to sleeping on the ground that he couldn't stand a bed for a long time. When he came back to Haskell to visit after about ten years of roaming, they found him sound asleep on the floor in the morning, the same floor we knew in the brick house on Avenue H.

In 1963, Uncle John wrote to my Uncle Marvin Post that he was "sitting on the side track watching the world go by—a world that is now new and strange and hard for a man who has spent his life on horseback to comprehend." I met Uncle John in July 1968 when I was finishing my PhD at Stanford. The Ballard family reunion was held in Reno to honor his ninety-six years. By then, he claimed and, no doubt, held the title of "last living herd drover of the old Texas trails." If I had guessed as a graduate student what I'd be writing after retirement, I would have finagled a day for recording his memories. He died two years later.

Leaving the Texas Trail, I remember the end of the Two Creek Ranch cattle drive in May 1990. When we finished sorting cattle into different pastures—cows and calves in one, steers in another, and heifers and bulls in another—Dennis said, "You all ride on back to cow camp. I'll meet you there after I check a few things."

We started out at a trot and then moved to a lope. Soon, we saw the peak of the roof at cow camp over a mile away. We knew there were no fences ahead. My friend Mitch and I and several others began to gallop. Our horses, smelling liberation and oats, broke into a full-tilt run. We whooped and hollered, sounding like Montgomery Clift and his companions in *Red River* as they start the herd on the first day of their drive.

But our "yahoos" did not come from movies. They came from a spontaneity as elemental as anything human can be. We were intoxicated by freedom, accomplishment, camaraderie, and riding in open country. Put simply, with apologies to my family, I cannot remember such pure joy before or since then.

In Lusk, I cross the old stage route from Cheyenne to Deadwood. From a rise west of Lusk, I spot smoke in the Laramie Mountains south of Douglas. A Union Pacific freight train rumbles east on the line that parallels U.S. 20 and U.S. 18 from Lusk to Orin. The train is over a mile long. Made up entirely of coal cars, it's pulled by two diesel engines and pushed by another two. Another coal train passes, having the same length and same number of engines as the first. I slowly overtake a westbound train of empties. Still more trains file their way along the narrow path, back and forth, all the way to Orin.

As much as I love trains, I can't help resenting these. How can you say "yonder" about such behemoths? They are all the more conspicuous because the land has turned arid and sage-brushed since I crossed the line of buttes near Lusk that marks the western edge of the Pine Ridge Escarpment and good grass in southeastern Wyoming. On this side, fewer cattle catch the eyes of travelers looking for signs of life.

In addition to coal trains, I observe chemical trucks and an oil field. Except for Miami, Arizona, I have just seen more signs per mile of the removal of minerals in Wyoming than anywhere else on my trip. I'm angered, thrown off balance by this evidence of the overnight transformation of eons. Basins with beds of coal and oil shale cover much of this state, including Powder River, Big Horn, Wind River, Green River, Great Divide, Washakie, and Hanna. These were Eocene lakebeds during the latter stages of what geologists call the Laramide Orogeny (or Revolution) when Cretaceous marsh and flatland became the Rockies. Now, trucks, trains, and pipelines empty these basins to fuel civilization a long way from where open country is shrinking and modest family ranches are vanishing.

Most of the coal now comes from the Powder River Basin, the final hunting ground taken from the Lakota and Cheyenne. North of Casper, industrialists plundered the Teapot Dome naval oil reserves in collusion with President Harding's Secretary of the Interior in the early twenties. Years after the oil boom came the strip-mining of coal and, most recently, the production of methane gas from coal beds. The effects are devastating, both visually and environmentally. Strip mining defaces the land and deracinates the soil. In coal bed methane extraction, thousands of wells pump water from the ground, depleting aquifers and polluting streams with salts. Thousands of compressors screech as they force the gas into pipelines. If Uncle John Ballard crossed the Belle Fourche today near Gillette, he would see gas bubbles.

The Stock Raising Homestead Act of 1916 gave the mineral rights for much of the homesteaded West to the federal government. The U.S. government now leases millions of acres of public land to energy companies. Washington also encourages them to drill and pump on private property. Making environmental matters worse, Wyoming has become virtually a one-party state run by energy companies and their political allies. Many ordinary voters would rather have the state depend on revenues from minerals than taxes. The large Republican majorities in most of the Rocky Mountain West are a far cry from the reformist and third-party movements that many ranchers and farmers supported in the late nineteenth and early twentieth centuries, such as Farmers' Alliance, People's Party, and progressives. Today's majorities far outweigh the encouraging reformist activity found in alliances between ranchers and environmentalists, decisions by certain counties to reduce or ban coal bed methane operations, and efforts of the Northern Cheyenne to prevent methane drilling from polluting the Tongue River.

In the two centuries since the Corps of Discovery, Americans of many political shades have taken full advantage of their freedom to strip the West of beaver, buffalo, prairie, timber, metals, and minerals. Today, it is those Americans who yelp "liberty" and "natural rights" the loudest while counting on the federal government to help them despoil some of the most beautiful land of the free. What the administration of President George W. Bush calls "balanced science" does not come from level heads. Applying that sort of science out here does not rest on balanced politics, let alone natural laws of conservation. Skullduggery is easy to spot in open country. So is excess.

A clear-eyed look at Wyoming will reveal the direct connection between the amplitude of full loads and the debris of free enterprise. Liberty has been stretched too far to justify the debris. Especially on lands that we all own, the freedom of the few to extract subverts the right of the many to experience what John Muir called "a good practical sort of immortality" (Muir 1911).

Extraction is out of control, and Wyoming is losing its center. You can't see this from large estates outside Jackson or from hermetic offices or official vehicles with closed windows and open cell phones. Thus, I propose chartering a fleet of old Bugs for a tour by prominent politicians and industrialists. I shall foot the bill and urge them to go slowly.

Pretend you are discovering Wyoming, I shall say. See how the land fits together, even as it changes. Suspend your belief that earth is an inanimate commodity. Collect the raw intelligence that good stewardship demands. Stop often. Aim your senses at the wonder of open space and the echoes of history. Listen. Walk the land. Smell it. Honor it as my Uncle John Rike did every time he left the pickup to look at wildflowers. Consider what traces you leave on earth that has been marked by trails, grazing, homesteads, and bloodshed.

To prepare for your tour, read Muir. "When we try to pick out anything by itself, we find it hitched to everything else in the universe" (Muir 1911). Then go on to Emerson, Thoreau, Luther Standing Bear, Teddy Blue Abbott, and Buck Ramsey.

I shall arrange to meet the group for dinner on the last day of their tour, let's say in Pinedale, a Green River Basin town that is booming on gas and losing its soul. I'll bring a chilled Brut Champagne from the vineyards of Anselme Selosse, who believes that "no one owns a *terroir* [a piece of earth]. I can work with its fruit and pass that on to my children, but I don't consider myself a proprietor" (quoted in Jefford 2002).

If any finish the tour and join me for dinner, I'll be surprised if they have opened up enough to feel hitched to the universe. Even if they regret the manner in which land was taken from Native Americans, they will not see that land is life itself, ours.

The Plains Wars began around here because the Lakota and Cheyenne, as Red Cloud put it, had "but a small spot of land left." Although this land had been recognized as theirs in the Fort Laramie Treaty of 1851, whites wanted it. By the end of the Civil War, the Bozeman Trail had become the most volatile and symbolic issue.

John Bozeman, Jim Bridger, and Allen Hurlbut established the trail in 1864, the year of the Sand Creek massacre in Colorado. Bridger knew the route best. He had first seen the Powder River forty years earlier as a nineteen-year-old trapper with the Rock Mountain Fur Company. Most of the Bozeman Trail, like much of the Oregon Trail, had long been a corridor of transportation from Paleo-Indians to historic tribes, trappers, explorers, missionaries, and settlers. In 1864, Bozeman and the others wanted to link the North Platte (Fort Laramie and the Oregon Trail) with the booming new gold towns of southwestern Montana, notably Virginia City and Bannack. A year later, the army completed the Minnesota and Powder River Road.

Against repeated warnings from Red Cloud, Dull Knife, and other Indian leaders that whites must not settle in the Powder River or Big Horn country, the

United States Army built a chain of forts there from 1865 to 1867 to protect the Bozeman Trail. The last was Fort Fetterman, situated on the North Platte near today's Douglas. Fetterman served as a major supply depot for forts to the north, including Reno on the Powder River, Phil Kearny near today's Buffalo, and C. F. Smith on the Big Horn River in present Montana. After losing Red Cloud's War, the United States pledged in the Fort Laramie Treaty of 1868 to abandon the Bozeman Trail and the Powder River Basin.

The army evacuated its three forts north of Fetterman, which remained in use as a base for military operations. But the treaty would not survive while men like General William T. Sherman, a reluctant peacemaker in 1868, intended to act against the Sioux with "vindictive earnestness" and exterminate their women and children if necessary. In 1870, hundreds of Oglala assembled near the fort to send Red Cloud and other delegates on their way to Washington to discuss violations of the recent treaty with the Great Father, President Grant. Custer followed portions of the Bozeman Trail in 1874 when he led the Black Hills reconnaissance expedition, whose enthusiastic report of rich gold deposits sealed the fate of sacred land that Washington had recognized unconditionally as Sioux. The Lakota called Custer's route "Thieves Road."

In the spring of 1876, General Crook followed the Bozeman Trail north from Fort Fetterman in pursuit of Crazy Horse, Sitting Bull, and their allies who, unlike Red Cloud, had not resigned themselves to peace after the Fort Laramie Treaty of 1868. Crook missed out on Little Big Horn in July. His withdrawal south along the Bozeman Trail after the Battle of the Rosebud a few weeks earlier deprived the army of one of the three forces that General Sheridan had ordered to converge on hostiles in southeastern Montana. After Little Big Horn, the army crushed armed resistance by any Lakota and Cheyenne bands that refused confinement to reservations, now the only spots of land left to their tribes.

The key to that short span of history seems clear as I drop into the valley of the North Platte. The Fort Laramie treaties had *wakan* insofar as the spirit of moderation and reconciliation resided at the center of negotiations. The treaties failed largely because of the excessive appetite of white Americans for land that was worshiped by people they considered uncivilized.

Looking south, I can tell that the smoke in the Laramie Mountains comes from a forest fire near Laramie Peak. The fire season has started early in the parched West. Laramie Peak has too little snow this June to chill cowboys who work nights along the North Platte. When I reach the banks of the North Platte at Orin, I have found my way back to mountain men I met at Arrow Rock.

Robert Stuart's small party of Astorians from the Pacific Fur Company came down the North Platte in 1812. They had followed the Columbia and Snake Rivers from Fort Astoria, and they discovered South Pass, or another very near it, over the Wind River Range. Twelve years later, Jedediah Smith and friends rediscovered South Pass. In 1823, Smith led a party of the Rocky Mountain Fur Company, including Tom Fitzpatrick, Bill Sublette, and Jim Clyman, up the White River from the Missouri, trading with the Sioux in the Badlands. They continued west to the Wind River, found South Pass in March 1824 thanks to directions from friendly Crow, and trapped along the Green River, which Indians called the *Seeds-kee-dee.* Clyman and Fitzpatrick returned to the Missouri late that summer by way of the Sweetwater and North Platte.

A year later, Smith came down the Big Horn and Yellowstone Rivers to the Missouri with William Ashley. In July 1825, Ashley had made Smith his partner in the Rocky Mountain Fur Company at the first rendezvous of mountain men and Indians on Henry's Fork of the Green. Their company's rendezvous system lasted into the early 1840s, and it shifted the fur trade's center of procurement from the Upper Missouri to the headwaters of the Wind, Green, Snake, and Bear Rivers.

Traveling eastward from the Columbia to the North Platte, Astorians and Ashley's brigade blazed much of what became the main highway west, the Oregon Trail. Over the plains, basins, and plateaus of today's Wyoming, geology had provided the easiest crossing of the Rockies between Canada and central New Mexico.

Smith saw more wilderness in a day than most of us do in a lifetime. But he could not have imagined how quickly the West would change during the life of septuagenarians born the year he first crossed South Pass. Today, between Interior and Orin, I have driven through five short periods in those seventy years, from exploration and fur trade to Oregon Trail and emigration, Plains Wars and extermination of buffalo, cattle drives and railroads, and settlements and fences.

Each period forms a distinctive part of the lore of the West. We tend to see ourselves in one or another, as I do in making my way back to Jedediah Smith or cowboys. Yet each period contains something of what precedes and follows it with effects and causes all over the place, people and land alike. I don't believe that determinism or predestination shaped the West. We did. Things might have worked out differently, even against doctrines as ordained as Manifest Destiny. Lore, at its best, leads you beyond one scene that may have become stereotypical and tells you a longer story full of permutation and choice. When lore does this, with history at its side, the Old West is still alive. Its players have had mythological status since their time, as did Achilles and Odysseus, but we continue trying to make them real by emulating, faulting, and warning, as Homer intended the Greeks of his time to do long after Troy.

The landscape of the West has also been overdrawn, as in early paintings that transformed the imperceptible divide of South Pass into an alpine extravagance. But we can still see, touch, hear, and smell parts of the West as Indians, trappers, and cowboys did. We can measure how much that West has changed or vanished, adduce the causes, and weigh the effects. We can tell we have already stripped too much of the West from ourselves.

Several years before *The Virginian* made Owen Wister and Wyoming iconic for the Western, Wister wrote *Lin McLean*. In the chapter titled "The Winning of the Biscuit-Shooter," Wister's narrator describes a Wyoming spring day of newborn greens, sage, willow thickets, and a snow-fed stream winding across meadows and vanishing:

> round the great red battlement of wall beyond. Upon this were falling the deep hues of afternoon—violet, rose, and saffron, swimming and meeting as if some prism had dissolved and flowed over the turrets and crevices of the sandstone. Far over there I saw a dot move (Wister 1897).

He saw a dot, not a coal train.

After a tough steak and overbaked potato at a friendly joint on the east side of Douglas, I drive through town and across the North Platte. A fly fisherman in waders tries his luck in the shallow waters. I take Wyoming 94 south. In ten miles, I spot the wooden sign over the front gate that reads, "Two Creek Ranch." I turn left off the highway, bump over the cattle guard, and remember the names of the two creeks. The La Bonte and the Wagon Hound flow into the North Platte a few hundred yards from each other, just after the river bends sharply to the east below Douglas. It has been twelve years since I helped Dennis and Nancy Daly trail cattle to summer grazing high on the Laramie Plains.

CHAPTER 10

▼

TWO CREEK RANCH

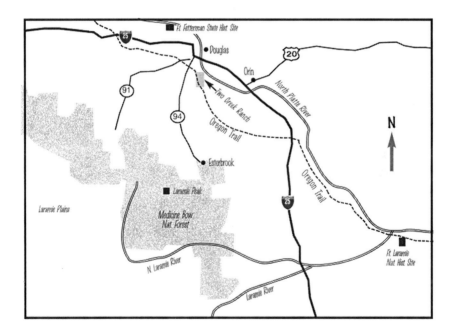

Shortly after buying Two Creek Ranch, the Dalys lost the old ranch house on La Bonte Creek in a flood on their wedding anniversary in June 1970.

"Where do you want your new house?" Dennis asked Nancy later that day.

They agreed on higher ground at the base of a hill overlooking Wagon Hound Creek. At an altitude of forty-eight hundred feet, they are about a hundred feet above the North Platte, which is out of sight a mile or so to the northeast. Sheltering the house and outbuildings, the narrow valley of the Wagon Hound sustains a green ribbon of cottonwood, willow, box elder, chokecherry, and buffalo berry.

Dennis and Nancy greet me as if it has been days, though the years show on us all. I join them and their teenage granddaughter, Skye, at the kitchen table. We fall into easy conversation. Dennis and Nancy still welcome paying guests to the spring and fall drives. Last month, they trailed over a thousand head, about two hundred more than we did in May 1990. They followed the same route to the Laramie Plains, but the rancher friend on whose land we spent the third night, a Yale graduate, has retired and moved to Chadron. Dennis says it's the driest he has ever seen the Laramie Plains. His cattle are already running out of good grass. He thinks they'll do okay if he gets a normal summer rainfall up there. He still runs mostly Red Angus. He has a few Black, which pay more per pound at auction. But he prefers the Red's combination of good value and excellent health.

After supper, we watch videos of cattle drives from the mid-nineties. I recognize two or three people from 1990 who became regulars. Nancy, Dennis, and I play a game of Shanghai, a form of gin rummy. I win, though Dennis skunks us on the last hand.

Wednesday, June 12

I rise early to give Dennis a hand with irrigation. We hop on a muddy ATV, my first time on one, and ride off to check the pipe on the uphill side of a large field of alfalfa and oats a mile from the house. The long white pipe measures about a foot in diameter with small valves every few feet for regulating the flow and the width of the area to be watered, leaving gravity to take care of the rest. As we approach the field, Dennis looks worried.

"Who's got all my water?" he grumbles.

Backtracking along the ditch that delivers water from La Bonte Creek to the pipe, he locates the problem, a gate that has been left open to a side ditch. We park the ATV near the pipe, and Dennis puts on rubber boots. While he checks the field for coverage, he wants me to walk to the end of the pipe, clearing any valves that twigs and grass have blocked, and adjusting them to reduce the flow. That done, we open more valves to begin watering the next portion of the field. Dennis finds a stick of perfect dimensions for adjusting the valves without having to bend over.

"High tech," he says.

He has me prop the stick against the fence, where he can easily find it. Meadowlarks have been singing since we left the house, and they sing all the way back to breakfast. I'm sure they do this for our enjoyment.

While Nancy finishes scrambling eggs, with her permission I read walls crowded with plaques, family photos, clippings, cartoons, postcards, and reminders. I concentrate on plaques. Dennis served on the Wyoming Game and Fish Commission from 1981 to 1987.

"Must be 'cause I was the only Democrat in Converse County," he told me in 1990.

His awards include Outstanding Young Farmer, First Place, State of Wyoming, 1973–74, "in recognition of exceptional progress in agriculture and contributions to the community" (co-sponsored nationally by the United States Jaycees, Chevrolet Motor Division, and Frigidaire Division of General Motors); Wyoming Game and Fish Commissioner of the Year, 1982 (presented by the Rocky Mountain Conservation Fund); Award of Merit, 1985, for "outstanding accomplishments in resource conservation" (Converse County); Outstanding Agriculturalist, 1990 (Wyoming Chapter of Gamma Sigma Delta, Honor Society of Agriculture); Outstanding Area Supervisor, 1990 (Wyoming Association of Conservation Districts); and Outstanding Cooperator (Dennis and Nancy), 1997, for "accomplishments in the conservation of soil, water, and related resources" (Converse County Conservation District).

A sign above his desk in a small back room reads:

> This is the beginning of a new day. God has given me this day to use as I will. I can waste it or use it for good. What I do today is very important because I am exchanging a day of my life for it. When tomorrow comes, this day will be gone forever, leaving something in its place I have traded for it. I want it to be gain not loss, good not evil, success not failure, in order that I shall not forget the price I have paid for it.

Nearby is this quote from Booker T. Washington: "No race can prosper 'til it learns that there is as much dignity in tilling a field as in writing a poem."

I don't always trust walls, but these tell the truth about Dennis.

Nancy spends much of her time being a traditional farm wife, washing, cooking, patching clothes, watching the budget, and supporting men. She keeps a clean house, but she doesn't mind clutter.

The message on a refrigerator magnet provides a clue: "Dull women have immaculate houses."

Their son Shawn, Skye's father, joins us for breakfast. Afterward, Dennis, Skye, and I saddle our horses and load them in the trailer. Mine is Roxy, a brown with a blaze and three socks. Dennis lowers the pickup's tailgate so his two old Border collies, Boots and Bandit, can jump into the back.

On the way south to one of his large pastures, I ask Dennis, "Why don't you carry a rifle in the pickup?"

"Don't need it," he replies.

"When did you quit hunting?"

"Around 1975."

"Why did you quit?"

"Oh, just got tired," he says.

I suspect other motives as well. He no longer puts up hunters for a few days at a time during season or guides them. There are no guns in sight at the Daly residence, no evidence of the NRA. Wildlife is the most popular subject on their bookshelves. Three mounted heads stare down from a wall in the living room, a pronghorn, a six-point buck deer, and a bighorn sheep. Dennis killed none of them.

The subject turns to ecology. Like most ranchers, Dennis resents the anti-grazing movement's accusation that ranching on millions of acres of public lands is ruining the West. He concedes that some ranchers abuse public land, but he argues that most of it was unwanted for homesteading in any case. He faults tree huggers for not giving farmers enough credit for conserving water, grass, and soil on the land they lease. Antelope and migratory birds use his water tanks on the Laramie Plains, for example, and he's careful not to overgraze.

"True," I reply, "but not all farmers are like you. If no one hugged trees, the best ones would disappear."

We agree on the need for more cooperation between environmentalists and farmers to defend open spaces against residential development, which is fencing in the West with ranchettes and paving it for SUVs.

Dennis does not hold the energy business accountable enough to suit me. Last night, he gave me a copy of Converse County's *Visitor's Guide*. I read this:

> The Powder River Basin sits just to the north of Douglas and is buzzing with natural resource extraction. Thousands of tons of coal leave the basin by rail each day. In harmony with those activities is the Thunder Basin National Grassland (Converse County 2002).

The guide omits discordant facts. For example, a rancher is suing the state's Department of Environmental Quality for allowing coal bed methane water to be discharged upstream from his property north of Gillette, near the northern section of the national grassland. I warn Dennis to beware of "balanced science" in the wrong hands, but he thinks I exaggerate the danger.

We do concur on the absurdity of allowing great numbers of motorized vehicles in national parks and near wild areas. "Buses and shuttles will work just fine," he says. "'Course I'd rather ride, and I reckon you'd rather walk."

"Yeah, usually," I reply. "But I'm a believer in pack trips since last summer."

I tell him I joined a terrific outfitter named Press Stephens, my cousin's son-in-law, for a ten-day trip in the Washakie Wilderness north of Dubois. We saw signs of wolves and grizzlies. The latter number enough in the Absarokas for Press to advise against backpacking there, but they avoid the smell and noise of a pack train.

Dennis shakes his head at the mention of wolves. He opposes their reintroduction to the Rockies because of the threat to cattle.

"I don't know who makes those decisions," he says, "but they're not ranchers."

He has no sympathy for millionaires who build trophy homes in the rural West and then complain about inconveniences and dangers.

"One of 'em," he says, laughing, "petitioned the game commission for reimbursement for a tree that a moose knocked down. Hell, that's the moose's home. Let 'im do what he wants to with that tree."

"Absolutely," I say. "But why not say the same for wolves, at least if ranchers are reimbursed for the calves they lose?"

"That's different," Dennis replies. "We're tryin' to make a living."

We find most of the cattle, over sixty head, around a water tank that he made by placing a gigantic tire from some sort of earthmoving machine atop a concrete slab. Inside the tire is more of Dennis' high tech. A toilet's ball cock regulates the level of the water piped in from the windmill on a nearby hill. After we move these cattle down the fence and through the gate to an adjacent pasture, I ride Roxy toward the windmill to look for the mamas of three bawling calves who stayed behind. No cows there, so I join Skye on the other side of the hill, where we search for the mamas and about thirty more head that are unaccounted for. We find them in several small bunches, or "magazine clubs," as my Uncle John Rike called them on his ranch. We move them to the other pasture, the three calves rejoining their mamas along the way. We do this after cutting out an intransigent bull and using several cows to lure him into the corral that Dennis built last year in the corner of the next pasture to the south. The Border collies, meanwhile, have done little more than pretend to help, but they love to run, and Dennis likes having them around.

I load Roxy in the trailer and drive back to the corral, where Dennis and Skye meet me. We lunch on egg salad sandwiches and Oreo cookies. The bull has settled down, but he still looks mean. Lark buntings hover over the grass and sagebrush. In flight, their trills are a light chorus compared to the meadowlarks' rich arias from fences.

Dennis and I begin talking about children and child-rearing. It's not the first time I have heard Dennis or Nancy allude to the disciplinary problems they had with Shawn. The tension I detect between Dennis and Shawn is not unusual between father and son. In this case, I can imagine Shawn's frustration at having to please one of the hardest-working men in the country.

"I 'magine you had better luck bein' a father," Dennis says. "Older and less uptight than I was."

"No, on the contrary," I reply. "I don't think age makes much difference in parents. We adopted our kids, loved them as our own. Kate was easy, but Daniel gave us fits. I'm still uptight from trying to raise him. But then I'd have been above average in the uptight department even without kids."

"Well," he says, "that's quite a gesture you and your wife made to do that. That's quite a service."

"I don't think of it that way. We wanted kids, just couldn't produce them ourselves. So, for us, adoption was selfish."

This doesn't convince Dennis, and I file away his point about service.

After lunch, Dennis lies down in the shade of the pickup with his hat off and eyes closed. In a few minutes, he sits up and puts on his hat.

"Well, boys and girls, our ridin' hasn't even started yet. What we did before lunch isn't what we were going to do today," he says.

"When are we going to start work?" I ask.

My legs and seat are sore, but my past reminds me that ranching often requires faking.

"Right about now," he replies.

There are no complaints from Skye, who happily seized this opportunity to ride with her grandfather. She'll return to her mother's place in Douglas this evening, having apparently adjusted to her parents' divorce about eight years ago.

We saddle up and ride along a ridge for a few hundred yards. Then we head west and split up. Skye and I ride together down a draw. Dennis and the dogs stay above us on a shoulder of the ridge before disappearing down the other side. Skye and I find about thirty-five head, gather them, and return to the ridge. Dennis soon appears with a larger number, and we trail them all toward a gate over a mile to the south, an easy ride along what has become his road through Lancaster pasture. This is one of the largest pastures on the ranch, about fifteen hundred acres. Its mixed grasses include green needle, needle and thread, wild rye, and his favorites for fattening cattle, western wheat for the "cool season" and blue grama for the "warm season." The views from high ground are stunning. Ahead of us and off to the southwest, the land slopes gradually upward toward the Laramie Mountains, which curve northwest from Laramie Peak toward Casper. Behind us, the land tilts downward to the valley of the North Platte.

Soon Dennis says, "Gaines, right here we're on the Oregon Trail."

I know from gathering cattle here in 1990 that the trail traverses the ranch, but only now do I recognize the faint twin tracks that approach the ridge ahead of us and leave it at a point we have just passed. The Oregon (or Emigrant) Trail usually consisted of several tracks. Leaving Fort Laramie, a major crossroads at the eastern edge of the Rockies since its beginning as a trading post, wagon trains could follow a doglegged stretch of the North Platte, but the preferred shorter route turned northwest at Horseshoe Creek and cut across country before returning to the south bank of the river near today's Glenrock, between Douglas and Casper.

Oregon, Mormon, and California Trails; Pony Express; northern routes of the Overland Stage and Pacific Telegraph: all left their marks on Two Creek Ranch. A mile or so downhill to the northwest was the La Bonte Stage and Pony Express Station, across the creek from what is now Dilts Ranch. Near us, we see the stumps of telegraph poles, left by shepherds who used the rest of the poles for firewood after the line was abandoned.

I have goose bumps. I had them as a boy when I saw the past as plain as day in the hollow of the Fitzgerald dugout in West Texas, the Civil War guardhouse at Camp Randall in Madison, and the ruts left by chariots in Rome. I have them whenever I lay eyes on traces of the Oregon Trail in Wyoming: along its main route from South Pass to Fort Bridger, on the Sublette Cutoff between South Pass and the Green River, and on the Lander Cutoff between Big Sandy and Salt River Pass.

"Have you gotten used to the Oregon Trail?" I ask Dennis.

"No," he replies. "Not entirely. Never will, I guess."

We continue along the ridge. I ask Skye about high school. I remember her as a four-year-old. Now she's a pretty blonde who is eager to start her junior year. She says she will have to reduce activities to allow more time for studies, but she doesn't know what to cut because she likes cheerleading, 4-H, student government, choir, and more. I spare her my qualms over the increasing amount of padding in the vitae of high school and college students. Skye has innocently overextended, so I offer compliments along with a nudge to trim the list.

I catch Dennis' eye and point toward Laramie Peak.

"The smoke looks heavier than yesterday," I say.

"No!" he exclaims. "Don't call that smoke. Try clouds or somethin' else."

Shawn is on call as a volunteer firefighter for Douglas. He might be summoned if the fire gets much worse. Dennis notices a sego lily by the trail, and I ride over to look.

"My favorite wildflower," he says.

"Mine is the gentian," I reply.

The cattle move slowly ahead of us, led by a gentle cow attentive to her calf and unperturbed by the occasional insubordination of others.

"Dennis," I say, "tell me about your brand."

"M Lazy C Bar," he replies. "Bought it from a local rancher for five dollars when I was gettin' started. Bought the brand and brandin' irons both."

The sun has sneaked under our hat brims by the time we reach the gate to Monument pasture, which contains a memorial for the Oregon Trail at the high point between La Bonte Creek and, to the east, Elkhorn and Horseshoe Creeks. Dennis counts seventy-four head, thirty-seven cows and their calves, as they trot eagerly through the gate to what they naturally expect will be better grazing. In this case, they are right. Nothing has been on this grass since early spring.

"We still lack eleven pairs," Dennis says. "Probably hidin' out on the west side and back there in the northwest corner where there's water and shade in the draws. I'll ride up to the corner and turn south. You all head west until you see the fence line and then turn north and look in all those rocks and draws. We'll meet somewhere in between. Get up high every once in a while so I can see you, and I'll do the same. Don't want to miss."

Skye and I split up, but we keep in view of each other. We ride up and down, through sagebrush and cedar, around rock, and into coulees and crannies. Dennis has larger pastures out on the Laramie Plains. Two of them are around five thousand acres each. All in all, he has twenty-eight thousand acres, owning about half of that and leasing the rest. Lancaster must be the roughest pasture of them all with the most hiding places. If anyone can find cattle here, it's Dennis. He doesn't. When we meet, he shakes his head.

"Don't know where they've gone to," he says.

He takes off his hat and mops his forehead with his sleeve.

"Well," he sighs, "let's head on home."

Back at the corral, the bull stands defiantly outside the new metal gate whose two upper bars he has crushed in our absence. Luckily, he has not yet assaulted the perimeter of fence that encloses the corral and several holding pens. We load our horses into the front part of the trailer and close its inside gate behind them. Then Dennis positions the trailer and orders Skye and me to open and close various gates while he drives the bull through a labyrinth that ends at the trailer, giving the bull no choice but to clamber in. I slam the trailer's rear gate shut a second later than Dennis had in mind. I was in time to hold the bull but not quick enough to prevent a fleeting look of reprimand. Dennis and I are the same age. We treat each other as equals. I have been around horses and cattle often since childhood, and he trusts me around his. Yet, I can still feel like the city boy who doesn't get it right in the country.

Inside the pickup, Dennis turns on the air-conditioner full blast and passes the water bottle around. I open and close gates on the way home. Dennis tells Skye she's smarter than the professor because she sits in the middle, but I've considered opening gates a privilege ever since Uncle John entrusted the job to the boy. At one of this evening's stops, it occurs to me that the gate might be as important a symbol for the rancher as the circle is for the Lakota.

Bad news awaits us at the ranch house. My Bug's engine is falling apart. Shawn had offered to troubleshoot when I described the clanking. He's an excellent mechanic who would rather work machinery than cattle, partly, I suspect, because this distinguishes him from his dad. Shawn is a few inches shorter than Dennis, stocky, and guarded around guests. But working on the Bug gives us something in common. I hear friendly concern when he says the problem isn't valve adjustment but it's serious, maybe a connecting rod or piston. The engine oil is gray, a sure sign that metal is wearing down metal. Tomorrow, I'll have to determine where to have the engine fixed, how long it will take, where to stay, how to get around, and so on. What a rude and discouraging development.

At supper, Dennis and Nancy offer strong moral support and invite me to stay as long as necessary.

"Only thing is," Dennis warns, "you gotta let us beat you at cards."

"Oh, the sacrifices," I moan.

We play Shanghai after supper, drinking most of the bottle of Australian Shiraz I have been carrying with me since Oconomowoc. I brought it to the supper table, but Nancy had already poured Kool-Aid. Dennis wins decisively.

"Just following orders," I say.

After saying good night, I walk over to the "Straw House," the bunkhouse they built two years ago. The walls are made of bales of straw, about one-and-a-half feet thick, covered outside and in with several layers of sprayed plaster. I let in the cool night air that the walls will shield from tomorrow's heat.

I go over the day. We spent at least eight hours in the saddle, moved over one hundred fifty head, and handled a bull that gave us fits. Good stuff. Dennis and Nancy are tops. He's a little over six feet tall, long-faced, and wiry. He needs a belt to hold up his jeans. His fingers are thickly calloused, their nails ragged. But there is softness in the way he holds bridles, cards, and the stub pencil he keeps score with. Nancy is a foot shorter, spectacled, and round-faced. She belongs to a national weight watcher group called TOPS, or "Take Off Pounds Sensibly." She's sensible, cheerful, generous, and unflappable.

"Just tell me how I can help," she said about the Bug.

Both have a ready wit, dry and benign, with facial lines that give it away. Both have faith, though we haven't discussed belief. We talked about terrorism while playing cards, and we agreed that religion, or citing God, has been one of history's major killers. They are equally offended by Muslim and Christian fanaticism. They suspect that terrorism has become a fact of life, and that declaring war on it won't make it go away. They think President Bush has begun using the threat for political ends. I wonder how many of the people I have met since leaving Claremont would agree. It's not an opinion that Americans are likely to tell strangers these days for fear of appearing unpatriotic. Is that one reason why I've heard so little about politics?

Thursday, June 13

I have always been impressed by the way that business gets done on a ranch or farm. Shawn comes for coffee, as do Jeremy and Sam, a couple of hired hands. Sitting around the table, and in no particular order, they sort out what needs doing today, who will do it, where to meet, what gear or supplies to fetch, and so on. The mood is low-key, practical, and goal-oriented. They plan one step at a time, as if they do this sort of thing every day (they do) and never quite catch up (they don't). They acknowledge Murphy's Law, but it does not daunt them. They persevere like good Stoics, tackling problems as they arise. The bull broke yet another gate early this morning, escaping the pen where we put him last night. After coffee, Dennis, Shawn and Jeremy go after the bull and load him in the trailer for auction later today. Solves that problem.

I planned on staying two nights with the Dalys ... three at the most. I don't want to wear out the welcome, but now I hope my schedule with the Bug works out so I can help Dennis tomorrow afternoon. He must find thirty heifers that have broken out of the pasture he leases up in the Laramie Mountains.

I gingerly drive the Bug the half-mile to the front gate on State 94 and wait for the towing service. On the ranch side of the sign over the gate are carved the words, "see you later," upside down. Soon, I'm riding shotgun on the way to the VW dealer in Casper, about fifty miles west of Douglas on I-25. Since I haven't seen another Bug on the highway since leaving Wisconsin, I'm all the more conscious of how lonely mine looks on the platform of a tow truck.

Mr. Russell, sole owner of Russell Towing, has also been the sole operator since deciding he would rather maintain only two trucks and no staff. He doesn't crave company in the cab.

"Hauled many old Bugs?" I ask.

"Nope, not for a while," he replies. "Used to see 'em all the time. You know, hippies, college kids, and all that."

"See many foreign tourists?"

"Oh, sure, they come through here on the interstate. A lot of 'em think I'm trying to screw 'em. Guess not knowin' the language makes 'em uneasy."

He answers a call on his cell phone. It's his son. He smiles when he hangs up, puts a toothpick in his mouth, and says nothing further.

Powders Volkswagen does not impress. While I wait for the verdict on my engine, the Powders' paterfamilias, around seventy I would guess, putters at his desk in the showroom and shows nothing because no one drops in. A woman of about the same age, materfamilias I presume, runs the office. The son, RP, is in charge of service and the parts department. The garage is lifeless, and no one comes in for parts. RP assures me they have been in business for over thirty years and know old Bugs. I have the uneasy feeling I'm in the wrong place at the wrong time.

Enterprise Rent-a-Car has nothing to rent until evening because there's a rodeo in town. I ask Mrs. Powders how I can get to the airport, where other rental agencies have their offices.

"Take a taxi," she says.

"How far is it?" I ask.

"Eleven miles."

"Is there a bus?"

"No, this is Wyoming," she says.

I call Enterprise again and reserve a car. I kill time in a waiting area near the parts counter, reading my book on Oglala rituals and wondering what is *wakan* about a healthy Bug engine and what has knocked mine out of balance. During one of several leg-stretching breaks outside, I investigate the new cars on the lot.

A cottontail rabbit scurries between an Audi GT Roadster and a VW Passat. Now what would Red Cloud make of that?

Around three o'clock, RP confirms Shawn's tentative diagnosis. He has disassembled the engine and can salvage only the cylinder heads. He will make some calls and advise me by noon tomorrow whether to order a new engine or build one from scratch. He twists an arm at Enterprise so I can have a car shortly. I'm grateful for the favor and somewhat reassured about Powders, but my old Bug is family. I worry about hospitalizing it in a town without buses. Blue over separation, I drive an impersonal, white rental car back to Two Creek Ranch.

Dennis is pleased I can help him tomorrow. We can stay in touch with Powders VW using the phone that plugs into the pickup's cigarette lighter. Supper conversation ranges widely, perhaps because we know I will stay several more days and be part of the operation.

They like listening to National Public Radio, books on tape, and classical music. Nancy keeps the small radio over the kitchen sink tuned to NPR all day. Wyoming has an excellent network of affiliates and transmitters. Dennis has a tape deck in his tractor. When plowing fields in winter, he prefers long books on many tapes because that enables him to go all day and into the night. His classical taste runs to Brahms and Beethoven.

Jeremy returned to his home in town after work. Sam sits to my left. He lives at the ranch and takes his meals with the Dalys. He's about thirty, but he looks to be in his late teens. He's kind, polite, and usually smiling, but I'm relieved when he excuses himself after dessert and returns to his digs in the older of the two bunkhouses.

Nancy and Dennis ask what I think of Sam.

"He's a sweet guy." I hesitate, but their expressions ask me to continue. "A sweet fundamentalist. Lots about God and Christian values, but difficulty following the conversation or focusing on the job."

"That's absolutely right," Nancy says. "I'm so glad someone else besides us noticed that. He must think water will flow uphill, 'cause when we asked him to corrugate the ground on the downhill side of haystacks to help them shed water, why, he corrugated uphill as well."

We talk family and ancestors. I remind them that Jeanie saw the ad for "farm and ranch vacations" in the fall of 1989 and urged me to sign up for the most appealing cattle drive in the brochure. She knew I needed major help out of a long funk. I bring them up to date on her muscular dystrophy. They don't pry for details or gush solicitude, but they regret they may never meet her. I tell a few stories about the cowboys on both sides of my family.

"Boy," I conclude, "they must have wondered from their graves why I was fool enough to pay to trail your cattle."

"I'll bet they did," Dennis laughs.

Nancy's paternal great-grandparents came from Germany to Colorado in the 1890s and soon moved to Wyoming, where they leased a ranch between Wheatland and Fort Laramie. Her mother's family left England during the Great Depression and found work in Nebraska. In Dennis' family, the Sutherlands arrived in Wyoming in 1876, eight years after the establishment of the Wyoming Territory, the year of Little Big Horn, ten years before Douglas sprang up around the newly constructed depot of the Fremont, Elkhorn & Missouri Valley Railroad, and fourteen years before statehood. They lived briefly near Fort Laramie for protection and then homesteaded about fifteen miles up the Laramie River as the army forced the northern tribes onto reservations. Family members passed down stories about seeing Indian remains on scaffolds and staying up late when hundreds of Sioux, escorted by U.S. soldiers, spent the night on their way to the Rosebud Reservation in South Dakota.

The Dalys had come from Ireland to New York in the 1830s. Dennis' grandfather, the only Daly to go west from there, moved to Wyoming around 1890 and settled in the valley of the North Platte halfway between Douglas and Fort Laramie. He later married one of the Sutherland girls and bought her parents' ranch because she and her horse kept going back there. He figured he might as well own the place.

Dennis and Nancy speak sympathetically about Indians, condemning the government's duplicity in appropriating Indian lands. I mention some of my recent encounters with the Lakota, omitting my revelation at Red Cloud's grave. I don't know how to explain that, even to Jeanie.

Dennis complains about ongoing legal battles between Wyoming and Nebraska over water rights in the North Platte drainage. Anyone in Wyoming whose ranch touches a tributary is subject to regulations that help Nebraska by restricting consumption or paying compensation. A few years back, he was one of many ranchers to buy surplus acre-feet of water captured after a flood.

"I bought fifty acre-feet," he recalls. "Then I was told I could keep thirty, but I had to give twenty to Nebraska. That would be okay if they would send me some of their good feed in return, but that's not part of the deal. Doesn't seem quite right, does it?"

Dennis and Nancy do not wear any simple political label. Most of the issues facing them are too complex to warrant strict partisanship. They have little faith in bureaucrats and lawyers. They usually vote Democrat, but not always. They did not vote for George W. Bush. Among Bush's policies, Dennis resents none more than the erosion of America's civil liberties in the War on Terror since September 11.

"Some of what's goin' on just isn't right," he says.

Friday, June 14

I'm up at five thirty to help Dennis with irrigation again. We return to the same field, where he accepts the competition between oats and alfalfa because oats suppress weeds. Dry spots, he explains, are the darker patches of green with no dew. He sloshes down the field armed with a shovel to create new channels. I close valves along one length of pipe and open them along another. On the way back to the house, we detour to look at an irrigation pump on La Bonte Creek that has been acting up.

"I'll ask Shawn to adjust it," Dennis says. "I'm lucky my two creeks have more water than I thought they would in this drought."

Back on the ATV, my jeans still soaking wet from a maverick irrigation valve, I'm grateful for the efficiency of an off-road vehicle that doesn't have to ruin the countryside.

"How do you know when breakfast is ready?" I ask Dennis.

"I don't," he replies. "It's ready whenever Nancy puts it on the table. Sometimes it's seven, sometimes before, sometimes after. It all averages out."

After discussions with family and several phone calls, Dennis has planned the day. This evening, most of us will drive out to the "Little House on the Prairie," as they call their cow camp on the Laramie Plains. Tomorrow, we'll put a new roof on it. Shawn will fix the pump today and stay around the ranch over the weekend. Dennis and I will load our horses after breakfast and look for the cattle we didn't find on Wednesday. After lunch, we'll drive into the mountains, gather the thirty heifers, and then proceed to the Little House, where Nancy, Jeremy, and Sam will have set up for the weekend.

Dennis rubs his forehead and looks weary.

"It's gonna be a long day, Gaines," he says. "But then all of my days are long days."

I don't hint disappointment that I'll spend tomorrow on a roof instead of a horse. Little do I know, I'll do the best riding of my life before this day is done.

There's something about a pickup cab that releases ranchers like Dennis. Maybe it's just natural for the compression of work, family, politics, and ponder in a small place to seek an outlet in talk. Maybe that's why I often catch myself talking aloud alone in the Bug. This morning, I have little need for leading questions on our way to Lancaster pasture.

"Ranching is no picnic," Dennis begins.

He and Nancy barely eke out a living, even with the extra income from guests. When they bought a large amount of land with mortgages in the sixties, the lending bank assured them that the value of the land would appreciate about 5 percent annually over a fifty-year period. The land market tumbled soon thereafter. They are still paying off their forty-year mortgages. Only about ten years ago did the land return to the price they paid for it.

"We sure didn't cash in on appreciation," Dennis declares. "Look at it this way. When I started out in this business 'bout forty years ago, it cost me twenty-six calves to buy a new pickup. Now it would cost me eighty calves. That's just not right."

Two Creek Ranch is not agribusiness. For ranchers like Dennis, the catchwords of the business world just don't apply.

"In the eighties, when Reagan was president, we started hearin' things like cash flow," he says. "Shoot, in farming like this, you don't have cash flow. You average out over ten years if you're lucky, and you do okay. But, from one year to the next, you don't know what's goin' to happen. You might not get any cash. In the eighties, there was so much pressure from the Reagan administration to halt inflation and tighten up credit that, pretty soon, they were foreclosing on bank loans instead of rolling them over. So I had to sell some land and livestock in order to pay off my loans. That's not good for farming. That's not how farming works. Those bureaucrats and lots of bankers just don't get it."

Dennis grew up on a small farm that was not meant to support a family. His mother was a schoolteacher. His father worked for the state's department of reclamation. But land and cattle got into Dennis' blood early. He knew he would become a full-time rancher. He majored in agriculture at the University of Wyoming. Afterward, he taught agriculture in high school. He was good at it, but he and Nancy knew it wasn't right for them. In the late sixties, they bought the ranch and started a family. Dennis thinks they belong to the last generation that will stay on the farm.

"Younger people now just don't want to work hard," he complains. "Not as hard as you need to make a livin' on a ranch. So the family farm just isn't surviving over generations anymore. Lots of families are finding that out, and it hurts."

Dennis and Nancy are hurting, partly because they have high standards. They keep meticulous records, using numbered ear tags for every animal and every cow-calf pair. The purpose is not simply identification, but also to determine the best cows when their calves are about six months old, which is normally September. One measurement is the weight ratio between cow and calf. For example, a twelve-hundred-pound cow producing a four-hundred-pound calf gives a much better ratio than a fourteen-hundred-pound cow with a three-hundred-fifty-pound calf. Indexing all of the year's steer calves offers another comparison. If their average weight is four hundred pounds, four hundred is the "one hundred index" for that year. Thus, the index for a three-hundred-pound calf is seventy-five. For a five-hundred-pound calf, it's one hundred twenty-five. The Dalys will usually sell the cows whose calves give the worst weight ratio or fall below the one hundred index. They keep their own best heifers and some of their own bulls for breeding. They buy other bulls as needed. They aren't afraid of inbreeding because they have already established a healthy mix in the gene pool.

Dennis often refers to the genetics of cattle. He's proud to have built up the genetics of his herd. Bad times hit ranchers like him with both fists. First, drought combined with the high cost of feed forces them to sell and drives beef prices lower. Second, selling many head means surrendering or weakening the genetics.

Dennis recalls a fancy outfit in Oklahoma that was crossbreeding cattle and experimenting with grasses so as to increase yield. He agreed to let them observe his herd.

"They gave me some bulls and compared results across the herd. The results came out pretty good. Good genetics."

He considers it a high compliment to have been asked.

The gate to Lancaster pasture changes the subject. I unload Roxy and mount up.

"We're lookin' for eleven pairs," Dennis reminds me. "I still reckon they're somewhere on the west side or northwest corner. If you find any, just trail 'em to Monument pasture, same gate as the other day. I'll leave the pickup there."

Dennis will ride northwest from there, accompanied by Boots and Bandit. I'll ride west, keeping the northern fence line in view, then go south. "Double envelopment," the military historian tells the passing cowhand. I keep to ridges and shoulders, dropping down whenever gullies wind out of view.

I'm about to climb from one of these when a sixth sense warns me to go back and look behind a hummock that I thought was too low to screen cattle. I find four pairs. Most are lying in the shade of a clump of cedars in a low spot with good grass all around. I want to shout like a kid, as I did when I hooked my first fourteen-inch cutthroat trout in the Bridger Wilderness at the age of forty-nine. But you can't blow your own horn around cattle and expect them to stay around and listen. The "silent type" of cowboy is made, not born. The mamas and babies look at each other as if the party is over. They want to stay put, so I leave them and continue down the gully, expecting my luck to hold. No cattle have converged on the metal stock tank I remembered seeing on Wednesday. I ride another quarter-mile. Then I turn Roxy back, figuring I'd better settle for eight head in the hand.

They haven't budged. They slowly get to their feet when Roxy and I approach. The cows are agile for their size. The calves test their mothers' thesis that bovines unfold one set of legs at a time. Roxy is calm and steady. I alternate low whistles with calls I have picked up from Uncle John, Dennis, and experience.

"C'mon, babies. Oooooooh. Git on there. C'mon, mamas. Steady, babies. Hup! Hey!"

I add the occasional civilian exhortation like "Get with the program" and "Now you've got it." The idea, as with any organization, is to prod and pacify.

It's heartening to know that Dennis trusts me to gather cattle on my own. I think I did well on Wednesday, despite the split second with the bull at the trailer gate. And perhaps Dennis remembers my progress during the drive of 1990. In his "Dear Drovers" letter, thanking us a month afterward, he had added this note to me, "I believe you were really beginning to figure out the science of trailing cows. Maybe it's an inherited trait."

I had begun that drive riding drag, behind the herd where you eat dust and return the stares of calves that loiter and plot escape. He promoted me to swing and point for the last two days, where I helped control the herd's direction and speed. After we finished a sharp turn of about eighty degrees on the afternoon of what was usually the penultimate day of the drive, I rode over to see what was on Dennis' mind.

"Let's work as a team," he had said that morning when we knew we would be riding point opposite each other.

We had talked at lunch about the possibility of pushing on to summer pasture that evening. That would make fifteen miles for the day, our best so far.

"Well," he said, "let's do it."

The weather was cool and cloudy after a storm. The older cows were eager to reach their summer home. Dennis asked me to send the word down my side of the herd.

"Good job riding point," he added as I turned to go.

When telling Dennis about my forebears, I had not mentioned that, after twenty-five years of teaching, writing, and deaning, I had never received a higher compliment than Uncle John gave me when we were working cattle in a large pen the year I got my PhD.

Not known for stroking egos, my uncle said, "Nice cut, son."

"It's in his blood," he later told Jeanie in the pickup while I opened a gate. I'll never outgrow wanting to prove that.

Roxy and I move the cattle slowly. We'll stick to the draw as long as it maintains the southeasterly direction that will take us gradually uphill either to the road or south fence. Both will lead to the gate to Monument pasture. I keep an eye on ridgelines, hoping to see Dennis. I imagine he expects me to go high for the same reason, but I'd rather not interrupt what's going well. The cattle and I are doing just fine where we are, in our own coulee.

On the skyline off to the right, a pronghorn watches us for a few minutes and then vanishes. Sentinel or loner? I wonder. Now there's a great dissertation topic in anthropology: "Who is watching whom? Ridgelines and reckoning since the ice age."

The cows low from time to time, and the calves stop whining. Roxy is easy. There is no wind down here where the stillness is deepened by the soft sounds of our passing. I hear the thunk of unhurried hooves, the swish of grasses, and the snap of twigs. I'm not lost in thought, just happily adrift:

> I find it suddenly good not to think any more but to mix with brown water and earth smells;
> to split the confining shell of the mind and relax on this oldest, most certain breast (Eiseley 1979).

In about an hour, the gully rises sharply to the south fence. We shift gears and the protests begin. Some of the calves stumble on the way up, and the second cow wants to turn right at the fence. But soon, we are all moving east toward the gate. In fifteen minutes, the four pairs enter Monument pasture. I let Roxy graze near the pickup while I have a swig of water and scan the ridges for Dennis.

There's no sign of him and the dogs, so I ride toward the northwest corner where I guess he will have found cattle that I missed. I find him with none. He's pleased to hear my report, but I sense I should have tried to signal him after gathering my eight head. We ride together for a while before Dennis asks me to return to the pickup and drive it back to the northeast corner. We'll meet at the corral, where we had lunch the day before yesterday. He'll check one or two more places on his way there, but he's baffled.

On my way back to the pickup, I pause on the Oregon Trail and imagine being new to the country back then. I don't like reminding myself that this trail was not the high lonesome. It was a thoroughfare, loud, crowded, and littered with as many as two hundred wagons a day passing this point between winters following the Civil War, which had only stalled westward migration. The fire near Laramie Peak has spread during the past two days, but Shawn has not yet been summoned. Nearing the pickup, I look back and see Dennis moving cattle up a distant draw. He's got five pairs. I turn back to join him. He looks happier as we move them into Monument pasture. We load our horses and head for home, but we're still two pairs shy.

Dennis hands me the phone and says, "Tell Nancy we're on our way to dinner."

It's mid-afternoon.

"Well, I was beginning to wonder," she says. "You tell him I baked two pies, apple and rhubarb!"

"Guess she wants us home," Dennis chuckles.

But two pairs weigh more than two pies. Dennis stops short of the corral for a final look in a jumble of small gullies in the northeast corner. We ride separately for a half hour and then link up and start back toward the pickup, empty-handed. We pass a patch of good grass under a clump of trees.

"Now that's where I would be if I were a cow," I remark.

"Well, Gaines," Dennis cracks, "maybe that's why you're not a cow."

My brother is a distinguished professor of philosophy, but he can't match Dennis for ontological clarity.

"Let's go get some pie," Dennis says.

We give up on this pasture for the day.

Nancy's rhubarb pie is worth a trip to Wyoming. It's tart just the way I like it but can't find in restaurants. After dinner, still the mid-day meal in farm and ranch country, I contact Powders VW. RP and I have been playing phone tag much of the day with Nancy relaying messages because I can't reach Casper from the pickup. It's settled. Powders will build me a new engine with parts that should arrive by Monday.

RP says, "Your car might be ready Tuesday evening, but no later than Wednesday. You can bet on it."

I thank him.

"That's what we're here for," he replies.

I tell Dennis and Nancy that his chamber of commerce tone is not right for that old Bug about to have major surgery in a strange town. They had heard RP before. They bought a New Beetle for Nancy at Powders and have taken it there for servicing.

"Well, it'll be okay," Nancy says, like a friend of the patient's family.

The Dalys expect me to stay over the weekend. I'll drive to Denver on Monday, call RP Tuesday morning, and hope to return directly to Casper that afternoon or Wednesday. My friends in Denver had asked me to come by on my way home to Claremont. They adjust to my revised schedule. I telephone Jeanie to give her the news.

"Well, are you okay?" she asks.

"Oh yeah," I reply. "Worried about the Bug, but very okay here. How 'bout you?"

"Everything's fine," she says, "but I miss you. I hope you're home in time to pick the apricots."

"Don't worry. Should be home on Friday. I miss you, too, but the Dalys keep me busy. Call you tomorrow from the Laramie Plains if the phone works."

Around four thirty, Dennis and I set out to find the heifers loose in the Laramie Mountains. It's going to be a long day. We follow the same route as the spring cattle drive of 1990. We drive west a few miles from State 94, cross the Oregon Trail near the site of Bed Tick Pony Express Station, and then turn south on State 91 some sixty miles to the Laramie Plains. Shortly after we turn onto it, State 91 begins following the old Fort Fetterman Road, which ran due north from the Union Pacific station in Rock Creek to supply the fort, a few miles upstream from today's Douglas.

Construction of Fort Fetterman started in July 1867 on a bluff overlooking La Prele Creek and its confluence with the North Platte. The fort's supply officer could have marked the westward progress of the Union Pacific Railroad according to the depots where his wagons loaded. In 1867, it was Cheyenne. The Cheyenne to Fort Fetterman freight and stage road stayed east of the Laramie Mountains. Depots appeared in quick succession at Rock Creek (today's Rock River) and Medicine Bow after June 1868, as the railroad, having struggled over Sherman Summit between Cheyenne and Laramie, laid track northwest from Laramie in a breakneck rush to beat Leland Stanford's Central Pacific to Ogden.

Although the Medicine Bow route was shorter than the Rock Creek road by a few miles, freighters preferred the latter because it was easier going through the Laramie Mountains. Either way, the Union Pacific greatly improved the army's logistical position for the Plains Wars after Red Cloud's victory in the Fort Laramie Treaty of 1868. At the same time, the Union Pacific enabled Andy's great-grandfather to travel for pleasure by rail from Wisconsin to California.

Fort Fetterman was named after the cavalry officer who, in December 1866, led a detachment of nearly a hundred men into a fatal trap near Fort Phil Kearney east of the Big Horn Mountains. No soldiers survived what whites called the "Fetterman Massacre." The victorious combined forces of Sioux, Cheyenne, and Arapaho named it the "Battle of the Hundred Slain."

Highway 91 soon turns to gravel and climbs the valley of La Prele Creek into the Laramie Mountains. We level off at about seventy-five hundred feet and follow a north-south passageway through the mountains with good grazing and hunting that served buffalo and Native Americans for centuries. After crossing La Bonte Canyon, the corridor's only major excavation, we enter the drainage of the North Laramie River, which flows south and then turns east to cut through the mountains before joining the main stream and emptying into the North Platte at Fort Laramie.

We pass souvenirs of the cattle drive, such as campsites where Dennis sang songs with gusto. His favorite, sung in the manner of Jimmy Dean, had the refrain, "Well, the moon is bright an' I'm half tight, my life is just beginnin'; I won't go huntin' with you, Jake, but I'll go chasin' women."

We pass lunch break landmarks, log homesteads from the 1880s, an old corral where we kept the horses one night, pronghorns and deer on long stretches of unfenced prairie between timbered ridges of Medicine Bow National Forest, traces of the Fetterman Road where it contoured across La Bonte Canyon, a creek bed where a calf died beneath red bluffs on our most dehydrated day, and a grove of pines where my new friend, Mitch Mitchell, who was born on a ranch in Oklahoma and worked in the defense industry near Los Angeles and sat his horse like the Marlboro Man, placed his sleeping bag one night.

"Boy, you have a good memory," Dennis says at one point.

"Well, you don't easily forget a trip like that," I reply.

Of all my memories of the cattle drive, one has made the deepest impression. When we broke for lunch on the last day of the drive, we had just made the northern edge of the Laramie Plains. I hadn't expected such a moonscape. Low buttes and arid grassland surrounded us. Not a tree was in sight. Dark storm clouds raced toward us from the south. I smelled ozone and saw the hair bristle around the ears of my horse, a large buckskin named Cheyenne. A driving rain hit us in the face as we prepared to tether our horses. I hesitated while others hurried into storm mode, turning up collars, lowering hats, throwing down, and finding shelter.

I remembered Granddad Post, sitting in the cowhide rocker on his front porch in Haskell and smoking his corncob pipe. While cicadas buzzed from the chinaberry trees, he recalled his worst teenage encounter with Saint Elmo's fire in a fierce electrical storm on the Western Trail to Kansas. The herd had been drifting slowly with the wind. Balls of fire danced above horns and then over his horse's ears.

Granddad put his fists together as he turned toward my brother and me. He raised and wiggled his thumbs to imitate the ears of a horse in grave quandary. He continued the story. He had stopped and dismounted, thinking he'd be safer leading his horse on foot.

The trail boss rode over and asked, "What are you doin' down there, Henry?"

"You'd be down here too if your horse was on fire!" Granddad replied.

"Hell, Henry, your slicker's been on fire for the last mile. Now get back on your horse."

So this is it, I said to myself on the Laramie Plains. All that's missing is Saint Elmo's fire. Everything else is what Granddad lived. Wind, rain, cold, cattle turning downwind, uneasy riders and horses, gray blanket pulled over the earth, lightning, and foreboding.

At that moment, I was closer to my grandfather than ever before. We understood teamwork. We knew there was an art to riding point, and we felt the rhythm of a herd on the move. We read the weather and hunkered down. We welcomed fellowship on the trail.

"Laugh Kills Lonesome," as Charlie Russell painted it.

Since that moment, forever moved by it, I have been haunted by memory's historical layers. I have always been nostalgic, yearning for what I had, missed, or might have done. Often, nostalgia returns us to idealized moments that release us from uncomfortable reality. But since the cattle drive, I believe that some of our most powerful memories grow where the senses touch ground. By returning us to where we were at instants of extraordinary awareness, these memories bring nostalgia down to earth and tell us who we have become. I urged my students to imagine being in the shoes of historical figures. Riding on the Laramie Plains in 1990, I no longer imagined being in Granddad's boots. I wore them.

After that, I drifted away from writing footnotes. What I began a few years later as a history of the Cold War in Europe evolved into my memoir about coming of age in the fifties and making history during the Berlin Crisis of 1961. By now, manuscripts and notes for short stories fill most of a file cabinet drawer. I read more about trails of the American West than origins of the Second World War. I am less skeptical than I used to be about the value of historical reenactments. The Fort Fetterman Road is part of my life. History, remembrance, and reality are connected by doing.

Many professional historians smell heresy in such sentiments, and colleagues begin to wonder what has gotten into old so-and-so. Not wanting to embarrass myself or my students with displays of apostasy made it easier for me to retire early. All of this is clear now as I remember meeting my grandfather on this road twelve years ago.

Dennis turns east off State 91, several miles before it enters the Laramie Plains. We drive northeast up the valley of the North Laramie River, just a creek here, and we park alongside a stock trailer near a tidy ranch house. I check my watch before leaving it in the pickup. It's six o'clock.

We ride our horses over to the house. A man comes out to greet us, the one who called Dennis about his heifers. He looks to be about seventy years of age.

"It's been a while, Dean," Dennis says. "You don't look too good."

"No. Got cancer. Lung cancer," Dean replies. "Had my first treatments last week. The pain is gone, so I've stopped taking painkillers, and that's a relief."

"Well, I didn't know. I'm real sorry to hear that," Dennis says.

"I guess you've gotta deal with what you're given," Dean says, shaking his head and smiling.

Dennis introduces me. The rancher comes over. We touch hat brims as he reaches up. His handshake is firm and warm. Up close, I would guess he's about my age. He tells us where on his land we are likely to find the heifers and how to get there. We thank him and turn our horses, nodding to his daughter and two grandchildren who have been watching from the living room. Wordless, we ride past the corral and into the trees.

Dennis changes the mood, thinking aloud as we consider options before locating the trail for climbing the ridge we need to cross. I overcompensate for things unsaid when I hail high-country wildflowers, lush grass, aspen, lodgepole pine, and fine spots for a tent. We cross a saddle and drop down to Beaver Dam Creek. Dennis thinks we'll find the heifers along its banks. We observe hoofprints near the creek. They go both ways. We head downstream in the opposite direction from Windy Peak, which overlooks his pasture several miles north of here. We pass dams and ponds, but we see no beaver. We turn back when we hit the fence that cuts across the creek and then angles upstream below the forest that marches up the next ridge. Dennis hesitantly accepts my suggestion that we look on the rocky slopes along our side of the creek.

"That's enough," he says shortly. "We don't have time to get too exotic here."

We return to the creek and continue upstream. Dennis teases Boots and Bandit.

"Boy, you dogs aren't good for anything," he says. "Now, in the old days, dogs would round up cattle without any help. They'd find their own food, too, so I wouldn't have to buy it."

I pick up the routine, and we recall how much better things were in the "good ol' dog days."

Soon, I stare at a spot in the pines about fifty yards ahead.

"What is it?" Dennis asks.

"Heifers. I think."

I add the qualifier because never on Uncle John's ranch did I see animals in the mesquite before he did.

"Well, sure nuff," Dennis says.

"That's what I'm here for," I reply.

He laughs. We gather fourteen head from their timbered powder room and start trailing them along the fence that has crossed to our side of the creek. Dennis looks up at the ridge to our left and reconsiders the exotic. He asks me to backtrack a half-mile, scour the ridge in this direction for twenty or thirty minutes, and then catch up with him.

"I'll stick to the fence," he says. "So just come on back down and follow it along and you'll find me. Don't get lost up there."

Roxy is superb. She takes over as we bushwhack around rocks and thickets looking for hollows where I would be if I were a heifer. No luck. Blue spruce appear among the lodgepole and ponderosa as I gain the top of the ridge and follow it to the right. Its shadow climbs the ridge across the creek, and I start to feel uneasy about time, terrain, and getting lost, or getting "cliffed," as backpackers say, above a precipice. I'd better head back down and find Dennis while light permits. Roxy and I must be above eight thousand feet. I gratefully button the oilskin duster that Dennis gave me back at the pickup.

"Better wear this," he said.

I'm about five miles in from the pickup, with another couple of miles to the pasture below Windy Peak. Days are long this time of year, but this is cutting it close. We'll probably have to ride out of here in the dark. If Dennis doesn't come across any more heifers, he'll be sixteen short and cranky. I let Roxy find her way down.

I follow the fence until Beaver Dam Creek disappears. Then the fence vanishes, and the woods close in. But the trail remains clear over an easy saddle to Stratton Creek. I have just seen a rare example of two creeks sharing the same cleft but running contrariwise. Stratton feeds Horseshoe Creek about five miles northeast of here, and Horseshoe flows on into the North Platte.

I hear Dennis call from far ahead, and I answer. We keep that line open as I close the gap.

When I catch sight of him, I yell, "Sorry! Nothing!"

"I got 'em!" he shouts over his shoulder, uncommonly jubilant.

"How many?"

"All of 'em!" he says. "'Bout fifteen minutes after you left. Been yellin' for you ever since, but the wind wasn't right."

I trot forward to join him, noticing the characteristic list of his hips and butt slightly to port when he walks his horse. The posture must have evolved to give his right hand more freedom to open gates, dally a rope, and point to wildflowers.

"Nice going!" I exclaim.

Dennis Daly and friends, Laramie Mountains, Wyoming

"Well, we finally did something right," Dennis says. "But then that's what we're here for."

"I know that, Dennis, but what's RP there for?" I ask.

"Whooie!"

The heifers have fattened up on mountain grass. Their russet coats are sleek, their briskets wavy. We trail them without incident, save for a bouldered downhill stretch that stymies them until a couple of student government types show the way. When the heifers clear the rocks, they frolic across a meadow, kicking up their heels as if they have finished a Friday afternoon exam and are free for the weekend.

"Kids," I remark.

"Yeah," Dennis says.

Soon, we push the heifers through the gate into Dennis' mountain pasture. Boots and Bandit look up at us for undeserved praise. Near the gate are the collapsed remains of a small log cabin. Dennis tells me a young man named Bob Newell built it around 1910.

"Can you picture homesteading back here in these mountains with no one in miles?" Dennis muses. "He would have ridden out that gap over yonder to get to town. Went off to war in 1917 and never came back. Buried in France. There's a meadow near here named after 'im."

I taught courses on the Great War.

"The poetry is in the pity," wrote the British poet, Wilfred Owen, a few months before he died in the trenches (Owen 1964).

A mountain bluebird lands on the gate beyond the decaying logs. The sun strikes the top of Windy Peak.

"Better get goin'," Dennis says.

We ride west, following a little used track over a wooded saddle. It's twilight when we reach the upper end of the valley where we left the pickup. We ride in the open between scarped ridges. Deer graze at the meadow's edge, brown shapes against the black fringe of forest. Coyotes signal from both ridges. The dogs scamper about, listening and sniffing. Above the sun's recent setting, gossamer clouds turn rose-violet. A slender crescent moon dips toward the evening company of Venus and Jupiter.

Dennis points to whorls in the grass and says, "Buffalo wallows."

Soon, we see hundreds of them all around us. We rein in.

"My God," I murmur.

"Yup," Dennis says. He turns and looks up the valley, leather creaking under him. "What if we came ridin' down out of the trees and here they were? Must have been thousands of 'em. Wouldn't that be somethin'?"

There is reverence in his voice.

As we ride through the quiet dusk, something works its way into my bones. It's made up of the wallows, the mountains, the beauty of the evening, the allusions to mortality, the pleasure of Dennis' company, the work we have done together, the fulfillment of doing well on Roxy, timelessness, and reverence. I don't know what to call this. Wonder? Luminosity? Transcendence? Those are ethereal. This is marrow.

We arrive at the pickup in near darkness and load the horses. Lights are on in the ranch house, but we don't want to intrude on this family at this hour. Dennis will thank them by telephone in a day or two. We see no more lights, except our own, until we approach the Little House on the Prairie an hour later. On our way there, the pickup cab generates fragments of talk about nothing of consequence. Tonight, we are far removed from politics. We keep most of today's ponder to ourselves.

Sam and Jeremy have already sacked out upstairs. Nancy reheats what's left of a casserole and the two pies. Dennis chooses blueberry. Nancy serves me rhubarb without asking. She's pleased we found all the heifers, but I'm too tired to embellish. Dennis wants to go over tomorrow's schedule for replacing the roof. We soon say good night. Having warned them of unkind rumors that I snore, I take my gear outside to the trailer that serves as an overflow bunkhouse. The stars are brilliant. The Milky Way is a broad spill deserving of its name. I have no need of flashlight or moon to find my way.

Saturday, June 15

It's Jeanie's birthday. I love her for understanding why I'm on the Laramie Plains without her. Nancy loads the breakfast table with pancakes, sausage, and coffee.

After a third cup, Dennis says, "We're burnin' daylight."

Coming from him, that's an order. He, Jeremy, Sam, and I start tearing off the old shingles. Dave, a friend from Douglas, soon joins us. It's hot work, and we welcome afternoon clouds. By suppertime, we have installed a corrugated metal roof that once covered a Cold War prefab on Warren Air Force Base outside Cheyenne. It's high enough tech for Dennis, and it cost him nothing except for shipping. Back in the eighties, he paid all of two hundred dollars for the Little House. He trucked it here from the Alcova Dam property on the North Platte above Casper. I had placed an unspoken bet on finishing the roof tomorrow afternoon, but I underestimated the ingenuity of these jacks-of-all-trades for which they have no formal schooling. I would have agonized over yellow page specialists, materials, estimates, and so on. These guys just got it done.

Nancy and Dave's wife fix the kind of ranch dinner that rewards a long morning and fuels a long afternoon. Except for pastries, Nancy's cuisine is not haute, but it is tasty and ample. She is modest about her cooking.

About her pie, she says, "Oh, it's all right."

Even in her own kitchen, she doesn't boss. She embraces. She returns compliments. She serves me the last piece of rhubarb pie without giving others the choice. We sit at a long Formica table that stretches into the living room, where the furnishings are frayed eclectic. I can't resist.

"I really like your Louis XIV furniture," I say.

"Yeah," says Dennis, "we got it from his dump."

Dave says little, except to report that he recently went "back east" to Kansas City.

In the afternoon, Nancy drives the pickup to haul the old shingles to a pit not far from the house. Little over five feet tall, she's barely visible in the cab, wearing a smile and a baseball cap, peering through the steering wheel. Everybody leaves after supper except Dennis, Nancy, and me. Our Saturday night in town is out here. We play Shanghai and listen to Garrison Keillor on NPR. Dennis skunks us again. I claim that my brain was shaken by twice hitting my head on a metal bar in their long, open trailer while climbing its side to reach the roof. The first time, the others had ribbed me; the second, they looked worried.

Alluding to the passage from Revelations we saw on Sam's sweatshirt, I confess I don't really care what religious beliefs anyone has as long as they leave me alone and don't tell me what I should believe.

"And that includes wearing the Bible," I add.

"I feel exactly the same way," Dennis affirms, relieved I put those cards on the table. "I don't really need a church."

"Our church is out here," Nancy adds.

"That's right," says Dennis. "Hell, ranchers depend on faith, and 80 percent of what we do is based on faith. Don't anyone tell me that you have to go to church every Sunday to have faith."

His family was Catholic a generation or two ago, but he doesn't practice. She grew up Baptist, but not the judgmental type I have known in Texas. Nancy and Dennis don't reveal what manner of God they believe in, but they profoundly believe in their own way. Their way includes the pantheism that enabled Teddy Blue to read country like the Cheyenne and see their side of things. If I told the Dalys about Red Cloud's grave, they would understand.

Before heading for bed, I ring Jeanie on the field phone to wish her a happy birthday. She's not there, probably out for a birthday dinner with Kate.

Sunday, June 16

As we finish breakfast, a friend of the Dalys stops by, pulls up a chair for coffee, and asks permission to shoot prairie dogs that have established a colony about a mile from the Little House.

"Sure," says Dennis. "Don't want those critters taking over. Don't have any cattle over that way."

The friend, one of the county's specialists in artificial insemination, tells a story about his three-year-old granddaughter. In nursery school the day after accompanying him on his rounds, she put her right arm inside a plastic bag and stuck it into one end of a hobbyhorse. The consensus around the table is that imprinting carries risks.

When Dennis and Nancy compare notes for the day, he apologizes to me for not having much work on the plate.

"You don't have to break your back every day," Nancy reproves.

"Well, I think I do," Dennis replies.

He seldom takes time to relax or celebrate. The closest I have seen him to such respites is in the evening after finishing a project. He is not explicit or verbose, but you can read his intonation and body language. I knew he was pleased to have found the heifers and finished the roof in shorter order than might have been the case. I heard lyrical notes in his account of Friday evening. He offered me a beer when we played Shanghai last night, another good sign.

Dennis does seem willing to make concessions to Sunday. He hopes to return to the ranch in time to clean up for a Wyoming Homemakers Sunday dinner.

"That's always a good feed," he says, failing to mention how important the organization is to Nancy.

The Wyoming Homemakers, affiliated with 4-H, teach the use of new products and techniques. Their nutritional program hopes to rid schools of soda vending machines. Nancy has been a member of the Converse County Chapter since 1967 and will serve as the next state president.

When I ask what she plans to do with her presidency, she replies, "Keep six hundred and ten women and a few men busy."

Dennis' respect and affection for Nancy are deep, though he won't express this in public. Again, this reminds me of Uncle John Rike, who used to say there were just three things that scared him: "snakes, lightning, and my wife." He adored Aunt Agnes, who was probably the least scary woman in Haskell.

Apart from generalizations about farming and small towns, I cannot explain mute or paradoxical endearment from men or why women accept it. My father inherited this reticence from his father, and I have it, too. My father's may have contributed to my mother's depression. Jeanie needs better from me.

The morning air is clean. The sun warms my neck as I walk to the trailer to collect my things. About fifty yards beyond the trailer, a bright red outhouse still serves as backup to the flush toilet in the Little House. On the southwestern horizon, fifty and more miles beyond the outhouse, are the white caps of Medicine Bow Peak and Elk Mountain in the Medicine Bow Mountains, country that inspired Owen Wister to write *The Virginian*.

On the Laramie Plains, Wyoming

Dennis and I spend most of the morning checking water points, fixing ball cock valves, and adjusting pumps as dictated by the water's level in the tire tanks scattered about the enormous pastures that he leases. Their elevation is about seventy-two hundred feet. Water drains in opposite directions to the North Platte, east by way of the North Laramie River and west down Sheep Creek and the Medicine Bow River. The dominant grasses are prairie June and western wheat. For grazing, he figures he needs about five acres per month per head.

By the time we return to the Little House, Nancy has left for home in the 4x4. Dennis and I hitch the stock trailer, load our horses, help the dogs into the pickup, and start back. After a mile or so, Dennis detours to show me a Swainson's hawk nest atop an abandoned metal water tank.

"Walk on over yonder and take a look at those little buggers," he says. The mother circles overhead. The fledglings heed her warning to keep absolutely still, and I dare not approach too close with my camera.

We take a different route back, northeast through the mountains to Esterbrook. On the way, Dennis stops at a ranch to see if his friend Jim is there. He isn't, but his daughter invites us in. She's working on ranch ledgers at the dining room table, and her teenage son wears a white-and-orange Texas Longhorns cap.

"Just wanted to bother Jim," Dennis says. "I want 'im to get that water line in soon."

Back in the pickup, Dennis looks at his watch and says, "Well, we're not going to make it to the Homemakers dinner. We'll grab a hamburger in Esterbrook."

Our road comes near the fire on the northeast slopes of Laramie Peak. It has spread above eight thousand feet and down into inaccessible ravines. Firefighters have encamped in and around Esterbrook, many of them Native Americans. Helicopters fly to and fro. We stop at the Esterbrook Bar and Café for lunch, the only eatery in this rustic mountain village. The proprietors tell us the fire is burning slowly this way, but it hasn't threatened the community yet. They had been feeding the firefighters, providing nearly four hundred meals a day. Today, a caterer has taken over. Our table, along with the entire dining area appended to the original log cabin, sags downhill. The place is full, and the portions are gigantic. Dennis seems to know everyone, including the district's state representative sitting at the table behind me.

A sign on the wall reads, "All work and no pay means a farmer."

Nancy returns to the ranch shortly after we arrive, looking proprietary in her New Beetle.

"You missed a good feed," she reports, throwing Dennis a glance that says she knew he wouldn't make it.

Shawn drops by. He doubts he will be called to the fire near Laramie Peak. I reach Jeanie by phone, wish her a happy birthday, and bring her up to date. After packing a few things in the Straw House, I walk down past the corrals and across La Bonte Creek before supper. I'm not eager to leave.

Monday, June 17

I help Dennis with sunrise irrigation one more time. After breakfast, I telephone RP.

"We've run into a glitch," he says. "I'll talk to my parts people."

There are no parts people, except for part of RP. I doubt Powders will deliver by Wednesday as promised. Dennis and Nancy invite me to come back in that case.

"That's what we're here for," Dennis adds, sounding like a radio ad.

I hug Nancy. The handshake with Dennis lasts a long moment.

Driving south on I-25 in the rental car, I'm a lucky man. My Bug could not have broken down at a more fortuitous time and place for a driver with my baggage. With a healthy engine, I would have left Two Creek Ranch on Thursday. I would not have had that Friday. The riding I did with Dennis was the most challenging of my life. He gave no seminars. He just sent me off on my own.

When I was twelve, Uncle John handed me the reins of a saddled horse and said, "Take old Doug for a ride." I had never ridden anything but bareback, and he had held no classes. There is method in such mentoring.

There are few things I would call perfect. One is Friday's ride with Dennis in search of the heifers. I can imagine Red Cloud nodding. He names me "Maybe Cowboy." He sees a red road from Pine Ridge to Two Creek Ranch.

Afterword

Two nights and a day with Walt and Sandra Whitman at their hilltop home west of Denver gave barely enough time to catch up on the years since Walt and I last saw each other at Cornell in the late fifties. Their own experience with illness and travel helped me review mine. I spent Wednesday night in Casper, picked up the Bug at Powders VW early Thursday afternoon, and headed for California. RP told me to take it easy on the new motor. Don't go over forty-five to fifty miles per hour for the first fifty miles, he advised. That got me to Independence Rock on the Oregon Trail, my last historical stop. I promised Jeanie I'd be home for lunch on Saturday. Then I'd start picking apricots.

The engine worked fine, all thanks to Powders. I pushed my speed up to sixty on I-80 from Rawlins to Evanston, crossing the Red Desert and the Green River. I passed north of Fort Bridger, where I had rendezvoused with John and Pat in the summer of 1993 before we backpacked in the High Uintas Primitive Area. Remembering that trip as I looked south to the snow-capped Uintas, I thought of going through my marble collection as a boy and picking out favorites.

On Friday, I drove through the ugly sprawl around Park City, Utah, schussed most of the way down to Salt Lake City in neutral, and faced a headwind south to St. George.

"Memories last a lifetime," said the billboard advertising Mesquite, Nevada. It pictured a woman having a massage at a spa. A chartered bus with a large pair of dice painted on its side slowed and honked as it drew even with me in the left lane. The driver, a young black guy with dark glasses, gave me thumbs up, pumped his fist, nodded a few times, honked again, and took off.

The evening news covered enormous forest fires. One of them was south of Denver. The Whitmans and I had seen its smoke from their home. Two infernos converged near Show Low, Arizona, my location on day two, four weeks ago. I left St. George before sunup Saturday morning and hit Las Vegas around six thirty. The traffic was already (or still) nasty. I decided to postpone breakfast until California, which Teddy Roosevelt rightly called "West of the West."

I reached Cajon Pass before noon. Jedediah Smith walked over it in November 1826 after two weeks in the Mojave and recuperated at the San Gabriel Mission. I could barely see the near edge of the San Gabriel Valley through the brown smog. Lanes multiplied, speeds accelerated, decibels climbed, fumes thickened, and drivers gave no quarter. How would I find my way through that?

*   *   *   *

Some time later, I wrote an essay that became chapter eight of this book. I sent it to Ansel Wooden Knife, asking if anything in my account offended him or his people. Here is his reply:

> I am honored by your writing, and not offended by it. I have taken it out to the wisest being I know, the Tree, and read it aloud. I waited for the answer. Now I will give you this. It is a prayer from my first vision quest in '87. It is what guides me, and connects my being to our Mother. So if you will accept this:

> So I sit, I have come out to these hills to learn my death.
> I must know my song or I cannot pass over.
> I sing backwards from where I now find me.
> And know that if sung true, I cannot be lost, for the song is my map.
> I must pick up the discarded things in my life and add them to my song.
> The animals sing with me, to help me with what I have lost along the way.
> After my song is complete, I may finally have my death.
> And my life.

References

Abbott, E. C. "Teddy Blue," and Helena Huntington Smith. *We Pointed them North: Recollections of a Cowpuncher.* Chicago: R.R. Donnelley & Sons, 1991.

Black Hawk. *Black Hawk: An Autobiography.* Edited by Donald Jackson. Urbana: University of Illinois Press, 1964.

Brown, Dee. *Bury My Heart at Wounded Knee.* New York: Bantam Books, 1972.

Brown, Joseph Epes, ed. *The Sacred Pipe: Black Elk's Account of the Seven Rites of the Oglala Sioux.* Norman: University of Oklahoma Press, 1953 (recorded by Brown in the winter of 1947–48).

Camus, Albert. *The Plague.* Translated by Stuart Gilbert. New York: Vintage Books, 1972.

Chatwin, Bruce. *The Songlines.* New York: Viking Penguin, 1987.

Converse County (Wyoming). *2002–03 Visitor's Guide.* Douglas, 2002.

Draper, John Ballard, comp. William Curtis Ballard, His Ancestors and Descendents. 1979.

Eiseley, Loren. *All the Night Wings: Poems by Loren Eiseley.* New York: Times Books, 1979.

Frémont, John C. *The Expeditions of John Charles Frémont.* Vol. 1, *Travels from 1838 to 1844.* Edited by Donald Jackson and Mary Lee Spence. Urbana: University of Illinois Press, 1970.

Garland, Hamlin. *A Son of the Middle Border.* New York: Macmillan, 1927.

Gregg, Josiah. *Commerce of the Prairies: Or the Journal of a Santa Fe Trader, during Eight Expeditions across the Great Western Prairies, and a Residence of Nearly Nine Years in Northern Mexico.* Vol. 2. New York: Henry Langley, 1844.

Jaspers, Karl. *The Question of German Guilt.* Translated by E. B. Ashton. New York: Capricorn Books, 1961.

Jefford, Andrew. *The New France: A Complete Guide to Contemporary French Wine.* London: Mitchell Beazley, 2002.

Locke, Charles O. *The Hell-Bent Kid.* New York: Popular Library, 1958.

Long, Stephen H. *The Northern Expeditions of Stephen H. Long.* Edited by Lucile Kane, June Holmquist, and Carolyn Gilman. St. Paul: Minnesota Historical Society Press, 1978.

McMurtry, Larry. *Lonesome Dove.* New York: Simon & Schuster, 1985.

Moulton, Gary E., ed. *The Journals of the Lewis & Clark Expedition.* Vol. 2. Lincoln: University of Nebraska Press, 1986.

Muir, John. *My First Summer in the Sierra.* New York: Houghton Mifflin, 1911.

Nicollet, Joseph N. *Joseph Nicollet on the Plains and Prairies: The Expeditions of 1838–39 with Journals, Letters, and Notes on the Dakota Indians.* Translated and edited by Edmund and Martha Bray. St. Paul: Minnesota Historical Society Press, 1976.

Owen, Wilfred. *The Collected Poems of Wilfred Owen.* Edited by C. Day Lewis. New York: New Directions, 1964.

Parkman, Francis. *The Oregon Trail.* New York: Random House Modern Library, 1949.

Rainey, T. C. *Along the Old Trail: Pioneer Sketches of Arrow Rock and Vicinity.* Marceline, MO: Walsworth Publishing Co., 1971.

Ramsey, Buck. *And as I Rode Out on the Morning.* Lubbock: Texas Tech University Press, 1993.

Shelley, Percy Bysshe. "Ozymandias" in *The Major Poets: English and American*, 2nd ed. Revised and edited by Gerrit Hubbard Roelofs. New York: Harcourt, Brace & World, 1969.

Steinbeck, John. *Travels with Charley*. New York: Curtis, 1961.

Stevenson, Robert Louis. *Travels with a Donkey in the Cévennes*. Evanston: Northwestern University Press, 1996.

Whitman, Walt. "Cavalry Crossing a Ford." From *Drum-Taps*. In *The Major Poets: English and American*, 2nd ed. Revised and edited by Gerrit Hubbard Roelofs. New York: Harcourt, Brace & World, 1969.

Wister, Owen. *Lin McLean*. New York: Harper & Brothers, 1897.

About the Author

Gaines Post, Jr., is professor emeritus of history, Claremont McKenna College. Educated at Cornell, Oxford as a Rhodes scholar, and Stanford, he taught European history at the University of Texas at Austin before becoming dean of faculty at Claremont McKenna College. His publications include scholarly books on Germany and Britain between the World Wars, a memoir about coming of age in the Cold War 1950s, and op-ed pieces for the *Los Angeles Times* and *San Diego Union.*

Born in Wisconsin, he has canoed in the North Woods, backpacked in the Rockies, worked on ranches in Texas and Wyoming, and served as a lieutenant in the United States Army in Germany. He has an eye for footprints, an ear for stories, and an appetite for adventure. He and his wife, Jean, now live in Santa Rosa, California, where he still drives his old VW Bug. They have two children, Katherine and Daniel.

978-0-595-46794-5
0-595-46794-6

Printed in the United States
109608LV00003B/172-174/P